The Way It Was
by Sam Wright

Dudley Court Press
Sonoita, Arizona

Published by Dudley Court Press, LLC
P.O. Box 102
Sonoita, Arizona 85637 USA
www.DudleyCourtPress.com

ISBN 9780983138303

Interior design by Suzanne Hocking/Trellis Editorial
Cover design by Jill Milton, Blue J Studios

INTRODUCTION

On approaching ninety
in the spring of 2009

The odds of our being are beyond comprehension.

"Miracle" is the only word that can come close.

Like "miraculous sunlight" that makes conditions for life to appear and develop here on this earth.

As a colleague of mine put it:

"Your parents had to couple at precisely the right moment for the one possible sperm to fertilize the one possible egg that would result in your conception. Right then the odds were still a million to one against your being, or the answer to the question your biological parents were considering or unconsciously posing."

And that's just the beginning. The same happenstance must repeat itself throughout the generations.

From the turn of the 12th century (mathematically speaking) each of us have about a million direct ancestors.

Remember, each of these ancestors had to live to puberty. For those whose bloodlines came through Europe (and there were similar tragedies around the globe) not one of your hundreds of thousands of direct forebears died as a child during the bubonic plague, which mowed down half of Europe with its mighty scythe.

Not only did all our human ancestors survive puberty; their pre-human ancestors did the same.

Then we have to go back further to our pre-mammalian ancestors. And from them to the paramecium, and beyond that to the pinball of planets and stars, playing out their diurnal courses, spinning back through time to the big bang itself (if there ever was one).

Mathematically, our death is a simple inevitability. Whereas our life is the miracle that hinges on an almost infinite sequence of accidents. The universe was pregnant with us when it was born (assuming a beginning).

So, if you find yourself feeling out of life's race, so far behind the pack that you can hardly see its dust, if the odds weigh against you, the odds against happiness returning to fill your days with joy, the seemingly overwhelming odds that you will never recover from whatever is beating you down – take a moment to ponder life's cosmic odds and how you have already beaten them.

Sam Wright, March 20, 2009
On the first day of Spring

PREFACE

To you who may read these letters:

They are not fiction or written to children. Every incident actually happened. And all persons named were as I knew them or as I knew of them.

I began writing these "Letters To Unborn Posterity" at the beginning of the twenty-first century as a personal reminder of how fortunate I was to have lived through most of the twentieth century and into today's adventurous and transitional time in history. Writing across several generations, I wondered what would be of interest in a future time and place that I cannot imagine. So, I decided to begin by telling those who had not been born what I first remembered and then go on from there.

I did not want to make my letters any longer than my fingers usually scribble one out, which is about three or four pages. And above all, I wanted to keep them as personal as if we were sitting down together and talking to each other. As I looked through them, with their attachments, I thought they should be put into a form that would make them easy to share. So here they are in the form of a book.

Early in the twenty-first century seems to me an appropriate time to tell you "the way it was" as I saw it during those last three quarters of the twentieth century and as I see it now at age ninety.

Your Great-Great-Granddad, Sam

FIRST

Dear Great-Great-Granddaughters and Sons,

When you read this I will be dead.

It is funny, my writing about being dead. Right now I am very much alive and you are dead. At least you have not been born.

I wonder if you were dead before you were born like I will be dead when you read this? Anyway, I am writing to you before you are born and before I am dead.

I'm writing you letters so you will know a little bit about what it was like to be alive at the beginning of the century 2000.

I am going to try to tell you what it is like for me to be alive at this time because I would like to have known what it was like to be alive before I was born. At least I would like to have had a great-great-grandfather or great-great-grandmother tell me the story of how it was for them before there were paved highways and airplanes, or how it was before there were telephones or before women could vote.

Most of my life I can remember. But when I was about five years old I was knocked unconscious by a big rock and I cannot remember what happened before that.

My father was a minister. He was minister of the Union Congregational Church in a little town called Hurley. Hurley was a copper mining camp in the Santa Rita Mountains of western New Mexico. The mining company's church served all Christian denominations except the Roman Catholic. I remember the Catholic Church was in Mexican Town across the railroad tracks. It had two tall belfry towers.

Whenever someone in Mexican Town died, the bell in the Catholic Church tower would slowly ring one long bong at a time. My dad, whose name was Sam, the same as mine, was also the Boy Scout Master. He took the troop on hikes into the craggy cliffs of the Santa Rita Mountains on occasional weekend outings.

This is how I lost my memory before I was five years old. It was on a Saturday hike. Because my dad was the Scout Master, I was allowed to go along with the older boys as a kind of mascot.

Anyway, we were a couple of miles from town, climbing single file up a rocky cleft, when a boy in the lead loosened a rock about the size of his head. It came bouncing down the slope to where I was scrambling over a rocky ledge. The boulder hit me a glancing blow in the forehead and knocked me backward over the low precipice. I landed among the rocks below, unconscious.

My father said he thought I was dead because there was so much blood. He said I was bleeding not only from my forehead but when I was knocked backward into the boulder-strewn cleft, the back of my scalp had been cut open by the rocks on which I fell.

My dad carried me the several miles to town at a half-run. The boys fetched the mining camp doctor. The doctor told my parents I had a concussion, and if I did not gain consciousness by morning, "The odds are Sammy will probably not survive."

This was my first experience with what I think death might be like. I had beaten the odds! It wasn't scary at all. It was like being asleep and not dreaming.

I remember waking up the next morning with my mother and father, a nurse and Doctor Hanks standing by my bed.

Dr. Hanks had helped bring me into the world when my mother gave birth to me five years earlier in the mining company's hospital in the town of Santa Rita.

As I said, everything that happened before this particular morning was told to me. I can't remember anything before that. But on this morning I do remember that Dr. Hanks was wearing a stethoscope. This is when I first learned that the way to identify a doctor is by his stethoscope. It was his symbol of authority.

Later on, when I was a pre-medical student in college, I was an aide in a hospital in Phoenix, Arizona. The patients thought I was a doctor because I wore a stethoscope around my neck. It gave me authority I hadn't earned. I also wore a white jacket.

A lot of people today wear authority they haven't earned. They wear costumes and other symbols to give them status they haven't earned, like climbing boots and cowboy hats.

Today, I don't wear a hat. I find it a nuisance. But when I was a young cowboy working in New Mexico I wore a Stetson cowboy hat because it was the style. It also kept me from getting sunburned. But I wore it mostly because it was the style and it made me feel I was properly attired.

I later wore a cowboy hat when I was working as a surveyor in the Sierra Ancha Mountains of central Arizona in the summer of 1938. I had just graduated from Phoenix Union High School.

On horses and mules we packed into the mountains surveying and marking sections of land for the government where it had never been surveyed before. I wore eight-inch high leather boots to which we nailed iron burro shoes backwards on the heels. We cut the tread from old automobile tires and nailed these extra soles beneath our leather ones. This was not done for style. We needed sturdy boots on our feet in the rough rocky terrain.

However, I did dress for style when I worked for the Fred Harvey Company at the Grand Canyon National Park one summer. I wore high-heeled cowboy boots and a big hat and leather chaps and spurs and rolled my own cigarettes from a sack of flaky-brown Bull Durham tobacco.

The tourists I took down the canyon trail on muleback recognized my garb as a symbol of authority but the mules didn't. No, the mules only recognized a kick, swat and the tone of my voice when I hollered at them.

Today I have authority because my hair is gray and I have written a couple of books and have titles like "reverend" or "professor" and can use long words like "hermeneutics" or "disestablishmentarianism" even if I don't understand them.

Enough for now, but I'll see that you hear from me again soon.

Your Great-Great-Granddad, Sam

SECOND

Dear Great-Great-Granddaughters and Sons,

Today I want to tell you more about what I remember when I was a young preacher's kid in the mining camp in New Mexico in the 1920s.

As I said before, we lived in Hurley. Hurley is where the copper mill was located five miles from the open pit mines in Santa Rita. Railroad trains pulled ore cars from mines to the mill. After the ore was crushed and milled, the copper was then shipped by railroad to smelters on the Mexican border in El Paso, Texas. In El Paso it was smelted in furnaces to get rid of the impurities and then poured into heavy oblong blocks called ingots.

It seems to me that all day and all night ore trains were bringing their carloads of rock from the mines in Santa Rita to be dumped into the giant ore crushers in the mill at Hurley. The huge iron railroad engines burned coal. Mexican boys would throw rocks at the engine and the Engineer and Fireman who would throw coal back at them from the engine's coal car. The Mexican kids would then pick up the pieces of coal to take home to burn in their stove. This was how I met my friend Ernesto Garcia.

Ernesto lived in an adobe and rusty sheet-iron house in Mexican Town. When I was in the fourth grade I joined him after school in throwing rocks at the ore train. I helped him fill a gunny sack in which we carried to his home the black lumps of coal thrown back at us. He invited me to stay for supper. His mother fixed corn tortillas with meat and chili on them.

Homegrown New Mexico chili sauce is delicious. It is also spicy hot. It brought tears to my eyes and my scalp itched with sweat. I tried to act like I didn't notice it. People today are always trying to act like they don't notice things, like what they look like reflected in storefront windows.

Because Ernesto was my friend I learned a lot about the lives of the Mexicans who worked as laborers in the mill and the copper mines.

Ernesto Garcia's father worked as a sweeper in the mill. That is what I heard he did. He would sweep with a broom after the ore had been crushed and removed. Ernesto's father was killed under tons of rock one night when an ore car dumped its load in the crusher where he was sweeping. Because Ernesto and his mother had no other support, a hat was passed among the workers at the mill for contributions to help Mrs. Garcia buy a coffin. My father went among the workers in the copper mill for contributions. I went with him to Mrs. Garcia's when he gave her the money.

I never thought about how poor the Garcias were until then. Their little adobe and corrugated iron house had a dirt floor which Mrs. Garcia swept every day, and on which she poured water to keep it packed hard. One room was made of adobe bricks, which had been plastered inside with white clay. The other room was made of used corrugated sheet-iron. It was once part of a torn down storage shed that belonged to the copper company.

There was no running water. Water was carried in a galvanized bucket from a hydrant near the railroad tool shed. Drinking water was kept in a terra cotta "olla" that was suspended from a roof beam. A tin dipper hung from its side. The "olla" and sheet iron stove were in the room that was built of adobe bricks. The other room, made of sheet-iron, was for sleeping.

Before he was buried, Ernesto's dead father was in a wood coffin placed on two sawhorses just inside the door. Candles were burning at both ends of the oblong box, covered with a dark cloth. Everyone talked softly or whispered. I walked outside with Ernesto and asked him what his father looked like after being crushed. He said he didn't know because the coffin had not been opened, but we talked about what might have been in it. I think I was seven years old then. I still wonder what he looked like after he was dead and had been crushed.

Later I had a dream in which Ernesto's father came back alive. I knew he was alive because somehow in my dream the tolling of the bell in the Catholic Church in Mexican town meant that he was not dead. With Ernesto, I crept through the great doors into the dimly lit church. There, his dead father was walking toward us. In my dream his face was horribly twisted and he smiled at us with mangled teeth. I woke up scared.

When I was a kid I had some bad dreams like that one about Ernesto's father. Then I learned to know I was dreaming. I would wake myself up. I wonder if you have learned how to do that too? I'll write more later.

Although we are far apart in time, I send my love to you.

Great-Great-Granddad, Sam

THIRD

Dear Great-Great-Granddaughters and Sons,

Since I last wrote, I decided to tell you about another unique experience as a young boy in New Mexico which gave me some bad dreams. It still does once in a while. It was a lynching. A Mexican man was lynched for rape.

Since I was only eight years old, I was not quite sure what rape was. I knew it was a terrible crime against a woman. And that in some way it had to do with perverted sex. I never knew who the woman was. Because the rapist was a Mexican and Mexican weapons were knives, I thought maybe he had cut her breasts or stabbed her genitals.

At eight I was aware of sex, particularly among animals. Cattle and horses were bred. I remember my piano teacher, Mrs. Robins, interrupting her piano lesson to throw a pan of water on a couple of dogs attached back to back in coitus in her front yard.

Anyway, this Mexican was being held in the town jail and I remember my dad speaking of his concern to my mother about the talk of a lynching. However, it was the morning after the lynching that is the most vivid.

The prisoner had been taken by a mob from the jail during the night and was hanged from the arm of a street light pole.

Because my dad was the minister, and the unofficial coroner, he had to see that the body was properly removed. I wanted to go with him but mother objected.

I learned a lot from their discussion about how terrible a lynching was and how uncivilized mother thought it was to raise children in a New Mexico mining camp. My two sisters were four and six years old then.

The upshot of the talk was that I could go with my dad but my sisters were far too young. Dad said I should know what the real world was like. He said perhaps some day I might help change it.

My parents were unusual people. I was a lucky kid.

I'll never forget that windy morning with tumbleweeds piled against the fence. My dad and I walked around a downtown corner to where we could see the body, head askew, turning slowly as wind ruffled the dead man's hair. His feet were bare and his hands were tied behind him as he hung by a dirty yellow rope from an arm of the street light pole.

Standing near the lamppost was Deputy Roberts. Sheriff Chapin was sitting on his great white horse talking to him. I remember how the sun made the pearl handle on Sheriff Chapin's pistol glitter where it stuck out of his holster. I remember how his big gelding horse kept stepping left and right, nervous at being check-reined while Sheriff Chapin talked down to us.

To this day, when I hear the phrase, "Get off your high horse," I remember that morning.

I remember that morning because my father said, "Get down off your horse, Chapin... I want to talk to you!"

What else was said is not in my memory. But the mood on that bleak, windy morning was clear. My father was an angry man. It was the first time I had heard this tone of voice from him. His anger was directed at the lawmen for permitting this atrocity.

As I say, I do not remember what was said but I do recall the whining tone of excuses. It was strange to hear the sheriff, whom we kids admired, making excuses to my dad.

When I was young I did not think of my dad as important. He was just the minister in the town. The doctor, the sheriff and the superintendent of the mill were important people. So, when I heard Sheriff Chapin making excuses to my dad it seemed strange. It was later that I discovered the importance of my father's authority in a frontier community.

This happened one morning when I was walking with him on his way to the Masonic Lodge where he was a member and earned extra income as the janitor.

There was a large crowd of men in the middle of the unpaved street shouting and making bets with each other. My dad pushed through the crowd. I was at his heels. In the center of the circle of men were two dogs. They were bloody and so fatigued that they lay there chewing on each other.

My father stepped through the circle and gripping one dog by the collar, then ordered one of the other men to pull the other dog away. He then turned to the crowd, which had become silent.

"Whose dog is this?" He said. "I am ashamed of you. Grown men like you!"

His face was white and his voice strange.

Holding the bloody pit bulldog, which was still trying to get to the other dog by the collar, he looked around the circle of men and repeated, "I'm ashamed of you."

"It's just a dogfight, parson," somebody said.

"The hell it is! Look at these animals. This is sadism."

That was the only time I ever heard my father use an oath. He handed the collar of the dog to one of the men and turned around facing the circle of mill hands and miners.

"Don't you men have jobs you're supposed to be at?"

I recall the men sheepishly walking away. I learned what sadism was. I also learned the power of moral authority as well as pride. I was proud of my dad. I was proud of him, not because of moral authority, but because he was tough. He was tough in a community where toughness was held in respect.

As the preacher's kid in a mining camp, I, too, had to learn to be tough.

Learning to be tough was easy. Learning not to be tough when I was older was hard.

Will write more soon.

Love, Great-Great-Granddad Sam

↳ FOURTH

Dear Great-Great-Grandsons and Daughters,

When I was young, one thing I tried to be tough about was carsickness. It didn't work. I still hate to throw up. It is embarrassing when others are around.

All of the roads in the part of New Mexico where I lived in 1928 were winding and unpaved. If I had to sit in the back seat of an automobile, and didn't have plenty of air from an open window, I got terribly nauseated. That is what happened when I drove with the Doctor Hanks' family to Lordsburg, New Mexico.

We drove through the Burro Mountains to Lordsburg to see Charles Lindbergh land there in his plane, the "Spirit of Saint Louis." It was the airplane in which he had flown alone across the Atlantic Ocean to Paris, France the year before. Because clouds of dust boiled up from the rough, dirt road, the car windows were tightly shut.

Near the mining town of Tyrone I could not hold what was in my stomach any longer. I got the window rolled down just in time to make a mess on the side of Dr. Hank's new Buick. At least I didn't get it on the shiny leather seat.

After we arrived at the dirt airstrip outside of Lordsburg, cars were lined up waiting for Lindbergh to fly in. I was feeling better. Expectations were high because Lindbergh was famous and was landing outside this small town for fuel. A flatbed truck with red, white and blue bunting cloth around it was awaiting the flyer. People kept squinting into the bright afternoon sky to be first to see the airplane coming.

Then we heard it. The small speck grew larger and soon circled above us. People tooted the horns of their cars and others waved, but it was not the "Spirit of Saint Louis." This plane was bright red and we knew that the "Spirit of Saint Louis" was silver. This was the advance plane.

And then, as it was landing in a cloud of dust, here came the "Spirit of Saint Louis!" It circled twice before it too dropped down to the dirt runway. Everybody cheered.

Charles Lindbergh was invited up a stepladder on the decorated flatbed truck. Official greeters were gathered there. Words were spoken.

I was just tall enough to see above the truck bed, and while Lindbergh was talking I drew my initials on the toe of his dust-covered shoe. He looked down at his foot. Then looked at me and smiled.

I don't remember anything that was said, or whether I was sick on the way back to the town of Hurley. But I vividly recall throwing up on the doctor's new Buick and seeing my S.A.W. initials through the dust on the famous flyer's shoe. Then seeing his smile when he saw what I had done.

Years later I saw the "Spirit of Saint Louis" hanging in the Smithsonian Institution in Washington DC. Lindbergh was dead then, and buried in Hawaii. To me that silver plane, hanging in the museum, was also dead and lifeless. But that day at Lordsburg, New Mexico is as vividly alive as if I'd thrown up yesterday.

More to come from me later.

Your Great-Great-Granddad, Sam

FIFTH

Dear Great-Great-Granddaughters and Sons,

When I wrote you about carsickness I remembered another time I felt sick when I was young. It was caused by falling in love.

I was in the second grade. She was the dentist's daughter who sat in front of me with golden ringlet curls. She turned around and gave me her dimpled smile. I could not take a deep breath.

In the third grade I felt sick with love also. Her name was Lavon and we were going to ride off together to some exotic place in a hidden valley of the mountains of New Mexico. We entwined our initials L and S in a form we would use to brand our cattle. I carved it into the rail on the front porch of her house and her parents ceased to approve of me as a proper suitor.

This was not a tragedy because at that time Madge moved to Hurley from Denver, Colorado, replacing Lavon. Madge had black, pageboy hair and could do the Charleston, a dance that she taught me. I can still do it today.

I was also sick about Madge until one of my Mexican friends loaned me a burro. This donkey was a young jenny with which I could explore the surrounding hills and to whom I gave my affection without that sick feeling.

Anyway, when I was in the fourth grade our family moved from New Mexico to Arizona. We moved to Phoenix. We were not really in Phoenix because we were over five miles south of the city where orchards of grapefruit had been newly planted.

My father was called to be minister of the Neighborhood Congregational Church that met in the Neighborhood Community House. Neighborhood House was a meeting hall, which was used by the Roosevelt Grammar School as well as the church and other community organizations.

I have a vivid recall of the day we arrived in the Salt River Valley. It is interesting how some things are easily remembered and others are lost in time.

It was the first day of May in 1929. We drove along Southern Avenue beneath huge cottonwood trees. They overhung and shadowed unfamiliar, narrow concrete pavement with its tar strips. Our Chevrolet sedan thumped rhythmically as its wheels passed over them. Mockingbirds were singing in the cottonwood trees. I remember the fragrance of alfalfa blossoms and newly mown hay.

Even now, when I recall freshly cut alfalfa I remember that May morning and the singing of birds. It is interesting how odors recall memory. Is it the same experience for you?

As we arrived, the parsonage that was next to the Neighborhood House was still being repainted for our arrival. It had been enlarged with the addition of an enclosed back porch on which my two younger sisters and I slept. The upper half of the porch was screened to let in air. Wood framed canvas flaps that were hinged on the outside could be let down with clothesline cord from inside the porch. They could be dropped for protection from summer dust storms or rain. Houses did not have air-conditioning then.

Because there was no air-conditioning, nearly everyone slept outdoors in the summer. We slept under chinaberry trees in the back yard on folding canvas cots. Sometimes it was so hot in the summer that people would put a watering hose into the cot to run slowly while they were sleeping. It was funny in the morning because you could be wrinkled like a prune.

It was really interesting if you were up early in the morning like I was the year I had a paper route. I was out each day at four a.m. delivering the morning paper. People were asleep outside everywhere in the rural area where we lived. I saw a lot of naked people as a paperboy.

Delivering the *Arizona Republic* by bicycle on a four-mile route each morning wasn't easy because of the dogs. It seemed that every citrus grove and farmer's house had a dog that did not like anyone on a bicycle. I still have a couple of scars on my leg from a dog bite. I solved the problem with a squirt gun loaned from another paperboy.

I filled a squirt gun with household ammonia. When a snarling dog was close enough, I gave it a shot in the face. After a couple of these episodes, all I needed to do was point my finger at an attacking dog as I peddled along. If the dog was one I'd treated, when he saw me point at him he would stop, drop his tail between his legs and retreat back to his yard. I often wished I could point a finger at some of my disagreeable customers with the same result.

Love, and more later, Great-Great-Granddad, Sam

SIXTH

Dear Great-Great-Grandsons and Daughters,

As I write you today, I want to go back to when I was a kid in New Mexico to tell you about a baptism before I forget it.

As I had said, my dad was the minister in this mining camp in New Mexico when I was eight. And because it was the only church allowed in the town, it was called The Union Congregational Church. My father was the minister for all the Protestant denominations, somewhat like an army chaplain.

Congregationalists did not practice total immersion in their baptism ceremony. They were known as sprinklers, like Presbyterians, Methodists and Episcopalians. However, there were many Baptists and once or twice a year the congregation would meet beneath the sycamores and cottonwood trees several miles out of town at Warm Spring Ranch for immersion on Baptism Sunday.

Warm Spring had once been an ancient Indian camping place. There was a large natural basin of clear, warm, fresh water bubbling out of the ground. A small stream carried the water to a large pond that had been scraped out as a watering place for cattle. On Baptism Sunday, people would drive to Warm Spring to picnic and afterward those who were to be baptized would wade out with my father into the warm, clear water to be dunked, "In the name of the Father, the Son and the Holy Ghost, Amen."

One lady stands out in my memory as she was dressed in a white robe that was more like a tent to me. She was an enormous woman. When she waded out into the basin, the water rose several inches around its sides. She held her nose and my dad put his hand behind her head. She lay back to submerge, "In the name of the Father, Son and Holy Ghost, Amen," but at the Amen, when she was supposed to rise up in the new spirit, she didn't.

She somehow lost her footing, or my dad did. Both of them went under. There was a great splashing of water and floundering around until one of the parishioners jumped in and helped my father rescue the great dame by pulling her to the edge. There, several others heaved her onto the grass.

I remember one other baptism from these early days in New Mexico. This was also immersion but not traditionally total. I guess I remember it because, like the fat lady, it too had a sense of the dramatic.

It was late afternoon and my mother and two younger sisters had driven the winding dirt road with friends to shop at the new Piggly Wiggly grocery store in Silver City. Piggly Wiggly was later called Safeway. In 1928 self-serving was a new way of grocery shopping. It was exciting to be able to help yourself from the shelves and not have to be waited on by a clerk.

Anyway, my dad and I were home alone when there was a knock on the door and a cowboy in fancy boots and a big white sombrero asked my father, "Are y'all the preacher?"

Dad invited him in and I noticed that the man had a black eye and his face was badly scabbed beneath it. He had a bandage taped over one ear. He said he had come to be baptized.

While sipping a cup of hot coffee, he told my father his story.

He was a cowboy working at roundup for the G.O.S. Ranch on the Mimbres River. A few days before, the cattle had gotten away from the cowhands. The herd had stampeded and his saddle had not been tightly cinched. He was riding herd at a fast gallop when the saddle slipped beneath his horse and his foot was caught in a stirrup. He said that while he was being dragged over rocks and brush he prayed as he had never prayed before. He prayed that if God would save him he would follow the wishes of his devoted mother and be baptized in full immersion as a true Christian.

He had just been released from the company hospital in Santa Rita, but before he rode back to the ranch, he wanted to know if "Mr. Preacher" would baptize him?

The problem was where to find enough water close to town for total immersion. Warm Spring was too far from town to go there this afternoon. However, the cowboy said there was a cattle-watering tank about a mile outside of town if my dad would consider it. So the three of us drove to the place of baptism.

The cattle tank was a typical water hole for cattle in the southwest. A dam had been scraped up across a shallow arroyo or drainage to form a pond to catch rainwater run off. This particular tank had dried to where the muddy, shallow water in the center was surrounded by twenty feet of gooey clay. This gunk, which was indented with the hoof prints of cattle and mixed with their droppings, had to be waded through to get to the chocolate colored water.

My dad and the cowboy took off their shoes, boots, shirts and trousers, then waded through the mud and out into the brown water which was about knee deep. I could not hear all that was being said from where I stood on dry ground, but their voices increased as they floundered about in the water. Apparently the problem was getting the cowboy completely under. I remember hearing, "Have you had enough, Preacher!" And my dad's response, "I think the Lord will accept it."

As my dad told my mother while we were laughing about it later, "I'd get his head under but both knees would come up. He was just too big for that water-hole!"

Anyway, when the two of them waded back through the muck, they were covered with mud. Flies followed the smell into the car with us. Even now, when I smell cow dung and mud, I live again that day I went with my dad to baptize the cowboy.

Love from your Great-Great-Granddad, Sam.

SEVENTH

Dear Great-Great-Granddaughters and Sons,

As I said when I wrote you before, our family moved to Arizona where my father was minister of the Neighborhood Congregational Church south of Phoenix.

Because the weather was sweltering in summer and dry air-conditioning was unknown, the church closed during the month of August.

At that time, the southwest district of Congregational churches had just leased twenty acres from the United States Forest Service for a conference ground at Mormon Lake in northern Arizona. It was cool in the pines at 7000-foot elevation. The lake was located about 25 miles south of the town of Flagstaff.

It took us a long, full day to drive to Mormon Lake from Phoenix. On this trip we had two flat tires and repaired them beside the road. One flat tire was on Yarnell Hill north of the town of Wickenburg where the engine of the car had overheated from the climb. We had a canvas water bag hanging in front of the radiator but the engine still boiled out clouds of steam. The flat tire came at the right time to cool the overheated engine. The second tire repair took place where it was cooler in the shade of the pines beside the dusty dirt road bordering Lake Mary south of Flagstaff.

To repair a tire back then meant unloading suitcases, canvas cots and bedding from the running board in order to get at jacks and tools. Then, after the inner tube was patched, we took turns at the hand pump after the tire was assembled. We then repacked all the stuff we had stacked under the trees on the side of the road.

Today, automobiles do not have flaring fenders and running boards like they did when I was young, nor is the highway from Flagstaff to Mormon Lake the winding dirt road that turned into a muddy quagmire when it rained. Most highways are hard surface now. But when I was young, paved roads were in or near cities.

Compared to the heat of the desert, the summer at Mormon Lake, beneath the Ponderosa pines, which scented the mountain air with fragrance, was paradise for my two sisters and me. For ten years, as soon as school was out, we would all pack the car with bedding and groceries and leave the heat of the Salt River Valley for the northern mountains. My dad would then have to drive back to Phoenix, as his vacation did not begin until August.

In the mountains, all of our heating and cooking was done on a wood-burning kitchen stove. Cutting wood with a bucksaw and splitting it for the stove was one of my daily chores. On Saturday night we would heat water on the stove to pour into a galvanized, steel tub. Then, beginning with my younger sister, Alice, and then Delcina, each of us would have a turn taking a sponge bath. We left the oven door open to keep us warm while we dried ourselves.

Once a week I cut extra wood for baking. I would help my mother knead a great wad of flour-dough and she would bake four loaves of bread in the oven. Baking day was a treat because mother would keep out some dough to make scones on top of the stove. We ate them hot with melted butter. Today, people don't make scones like we did. Instead they buy English muffins, which are like scones, but not really. Not for me. Real scones have to be made with bread dough fried on top of a wood burning stove and eaten hot and fresh with real butter.

We ate a lot of fish in the summer. We ate catfish, ring perch and sometimes large-mouth bass that we caught in the lake. I also hunted rabbits and squirrels, which we ate, fried or stewed. Several times we had porcupine. In the 1930s it was believed that porcupines were harmful to the forest and hunting them for food was encouraged. Today we know better.

Anyway, I learned a lot about hunting and fishing in the mountains of northern Arizona while I was growing up. It was there I first tried trapping. Years later, in Alaska, I became an expert trapper, which I will write you about some day. However, as a young teenager in northern Arizona I trapped my first skunk and learned how potent their scent is. Here is what happened:

This particular skunk was caught by the leg in a spring trap set behind a large ponderosa pine log. I made the mistake of jumping up on the fallen tree when I came to check my trap. The beautiful skunk, with white stripes, quickly turned his backside toward me and sprayed. Its stench hit me in the chest and I felt suffocated, unable to breathe. With my .22-rifle, I quickly shot the animal and removed it from the trap.

By then I was sick to my stomach and took off my shirt. I kept trying to breathe fresh air by facing the slight breeze. It did no good. I threw up and trotted home. It was worse than being carsick. It was awful. I felt I couldn't breathe.

When I came in the door, my mother quickly sent me back out of the cabin to remove my clothes while she filled a tub with water. The soap and water helped. Then she put some fragrance in the tub to change the odor. The smell of the perfume was intolerable! It seemed suffocatingly like the skunk's scent. I was sick again.

For weeks afterward, odors which in any way resembled the smell of skunk scent made me nauseated. We dug a hole in back of the cabin and buried my shirt. Even after they were well washed, I was sure I could smell skunk in my trousers. I refused to wear them. Months later, when we drove past a skunk which had been killed by a car on the highway, I held my breath as long as I could until we were well beyond it in order to keep from throwing up.

Even now, many years later, I dread the smell of skunk and cannot tolerate the smell of many perfumes and fragrances.

On a recent camping trip, a skunk tried to crawl into my sleeping bag where I was sleeping on the ground beneath the stars. I was very careful to make no aggressive moves and said, "shoo" in a gentle voice. Fortunately, it continued on to another campsite. To this day I treat skunks with great respect.

My love to you. Your Great-Great-Grandfather, Sam

EIGHTH

Dear Great-Great-Grandsons and Daughters,

Arizona was a wonderful place to live while growing up. It was a world of adventure. I took delight in both the southern deserts and the northern mountains.

Among the pines and aspen in the mountains of northern Arizona, it was not only cool in the summertime but there was always the exciting possibility of finding an arrowhead or a piece of beautifully marked black and white pottery left by Indians who once lived here hundreds of years before.

In the winter, when snows closed the northern mountains, we went to school in the Salt River Valley on the outskirts of Phoenix. There, in the Valley of the Sun at Christmas time, the Bermuda grass had turned brown. However, winter rye grass was green like the glossy leaves of grapefruit, orange and lemon trees with their colorful fruit.

In the newly plowed fields along the ancient Indian canals, there was always the expectation of finding a polished stone ax-head, which was once used by the Hohokam Indians. I found my first one when I was ten years old. I still have it.

Today, when I climb the hills around Pleasant Valley, where I now live in Arizona part of the time, I still keep an eye out for artifacts from the ancient past. Today it is illegal to disturb them.

I am writing to you this morning in Pleasant Valley.

Here, beneath the Mogollon Rim in central Arizona, is where I built an Indian style house with local rocks and logs that I had sawed into boards. I purchased the timber from the Tonto National Forest and cut the trees from among the ponderosa pines in the forest that surrounds us. When I say Indian style house, I mean that it is like a Navajo hogan. It has six sides, which makes it more or less round, and a door faces the rising sun. Of course, you and I know that the earth turns into the sunrise and the sun does not actually rise.

Anyway, the door faces east and the rock house also has a door to the north and many windows, which the ancient hogan's did not have.

As I said, I am writing you today from this valley in the Sierra Ancha Mountains of central Arizona while I sit in the morning sun under a juniper tree by the front door. I have not always lived in Arizona. When I was a young man I was married a week after my twenty-first birthday. I left Arizona to live in Albuquerque, New Mexico and enrolled there in the University of New Mexico. Albuquerque was where my new wife, Jean, grew up and her former home in Albuquerque was available to us.

It was more than forty years before I again returned to Arizona. In the meantime I had traveled to Europe and other foreign places and lived and worked in Texas, California, Massachusetts, Washington, Oklahoma and Alaska.

I still think of Alaska as home, as well as Arizona, but wherever I am is home. Yes, home is wherever I am. I hope you feel that way too. And although I built this hogan home in Pleasant Valley, I still consider Koviashuvik in Alaska home. Koviashuvik is the Eskimo word for my home in Alaska. It is north of the Arctic Circle in the Brooks Range. I guess I consider it more home than any other.

Anyway, one of the reasons I wrote the book *Kovianshuvik: A Time and Place of Joy* was to tell how I discovered the meaning of home. *Four Seasons North*, by Billie Wright, was another book about the meaning of home and our life together in the wilderness of northern Alaska. Billie was my second wife.

I am now married to Donna Lee. She was Billie's friend. Donna shared in conducting Billie's memorial service and went with me to scatter her ashes at Koviashuvik in Alaska. Billie died at our home in Pleasant Valley, Arizona on Pearl Harbor Day, December 7, 1987.

Pearl Harbor Day is hardly remembered anymore. The Korean War and the Vietnam War and the Gulf War have happened since then. Pearl Harbor was once remembered as the day the Japanese bombed Pearl Harbor in Hawaii and projected the United States into World War II in 1941. That was over sixty years ago. Because it was so long ago, you will learn about it as history of the past. But history is going on right now. I wonder what is going on right now where you are? I guess I can never know because it hasn't happened yet.

In Pleasant Valley, when Billie was dying of cancer, she chose to leave on Pearl Harbor Day because, as she said, "It might be the beginning of world peace as Gorbachev, Premier of the Soviet Union, is visiting the President of the United States." With our satellite dish we watched Gorbachev arrive in the United States on television. We then drank a toast to the beginning of world peace and she died in my arms. As I write this, there is still no world at peace, and assisted suicide is illegal. I hope you are living in a time when people who choose to avoid terminal misery can legally do so. But mostly I hope you are living a world without war.

I'll write again soon across these years. My love to you.

Your Great-Great-Granddad, Sam

NINTH

Dear Great-Great-Granddaughters and Sons,

To give you some follow-up on my last letter, I was married to my first wife, Jean, at Mormon Lake in northern Arizona in June 1940. That same month I celebrated my twenty-first birthday and was eligible to vote.

The wedding took place at the Congregational Church's conference grounds among the pines. It was called Pilgrim Playground. Today the camp is owned by the Four H Club and has a different name. Kids from areas in the state go there for summer programs.

One of the cabins, which I helped construct for the Henry Austin family, is still there. I nailed on the wooden strips that covered the cracks between boards. We called them battens, and the cabin types were called "board and batten."

I recall how disappointed I was when I first saw one of these cabins when I was about nine or ten years old. I expected it to be made of round logs. The word cabin meant "log" cabin to me. I guess it is because I first heard the word cabin referring to the log cabin in which Abraham Lincoln was born. Since then I have built three real log cabins in Alaska.

Anyway, at our wedding ceremony at Mormon Lake, all the church conference attendees from Arizona, Texas and New Mexico were present. The minister from Jean's church in Albuquerque took part in the ceremony, along with a missionary uncle of hers. There was also the conference minister and my dad. So, with four clergymen participating, it was assumed that we were well hooked. I guess we were. Our formal marriage lasted twenty-seven years. We produced four children, two girls and two boys who are now grown-up adults. It is wonderful to have four kids grown up because I can remember them as children.

I do not know how to think of you since you are not born yet. I have to use my imagination. For you, however, they are either a great-grand-parent or a great-aunt or uncle.

Following our wedding ceremony at Mormon Lake, Jean and I stepped outside the board and batten meeting hall among the pines for photographs. Just as we were getting ready to pose, lightning flashed down on a great ponderosa pine tree under which we were planning to stand. Pieces of steaming bark showered over us, and our ears rang from the blinding crash of the explosion. Then rain began a downpour, which soon turned to large hailstones keeping everyone inside.

A cabin, which had been offered us for our wedding night, had not been checked out after the winter. It leaked. Our loving was more mechanical than romantic. I remember spending most of the night moving pans from drip to drip as new leaks developed. We laughed a lot.

The next morning was bright and clear as we drove south from Flagstaff through Prescott and down Yarnell Hill into Wickenburg, and then into the heat of the desert valley.

I had bought a used 1937 Studebaker coupe the year before. With bruised knuckles and grease under my fingernails, I had completely overhauled the engine. So now, being just married, old enough to vote, and with six new pistons purring under the long shiny green hood in front of us, I felt I had complete control of my destiny.

The reality was something else because Hitler's troops were marching across Europe, and events that I could not foresee were already shaping my future and everyone else's, including yours. And you were not even born.

At this time I was employed by the New York Life Insurance Company in their Phoenix office. The economic depression had made jobs scarce. I could not get time off for my wedding, so it was a short weekend. I left work Friday night and drove the hard miles from Phoenix to Mormon Lake. On

Sunday we were married and I had to be at work at eight o'clock Monday morning.

Like me, people at that time were still afraid of losing their jobs. The country was just coming out of the depression of the 1930s and to have a job and keep it was important to me. In fact, having a job at that time was so important that I worked under conditions I would never tolerate again.

My boss, the office manager of the New York Life Insurance Company's center in Phoenix, was called "Little Caesar" by the five or six employees. He demanded our time so that I was seldom free to leave before six or seven o'clock in the evening when we were supposedly hired from eight to five.

We never openly complained. We could be replaced overnight. Jobs were not easy to get. There was no overtime pay. I was both the mail clerk and did secretarial correspondence. I was even bonded so I could sign checks. Most important to me was the privilege of selling life insurance after hours. However, trying to sell life insurance on the side to make up income beyond my salary of sixty-five dollars a month was a lesson in futility, which I quickly learned.

At that time, the economy was only beginning to come out of the Great Depression. Like others, I had trapped myself in the idea that to have a steady job that seemed secure was worth intolerable conditions and poor pay. What I learned from this experience was that I was wrong. The search for security leads into an endless labyrinth of illusions. To keep myself reminded of this I have carved on the log roof purlin of my cabin in the northern wilderness of Alaska, as well as on a support beam of our home here in Arizona, "SECURE US FROM SECURITY NOW AND FOREVER. AMEN."

I soon left the insurance company to go to work for Standard Stations Incorporated. This was a chain of automobile service stations with headquarters in San Francisco. It was part of the Standard Oil Company. Within a year I was a top employee of the largest service station in Arizona on the corner of Central Avenue and Van Buren Street in Phoenix. We were open twenty-four hours a day with eight employees who wore starched, white uniforms and black patent-leather shoes. When a car came in for gasoline, an attendant washed the windshield and swept the floor mat while another was filling the tank and checking the oil level. If the customer was not in a great hurry, the air in the tires was also checked. All of this for the twenty-three cents per gallon price of gasoline.

Then we had a baby. Rather, Jean gave birth to a little girl in the hospital where I had been a medical aide when I was a pre-med student. We named her Patricia Jean. We sold the Studebaker to pay the doctor and hospital.

Patricia was seven days old when, on a Sunday morning, a customer pulled into the gas pumps of the service station with a worried look on his face. He said, "Listen to this," and turned up the radio in his car. "The Japanese have bombed Pearl Harbor."

I remember standing there while his engine was running, listening to the national broadcast. The reporter was saying that President Roosevelt was calling an emergency session of congress. It was like a dream, standing there in the December sunshine, leaning on the sill of the car door and wondering what the future might be for me, and all of us. It was both scary and exciting.

It was scary because the future seemed to have been taken over by events beyond anyone's control. And in a way, it was exciting for the same reason. It was exciting because the future seemed now to be unknowable and adventure lay ahead. This funny mixture of anxiety and excitement is still when I feel the most alive. I wonder if it is the same for you?

I'll write more later. My love to you.

Great-Great-Granddad, Sam

TENTH

Dear Great-Great-Grandsons and Daughters,

In my last letter I told you how I felt when I heard of the bombing of Pearl Harbor.

At that time I was riding to and from work at the service station in downtown Phoenix on a used Indian motorcycle that I had reconditioned. When my work schedule ended, I roared out into the desert hills south of Phoenix and careened along the sandy tracks for more than an hour in an attempt to settle the anxiety I was feeling. It didn't help.

With a new baby and the world at war, I spent a sleepless night listening to the radio and all of the rumors that were being broadcast, such as, "It is believed that the Japanese have an invasion fleet on the way to the Hawaiian Islands." And, "Seattle, San Francisco and Los Angeles fear the possibility of being bombed."

What began on this seventh day of December in 1941 not only dramatically changed and conditioned my life, but the lives of everyone else I knew. I left my job with Standard Stations Incorporated and decided to go back to college.

It was the next month, in January of 1942 that I arrived in Albuquerque, New Mexico with a wife, a month-old baby and driving a well-used 1937 model Dodge Coupe. In Albuquerque we had a place to live in Jean's old home on Gold Avenue. Several years earlier, Jean's mother had her home redesigned to include two rentals. We became caretakers, as her mother moved to a retirement area at Claremont in Southern California.

That same month, at the beginning of the semester, I drove up to the University of New Mexico to enroll in the biology department. I had been a pre-med student when I graduated from Phoenix Junior College and thought I might continue in medicine some day. I had no money for tuition. When I tried to register, I told the comptroller that I was available to work for it.

I remember the amused look on his face when he said, "You can't register without tuition."

He then asked, "Are you a native New Mexican?" Since I was born in New Mexico, I said, "Yes."

"Do you know about the Two Percent Scholarship?"

When I said I didn't, he told me there were funds for tuition for two percent of deserving New Mexicans. And if I wished to apply, he would consider my application.

I said, "What do I do to apply?"

He said, "Fill out this application for admission." And that is how I entered the University.

In time I got to know the comptroller, Tom Popejoy, as a friend. Years later he became President of the University of New Mexico.

While the world was at war, I was a full time student in the biology department of the university and got an outside job as housepainter with a contractor. My wife, Jean, also got a job as a music teacher in a consolidated high school twenty miles south of Albuquerque in the town of Las Lunas. She was the band director and also taught English in the Spanish-American community.

I took our two-month-old baby, Patricia, to school with me. On a Bunsen burner in the biology laboratory, I heated her bottle. She spent time in her basket crib in the Dodge Coupe, which was parked at the curb with the engine running to keep the car warm.

Several days after this, Dr. Koster, my embryology professor, discovered I had the baby with me and had me bring Patty into his office during class. Later, we hired a young Hispanic girl to stay home with the baby. She was our live-in house sitter while Jean taught school and I was working and attending the university.

Her name was Emma Salge. To us this sounded strange because Emma did not seem to fit her Spanish language and Hispanic background. Emma would make beds and wash dishes but would not clean a toilet. Although she had used an out-house where she grew up, she was very particular and fastidious about many things. She would not make a bed with sheets that were not ironed, nor would she taste or eat anything that was not familiar to her.

As I said, Jean was teaching school at Las Lunas and I was attending the university, so Emma would on occasion prepare dinner for us on days when we were late getting home.

By this time I was also employed as a laboratory assistant in the biology department where I was responsible for purchasing embalmed animals for physiology and anatomy classes. Because the nation was at war, many laboratory specimens were not available.

I acquired alley cats from the pound and embalmed them.

At that time I was also interested in falconry and had a large red-tailed hawk I called Acoma, named after the Indian pueblo, now called "City in the Sky," west of Albuquerque.

Meat was rationed because we were at war, so Acoma's food was alley cat. When skinned and quartered, this looked like domestic rabbit, which was not rationed and was popular in the meat market. I had some of Acoma's food in a paper bag in the refrigerator and had written on it with a bold marking pen, CAT. I never thought to print it in Spanish.

While we were eating supper one evening with Emma, who had prepared it for us, Jean said to me, "Where did you get the rabbit? It is delicious."

I said, "Emma did a good job frying it. I thought you bought it."

Then we both looked up at each other across the table and I quickly got up and checked the refrigerator. The paper bag labeled CAT was gone!

What was left of my "leg of rabbit" I carefully placed on my plate and noted that Jean's face had turned white. With a sickly smile she excused herself and left for the bathroom.

Emma finished her piece of "rabbit" with fastidious nibbles and smiled proudly at the compliment to her cooking. Neither Jean nor I said a word. Emma was too valuable to us as maid and babysitter. Privately, we did admit to each other that so long as we did not know what it was, fried alley cat was not bad, even tasty.

More at another time.

Your Great-Great-Granddad, Sam

ELEVENTH

Dear Great-Great-Granddaughters and Sons,

I am sitting in Paradise Valley Mall near the entrance of Macy's Department Store waiting for Donna to complete her shopping. Here I can sit comfortably and write to you while the temperature in the parking lot outside is over one hundred and ten degrees Fahrenheit.

It is a great place to watch people and see what they are wearing in this late June morning in the year 2000. Most people are wearing cotton T-shirts, shorts and sandals. However, baggy trousers with a very low crotch and white tennis shoes dominate among the teenage boys. They seem to all wear their "baseball caps" with the bill facing backward, and all appear to be chewing gum.

When I was in my teens, here in the Salt River Valley, there were no shopping malls. However, we did have our tight-fitting blue jeans style and would not be seen wearing a hat. I wonder what "styles" dominate your time and place?

When Donna and I were backpacking in the Andes Mountains of South America, we were aware that people came to the Zocalo, or central plaza of the village to walk about, shop, see and be seen. Mostly to see and be seen. This seems to be what is happening here at the mall today as very few people are carrying paper or plastic bags, and no one is smoking. In the village plazas of Mexico, and other South American countries, nearly everyone appeared to smoke cigarettes, cigars or a pipe.

When I was a student at Phoenix Junior College, shortly before the Second World War, the school had built a Ramada for us to gather in pleasant surroundings out of the sun. There, we shared cigarettes, ideas and philosophical perspectives.

Smoking in public today is considered gross and ill mannered. It is interesting to me that today clandestine smoking of marijuana has replaced tobacco as "the weed of friendship." However, beer, wine, or cocktails still grace our meaningful occasions.

I was a cigarette and occasional cigar and pipe smoker until I was sixty-eight years old when my wife, Billie, died. She was a chain smoker and we rolled our own cigarettes together in the wilderness of northern Alaska for twenty years. I discovered that for me, smoking was a relational, social habit. I have never smoked alone, and like so many others today, I am an ex-smoker and do not miss it. I wonder what patterns, habits, and forms are used to help relate people to each other in your time?

Here in this mall today, one relational device appears to be the portable, hand-held cellular telephone. Even so, I find it strange that so many seem to be talking to someone somewhere else, while shopping, strolling, or just sitting with a drink at a table in the fast food restaurant section. It is interesting to me that here we are all strangers except for the few who obviously came to the mall together. We avoid eye contact to keep our privacy.

From where I sit writing to you, I can look overhead through a great glass skylight at fluffy clouds breaking the expanse of blue sky beyond. Among the hundreds of people walking by, no one looks up except a child being pushed in a stroller. It was his attention that caught mine, so I looked up.

And there it is – real sky! Sky, which was not windowed by the architect in order to be seen, but to admit sunlight. Sunlight, which in today's technology still has no comparable replacement. I wonder if you find this your experience also?

What is reality? This has always been an interesting question for me. I remember fingering the leaves of what I thought was a living plant in a fast-food restaurant this morning and discovered they were plastic. "Unreal," I said to myself. But they were "real" plastic, just not real leaves.

A store across from me displays shoes that appear to be made of real leather. I know they are not. The floor beneath me "appears" to be stone and the plastic, green carpet in a booth beyond presents itself as grass. So what is real?

Is this a question you ever ask yourself?

This is one of the reasons I built a log home and moved into it in the northern mountains of Alaska. Somehow, I felt I was closer to what was real where I had to hunt and gather wild food and build my own house out of the trees growing there.

As I think about it, here in this huge mall, would it have been any less real for me if there had been a road into the northern wilderness and I had pulled an aluminum sheathed mobile home to the shore of our lake? What if I could do the opposite? Haul my log cabin here into this giant mall?

What is reality for you where you are? I wonder if you ever think about it like I do?

Oh, oh, I see Donna walking toward me. She is carrying a cardboard box under one arm and has a plastic bag in her other hand, so I'll close this letter and write more later.

My love to you,

Great-Great-Granddad, Sam

TWELFTH

Dear Great-Great-Grandsons and Daughters,

I last wrote you from Paradise Valley Mall in Scottsdale, Arizona.

As you probably remember, the reality question carried me away. Some people seem to be born questioners. I wonder if you are? I have often wished I had letters from a "born questioner" who lived long before I was born. His name was Socrates. He has been dead a long time, but so have you because you have not yet been born. When you read this, I will be as dead as Socrates but you will be alive and we will be connected through these letters.

Today, writing letters is becoming old fashioned. Most people communicate in writing with electronic mail on the Internet and do not call it a letter. When the communication is printed on paper, it is called hard copy. You will probably read this as hard copy, but in whatever form you receive it, it is a way I can talk directly to you wherever you are.

Today is June thirteenth, my eighty-first birthday. Since I have been around this long, I've been many places and done a lot of things. One of the places, which I have mentioned to you in several "hard copy" letters, is Koviashuvik.

I think I wrote you that Koviashuvik is an Inuit (Eskimo) word, meaning a time and place of joy. It is what Donna and I call our isolated home on the shore of a lake, north of the Arctic Circle in the Brooks Range of Alaska.

Koviashuvik is also the title of a book I wrote, which you may want to read some day. It will tell you something about our life in the northern Alaska wilderness, and how we visited the United States back then.

I say "back then", because I wrote the book thirteen years ago, and though the University of Arizona Press reissued it in paperback, much has changed since then. I cannot imagine the changes that will have taken place by the time you read this.

Anyway, I moved into the isolated northern wilderness after seven years as a professor in a graduate theological school in Berkeley, California. It was a dramatic shift from an urban San Francisco Bay area life to that of a subsistence hunter and trapper. I also had a new wife.

Billie Rose and I met at Starr King School. This was the graduate seminary in Berkeley, California where I was teaching. She was a middle-aged, special student, taking courses to explore the liberal ministry. This was in the late nineteen sixties when Berkeley and the University of California were in turmoil over the Vietnam War. It was also a volatile time of unrest, with psychedelic drugs, protest marches, "sit-ins" and "flower children."

Both of us were recently separated from our former marriages, and together we moved into our new life in the far north. For Billie, our subsistence life in the arctic was a unique and compelling experience. As a professional writer, she was intrigued by our wilderness life style. Her account of our first year in the Brooks Range became an award-winning book.

If you want to know what daily life was like in building a cabin and making a home in the wilderness, look for *Four Seasons North* by Billie Wright, published by Harper & Row 1973. It is a great story, which is real and true. Sierra Club Books re-issued it in paperback twenty years later after Billie's death.

At the end of the twentieth century, I wrote another book from Koviashuvik, titled: *Edge of Tomorrow: An Arctic Year*, published by Washington State University Press 1998. All three of these books can be located in any public library today.

For your information, I just turned on our TV satellite dish for today's news. The two top leaders of North and South Korea are warmly shaking hands after years of no contact between their separate governments following the Korean War. By the time you read this I hope that destructive wars will have become past history.

This handshake today, at the airport in North Korea, is one of the best birthday gifts for which I could wish.

It is strange being eighty-one years old. I feel the same as I always have. I find it pretty funny when I look in a mirror and see an old guy with gray hair and wrinkles looking back at me, while the person looking into the mirror seems only thirty-five.

I've read that Sigmund Freud believed that whatever the physical changes, no matter what the calendar states, whatever people think and say, you subconsciously remain pretty much the same throughout your life. I feel I'm still the person that I have been and will continue to be.

Today's science of the brain holds that subcortical structures are heavily involved in feelings. These systems apparently change very little with aging. Maybe this is why in general I find so many old people dull and boring to be around. It is not because they are old. They are just the same dull and boring kids I knew when I was in my teens.

There were dull and boring people back in Socrates' time in ancient Greece, and they are here where I am today. I suspect it is not because they are old. It is what they have always been. I'll bet it is the same where you are.

Will write again later.

Your Great-Great-Granddad, Sam

THIRTEENTH

Dear Great-Great-Granddaughters and Sons,

One of the questions people ask when they first meet is, "What do you do?"

What they really want to know is "Who are you?"

What they mean is, "What is your job or profession? How do you earn your bread?"

The answer to this question usually defines you to the questioner. From then on you are a farmer, broker, stonemason, teacher, trapper, pilot, professor, writer or whatever you acknowledge at the time. This seems sad to me because a person's identity is not the source of income or a title bestowed by an institution or society.

When I was trapping in Alaska I was a trapper. When I was in school I was a student. I do not consider myself particularly reverent, but I receive a lot of letters addressed to me as the Rev. because I have a graduate degree in theology and was ordained by a church I served.

So when I was once asked to identify myself for publicity in a public appearance, I said, "I'm an epistemologist."

"What is that?" I was asked.

I said, "I am a person who explores how he knows what he knows."

"Oh," was the response, "I thought it had something to do with the study of certain insects."

"Ultimately it does," I said, "It's a branch of philosophy."

There the conversation stopped. Since then, when asked, "What do you do?" when someone is trying to pin down who I am, I say, "I'm an epistemologist."

For me, the hardest question I know is "Who are you?" I suspect one of the reasons I'm writing you these letters is a way of finding out who I am.

I wonder who you are? Who you will be?

As I write this I am aware that a lot of what we do is a way of finding out who we are.

One of the things I did was sail in a small boat from the coast of British Columbia across the Pacific to Hawaii. Here is a bit from my journal during that trip:

What was it that called me to respond so quickly and affirmatively to this adventure? I guess it is that beyond interest in research or scientific rationale, it is an adventure. Adventures are not as plentiful as they seemed to be in the past. Besides, there is something I don' t want to miss. What is it? What is it I don't want to miss? I seem to have no adequate words for it.

For me it is stepping out into the unknown and meeting the new, a kind of risk taking. It is that quality which gives sharp meaning to our brief existence. I think I would find it sad if, as I came to die, I had chosen the other way.

At another place in the journal I wrote this:

The three of us have now sailed two thousand five hundred and sixty-nine miles across the Pacific Ocean in this thirty-six foot Cape George's Cutter as of noon today when we determined our location in this vast heaving sea. Within four days we should sight snow topped, 13,825 foot Mauna Kea on the big Hawaiian Island where we will put into Hilo Bay. Daryl is our Captain and his brother, Neil, is Bos'n. I am the amateur in this sailing crew, although I share the duties of the other two.

Officially, I am the biologist. And as I write this, sitting on the cabin, leaning against the forty-five foot mast, a school (or should I say a "covey") of flying fish soared from the deep blue roller in front of me and with fluttering pectoral fins, skimmed across the great valley of a swell to crash-land in the following white-tipped ten foot wall of blue water. I have had no experience in salt-water sailing. When I was invited to replace the third member of the expedition, a biologist who was also an experienced sailor, the question was put to me this way: "How are you with terror?"

At the time this was said jokingly. But looking back to the nights we hove-to in heavy weather, the word "terror" might not be the right one. But it could be said that we were "exceedingly concerned." I say "we," for my fellow crew members acknowledged their amateur status on the open sea as we climbed and slid down great waves under reefed sails in howling winds. Although they were well read on the subject, I was informed that they had about thirty hours of actual sailing experience. The biologist I replaced was the experienced seaman!

Anyway, here I am writing this after twenty-five days on the world's largest ocean. I feel I can now call myself a sailor.

After I returned I did not call myself a sailor. I still don't. I wonder if it is because I do not earn my living this way?

Your epistemologist Great-Great-Granddad, Sam

[Epistemology: The branch of philosophy that investigates the origin, nature, methods and limits of human knowing. –American College Dictionary]

✿ FOURTEENTH

Dear Great-Great-Grandsons and Daughters,

In my last letter I wrote about my sailing trip to the Hawaiian Islands. It was on that trip that I remembered I had briefly been there before. It was just long enough for the bomber to refuel before taking off to Guam. That was during World War II.

I was with the wartime Office of Scientific Research and Development, OSRD, in Albuquerque, New Mexico. This was the summer of 1945. Our work and activities were classified as "Top Secret." At the laboratories in Los Alamos near Santa Fe, sixty-five years later, much is still secret.

I wonder if this is so when you read this. I hope not. I hope this kind of secrecy is no longer necessary. I shall never forget that early morning glaring flash of light that lit the horizon south of us at White Sands Proving Grounds near Alamagordo, New Mexico.

As we young scientists talked about it, we felt a deep anxiety about the future, not only for us but the future of everyone. That explosion of "Trinity" shifted the path of my life.

When World War II ended so traumatically, involving those secret weapons with which I was involved, it left me with a continuing backdrop of the brutality of our human species. So much so that when I was released from OSRD I left my post at the University of New Mexico and purchased a house trailer.

With our two-year-old and four-year-old daughters, Roberta and Patricia, my wife, Jean, and I drove south to El Paso, Texas. There, we started a diaper supply laundry service and I became the second faculty member in the biology department of what today is the University of Texas in El Paso.

El Paso is where my first (hand-built) adobe house sheltered the A1 Diaper Supply Service and us. Since then I have constructed other homes from the natural materials at hand, from log cabins in Alaska, to our rock hogan where I am sitting in the patio writing to you today.

I should not say "our" rock hogan. The hogan is being purchased by my grandson, Rene Henery. Some of you are related to him, as his mother is my eldest daughter. Today, daughter Patricia is now an Education Consultant and has her office in San Francisco.

When Rene was young, he and his sister, Celeste, helped me pick up and haul rocks with which I built our hogan. Today, Rene lives in Seattle, Washington. He is part of a fast-growing, successful Internet bookstore called Amazon. When he heard we were putting our hogan on the market, he asked the name of our realtor and negotiated its purchase. In the meantime, Donna and I have our home inside the Arctic Circle in Alaska where we return every summer. We can remain here while we look for another place to build a different kind of house. Maybe it will again be in Alaska, but farther south where stepson, Kienan and his sister, Melea, are looking for land with others. We find this possibility exciting. But back to El Paso: It was in El Paso I gave up motorcycle riding.

I once wrote you of my interest in motorcycles when I was first married and living in Phoenix, Arizona. In El Paso, our adobe was on the other side of the mountain from the university. I had purchased a large twin Harley Davidson motorbike to commute. I already carried scars from earlier motorcycle accidents, but these were caused by errors or misjudgments on my part. On this particular Sunday afternoon I was leisurely motoring alone on a scenic, paved back road over swells and dips where it was not possible to see what was coming. As I reached the top of a rise, a car loomed up on my side of the road and I barely had time to turn into the rocky wash to avoid a head-on collision. My leg was pinned under the bent crash-bar of the bike. The car never stopped. Fortunately, some people with tools in a pick-up truck were driving along that lonely road and pried me loose. I was badly bruised, but my leg not broken.

Up to that time, I felt I was pretty much in control of my destiny. This close call was a lesson I never forgot. You cannot count on people driving on their side of the road even though you do. I have not owned a large motorcycle since then. However, the lesson I learned can be translated into many other situations. My sale of the big bike was aided by a professional motorcycle racer who said, "Sam, it's like a bomb. Every horse-power they add shortens the fuse over what you ain't got no control over."

There were also other experiences in El Paso that gave me a nudge toward epistemology and the liberal ministry. As a biologist, I was fascinated by what today we call ecology. When I was teaching biological sciences in the university, ecology was a term used only by biologists for a minor area of interrelationships in the field of botany. Today, ecology has broadened to become such an inclusive term that nearly everyone knows the concept.

Back in 1948, I discovered that my ecological--biological focus had expanded into many interrelated fields. I was asked to teach a course in sociology, which led to psychology and philosophy. I was also Director of the Counseling and Guidance Program Center for the U.S. Veterans Administration for returning servicemen at the university. It was through this position that I indirectly discovered the religious movement called Unitarianism.

Because I was Director of the Counseling and Guidance Center, I had been asked to speak about problems of the returning service men to a small congregation called Pilgrim Church in El Paso.

Following the forum, I picked up a pamphlet on a table near the entrance. It had a red question mark, surrounded by large, black print that read: How Do You Know You Are Not A Unitarian? As I read the pamphlet later, I was intrigued to note that historically identified Unitarians included Joseph Priestly, discoverer of pulmonary circulation who, back in the 16th century, was burned at the stake for his Unitarian heresy. I learned that Unitarian history included the deists, Benjamin Franklin, Thomas Jefferson, Tom Paine and others in American history including Henry David Thoreau. Also, there were transcendentalists such as William Ellery Channing and Ralph Waldo Emerson, who were Unitarian ministers. I immediately began an exploration of this liberal religious movement, and I planned to continue this exploration while attending the University of Chicago in Illinois, where I had been accepted for a doctoral program in biological sciences. However, I never made it to the University of Chicago.

Soon after our son "Chip" (named after my dad and me) was born in El Paso, we sold our diaper service, put our house on the market, bought a small trailer, loaded it with our stuff and headed for the giant redwood country of California.

I had written to my dad that I would be exploring the possibility of ministry while at the University of Chicago that autumn. Through the clergy grapevine, the Community Congregational Church in Cloverdale, California had acquired my name and address. They wrote me that they needed a summer fill-in. The stipend would not be much, but they had a large parsonage so we would be rent free, and they wrote, "The fishing between here and the coast is outstanding."

That did it! We would have a summer in the redwoods before the long academic haul in Chicago. So, with three young children we became an intricate part of Cloverdale. We settled in the large parsonage next to the brown shingle church in the middle of town on highway 101, one hundred miles north of San Francisco.

I have to water our apple trees now so will write again later. The monsoon rains should be here by the fourth of July when I can relax the watering tasks.

In the meantime, I hope you are having a fun summer.

My affection, Your Great-Great-Granddad, Sam

FIFTEENTH

Dear Great-Great-Granddaughters and Sons,

A television story from the San Francisco Bay area this morning was about a whale that wandered through the Golden Gate into the bay.

This reminded me of the time I saw a whale there. It was when I was fishing for striped bass and flounder. The whale surfaced and blew out air about forty feet from our small boat. At that time I was minister of the Unitarian Church of Marin, living across the Golden Gate from San Francisco in Marin County. This was more that forty years ago. My fishing partner was Mike Rado, an old geezer who was born in the 1880s and grew up in San Francisco. As an avid fisherman, he was delighted that "his minister" also liked to fish. He had an outboard motor and we rented a small boat in the part of the bay we chose to fish.

At that time, we not only fished for fun but it gave us an excuse to be out on the bay in the early morning. We brought our catch back for a fish fry with friends. Today people do not eat fish caught in the Bay as the water is contaminated. A few years ago, Lake Erie was so contaminated it was considered a dying lake. Conservation measures today have saved it. Pollution is a major problem everywhere in the world. I wonder about you. Is it a concern?

Donna and I still drink water from our creek and lake in arctic Alaska, but here in Arizona many people will not even drink water from their faucets at home unless it is filtered. Here in Pleasant Valley, we have a hundred and fifty foot deep well. We do not have a pollution concern.

Anyway, I started writing to you about whales. When I was living near San Francisco Bay in the nineteen fifties, there was still a commercial whaling operation in the East Bay which I visited just before it ended. Whale meat was processed for dog food. Whales are protected today. Their commercial value now is to be seen and visited by tourists who are taken on whale viewing boats out of the San Francisco Bay, or on tour trips to Scammons Lagoon in Baja California, Mexico.

Gray Whales gather in the shallow waters of Scammons Lagoon after migrating from the northern Pacific. Nearly forty years ago, before today's whale watching era, I visited the lagoon with a friend. We were exploring the Baja peninsula in his rugged, modified four-wheel drive truck. I say "modified" because he had a seat welded on the front fender where one of us would sit to guide the driver as we drove over trackless areas and through dry boulder strewn washes. Today, tourists drive there on a maintained Mexican highway.

Years ago, we were camped on the shore of the lagoon. It was exciting to watch the whales rise out of the shallow water and slap the surface with their flukes. It was particularly exciting, as we lay in our sleeping bags in the stillness of night under the stars, to be awakened by a loud splash and the rasping, wheezing sound when the huge, barnacle encrusted leviathan released air from her lungs. Other than the sound of whales, the desert stillness of the night wrapped us in a sense of mystery. It is not easy to have this kind of first-hand, intimate experience today. I imagine it is even more rare for you.

This is one of the reasons Donna and I return to our isolated cabin in the Brooks Range of northern Alaska every year. We look forward to that life experience which has a quality of intimacy with the natural world, and a sense of mystery, which seems so second hand and symbolic in our urban society today.

When I first flew into northern Alaska in a small bush plane on floats and was left ashore at dusk in the empty silence, it was both an exciting and awesome experience to know the nearest pavement or road of any kind was many miles south, beyond the Yukon River.

I try to imagine your time. It would be great if you could write me back from the future and tell me how it is for you. Since you can't, I can at least write you from the past, which is my present. I hope it is interesting to you.

The winter I was exploring in Baja was during Christmas recess from my professorial role in the Graduate Seminary in Berkeley. It was during the Vietnam War when sit-ins, marches and public protests dominated the university community. I was glad to accept the invitation to explore Baja and shift my environment. I felt under scrutiny by colleagues and my institution. They had reasons.

In November I had received an invitation from Ken Kesey and the Pranksters to join them on the night of Halloween at a gathering in South San Francisco where he had rented part of a large warehouse. He had invited The Grateful Dead rock band to play for the occasion. Kesey, who was well known for his book and the movie "One Flew Over the Cuckoo's Nest," had also invited the Hells Angels who were a loose-knit motorcycle gang. We were to come in appropriate costume.

I knew Kesey would be there as Mister America, the popular cartoon character in red, white and blue, with stars and stripes. As I seldom dress formally, I felt appropriate in a dark suit with a white, reversed, clerical collar.

The moon was bright as I walked from where I had parked my car. I could hear the heavy beat of the band through the open windows. A dozen motorcycles and their riders were in a group in the moon's shadow by the door. The glow of joints and the pungent aroma of pot came from the group of lounging bikers.

"Hey, Father! Wan'ta take a ride?" came from a big heavy guy half-sitting on his big chrome plated Harley Davidson bike.

Needless to say, I was apprehensive. The circumstances were such that I felt a refusal inappropriate. And it was Halloween.

So, with my arms around Tiny's beer belly and my cheek pressed against the sequins sewn on the back of his leather jacket, we roared off down the street in the moonlight. I remember the sparks when metal touched the pavement as we screeched around a corner. Then I could see the moon above the top of a warehouse building and I pictured a piece in the San Francisco Chronicle: "Unitarian Minister, dressed as a Catholic Priest, injured in accident with Hells Angels in South San Francisco."

Anyway, it was a memorable evening. The academic underground grapevine passed the story around that I was motorcycling with Hells Angels and the tale grew by the telling. I had already acquired a reputation for my dissent to the Vietnam debacle. So, you can see that the invitation to head to the deserts of Baja and the whales of Scammons Lagoon at that Christmas break was welcome. More than welcome!

Isn't it interesting that a story about a whale in San Francisco Bay on television this morning kicked off all this other stuff? As I think about it, while writing you, this is the way most people put things together while talking about them. Maybe this is why personal conversation and communication seems so much more connected to human reality than the formal, linear form of the usual written communication of academic papers and books.

In the long run, it all comes together and makes sense. In other words, a story. What do you think? Wish I could get your response.

My warmest,

Great-Great-Granddad, Sam

SIXTEENTH

Dear Great-Great-Grandsons and Daughters,

Caves and caverns have always intrigued me. When I was eight or nine years old, my parents took me to visit the newly opened caverns near Carlsbad, New Mexico.

At that time we were guided down ladders through a great opening. We then hiked on a trail by flashlight and a gasoline lantern. Our guide, who had been a local cowboy, was the person who discovered what is now called Carlsbad Caverns National Park.

When we reached a huge area far below the dim stalactites hanging above us, our guide had the flashlights extinguished. He then turned off the hiss of his gasoline lantern. We were plunged into an awesome blackness and silence.

After an unbearable period of time, I reached out through the smothering black and total silence. There was the assurance of my mother's arm. Then, the grating sound of a struck match broke the silence. Our guide's face appeared beneath his white sombrero as he lit the gasoline lamp. I let go of my mother's arm. I could still feel the thrill of that silent blackness and at the same time I felt like a sissy.

Since then, I have visited many caverns and explored abandoned mines. None had the drama of this early experience. Maybe this is why caverns still intrigue me. Maybe I am looking again for that first time experience. There is a word for it: "Adventure" – that sense of a first time experience.

My American College Dictionary says adventure is, "An undertaking of uncertain outcome; an exciting experience." For me, as an epistemologist, this is what gives my life its zest. What about you? Do you keep looking for that first time experience where you are?

One of the reasons I am writing to you about caverns today is because Donna and I visited one of the newest caverns recently discovered here in Arizona. The Kartchner Cavern is part of a new State Park. New to us, but of course not to you.

The cavern was kept a secret by its two discoverers until they were assured it would be protected for the future. That means for you.

It was only a couple of months ago, before the turn of the century 2000, that the cavern was opened to the public and we were there. Great care has been given to this living cave to prevent damage to its ecosystem. Environmental instruments are placed throughout the cavern to monitor the high humidity and moderate temperatures. At the entrance great doors are open for tours to move into a transition area. Ahead, another set of sealed doors awaits a returning tour while the doors behind are closed. Every fifteen to twenty minutes a tour passes underground along a half-mile path beneath the hundred foot high ceilings dripping with multihued stalactites.

Before entering the cave, a documentary video was shown to provide a substitute for those who did not have the time or inclination for the entire cave tour.

I suppose that for some, this carefully tailored display was a first time adventure. I tried to see it that way. I was interested in its unique hidden lighting. It reminded me of a theatrical show. I don't remember if music was being played as a background but it could have been. However, one steps out of a theatre into reality. Not the other way around.

A few years ago I revisited Carlsbad Caverns. It was over seventy years ago that I was there for that first time adventure I just told you about. Today the cavern is well lit for a self-guided tour. At regular intervals speaker boxes inform you of what you are seeing. I can't knock it for what it is, but for me it was hard to make an adventure of it. I wonder if you can?

I find it curious that after forty years, I find this first-time sense of adventure whenever we head north to our lakeshore cabin in the Brooks Range of Alaska. When I step off the small bush plane's float to the shore, I have that same thrill of excitement as the first time. The unknown seems to always be awaiting our arrival. I wonder why?

Is it because a grizzly bear might have torn up the cabin, as has happened a couple of times in the past? I don't think it is this kind of apprehension. It is a positive sense of expectation of what might be. It is a sense of anticipation, a sense of joy. This sense is there the moment the plane sets down on our sparkling lake among the familiarity of our craggy mountains. This is why we call it Koviashuvik. It is an Inuit way of saying "a time and place of joy in the present moment."

I hope you are finding your own Koviashuviks. If so, you know what I am writing about is a verb, not a noun. It is a becoming.

I am writing these letters to you as you are a becoming that I cannot imagine any more than I could imagine what being without light in a cavern was really like until it was part of my experience.

Enough for now. I have to change a tire on the pick-up truck. It picked up a nail on the thirty-mile dirt road into Pleasant Valley.

Your epistemology driven,

Great-Great-Granddad, Sam

SEVENTEENTH

Dear Great-Great-Granddaughters and Sons,

I have told you that I was a teenager in Arizona. This is not quite true because I rode a bus from Arizona to New England to attend a prep school.

My mother had attended Northfield School for Girls and my dad graduated from Mount Hermon. This was the boys' school five miles across the Connecticut River in northwestern Massachusetts. When I completed the eighth grade in Arizona, I had received a tuition scholarship to Mount Hermon. This was through my parents' connection with the school. They wanted me to have a good preparation for college.

I looked forward to the adventure of a three thousand mile trip across the United States by bus. At age fourteen, I felt like a self-confident man of the world.

The All American Bus Line had the cheapest fare from Phoenix to Albany, New York. It was actually to Rensselaer, New York, where my mother's cousin, John Hodecker, was superintendent of a woolen mill on the Hudson River. The Hodeckers had a son my age and I was to spend a week with them before taking a bus from Albany to Mount Hermon.

I would be on the bus day and night with one stopover for a couple of days in Chicago to visit the World's Fair. This was in 1933.

In those days, there were no facilities of any kind on buses. My bus made only one stop between breakfast and lunch, then another in mid-afternoon. By the second day I had learned not to drink a second cup of coffee. At home, I was not a coffee drinker. On this trip, I was a man of the world.

I remember being in agony having to pee. Finally, the bus stopped for a mid-morning break at a service station and cafe somewhere on the desolate flats of West Texas.

There were two out-houses behind the cafe, a "his" and "hers." They could accommodate one person at a time. I was the first person off the bus and reached the John in record time. I had been restraining myself so long that I could not relax and empty my bladder. While I was trickling, a long line of men were waiting. A harsh voice said, "Come on kid, I gotta go!"

In embarrassment, I stood aside while the splashing sound of others recreated my misery. That trip and my return to and from the school the following year was an education never equaled in all my years in school that followed.

When I visited the World's Fair in Chicago I was most impressed by a "Believe It Or Not" Ripley's exhibit. It was composed of live characters on elevated platforms with whom you could interact. One was a man born without arms. He used his feet and toes like hands to comb his hair. With them he held a book to read to us. Then, using his feet, he lifted a harmonica to his mouth and played "Dixie." There were many other anomalies, including a live two-headed calf.

I also took in the science exhibits, and saw Sally Rand do her famous Fan Dance with a minimum of clothing. This brought me back to her show on my way east the following year to see her do the same dance with her fan replaced by colored balloons.

In Rensselaer, N.Y, my fifteen-year-old second cousin, Jack, was a neat guy. We had a lot in common. His home was just across the road from the Hudson River. We skinny-dipped after dark in front of the Bayer Aspirin headquarters.

When I arrived at Mount Hermon, I was introduced to my roommate. We were assigned to a cottage where freshmen were overseen by house parents who lived downstairs. I don't remember his name. He was pretty dull. He knew nothing about girls and had never heard a dirty joke. I do remember that he changed the room around about every week when I was at a class or at the gym in the swimming pool. At the pool, I remember how startled I was that the boys all swam naked. It made sense because we were all males. I wondered if it was the same in Northfield at the girls' school? I learned that the girls were more modest and wore swimsuits.

My second year at Mount Hermon was far different from the first. I returned from Arizona to this protected enclave with all the worldly knowledge of a western teenager. I smoked on the bus as we rolled east, and had my .22 rifle tucked in the bottom of my trunk. My trunk was with the other baggage strapped on top of the bus.

The year before I had acquired the name "Arizona" among my schoolmates. Even the coach called me "Arizona" but not the teaching staff. A couple of older students came onto the bus before we arrived at the school and I shared a cigarette with them. Smoking was strictly forbidden on the campus. If you were caught smoking a second time you were expelled. The three of us were in high spirits as we threw our cigarette butts out of the window when the bus arrived after dark at the campus gates.

Red, white and green lights were flashing at the entrance. Massachusetts State Police cars and uniformed cops swarmed around us. Two policemen came on the bus and required us to validate who we were and from where we were coming. No one would tell us the reason for this somber meeting. Everyone was very serious. Finally after urgent questioning by the older student, a non-uniformed person who seemed to be in charge said, "There's been a murder."

It was only after we arrived at our dormitory that we learned the Headmaster, Eliot Speer, had been shot through the window of his study in Ford Cottage. Ford Cottage was the Headmaster's residence. Other students, who had arrived early, told us that there would be a search of the campus for the weapon. It was believed to be a shotgun. I spent a fitful night knowing

I had a gun in my trunk. It was not a shotgun. But I knew if it was found I was in real trouble. It was in living up to my reputation as "Arizona" that I had the .22 rifle in my trunk.

The year before I had become close friends with a day student who was from a nearby farm and did not live on campus. He trapped rabbits and woodchucks and introduced me to chewing tasty black birch and how to make potent applejack from fermented cider. In the spring I participated in his family's tapping of maple trees and boiling off to make maple sugar.

In return, I shared my western lore that he identified from the cowboy movies he had seen. In nineteen thirty-four, a cowboy actor by the name of Tom Mix was popular from coast to coast in movies which were then in black and white. I took on a Tom Mix style. It was through this classmate I became known as "Arizona." Also, through him my reputation spread among the students.

One incident in particular, reported by my day student pal to other students, was my skill at knife throwing. It really happened, but it was only this one time. These eastern kids were eager to hear first hand about the Wild West. I was not reluctant to satisfy their curiosity.

I am sure that among some there was doubt about my skills at riding bucking horses, tracking mountain lions and knife throwing. In Chicago, at a knife display, when visiting the World's Fair, I had purchased a beautiful, leather handled hunting knife with its scabbard. My student audiences assumed it came from the "wild west."

One day, when I was hiking with my day-student pal, a woodchuck stuck its head out of his den and peeked over the mound of dirt at us. I nonchalantly withdrew my knife from its scabbard, and as I had seen the knife thrower at the carnival area at the Fair in Chicago, I flung the knife end over end. It pinned the woodchuck through the neck. It never moved.

My New England buddy looked at me wide-eyed. I felt the same surprise. But in my Tom Mix style, I sauntered over and removed the knife, saying, "I guess we'd better skin it while it's warm."

As you would expect, the word spread. I was asked many times to demonstrate my skill. My response was that I never wasted a throw unless the target was real and necessary. Fortunately, that situation never arose.

I was also fortunate that the weapon search that followed the killing of Dr. Elliot Spear did not include my trunk in the dormitory basement. We students aided the state police in scouring the surrounding woods for the murder weapon, and watched the troopers drag the Connecticut River for it. It was never found. Nor was the murderer, or his motive. The school's dean was rumored to be under suspicion, and the Springfield, Mass. papers and Boston Globe made his life so miserable he resigned and moved to New Hampshire. He was my father's friend, and had been his roommate in college at the University of Illinois. Years later my dad and I visited Tom Elder in New Hampshire. He was bitter that as an innocent man, the press had crucified him. This was also part of my New England education.

I flunked Latin and barely passed algebra, but I did learn to put fermented cider outside the window in winter to make applejack and how to keep out of trouble. Or so I thought!

I've written too long. Hope you're not bored. More later.

Great-Great-Granddad, Sam

EIGHTEENTH

Dear Great-Great-Grandsons and Daughters,

It is the fourth of July 2000 here in Pleasant Valley. The news from our satellite television dish is about the election of the new President, Vincente Fox, in Mexico. It is the first shift from the governing party that has been in power there for over seventy years.

The negative morning news is that the Japanese are still harvesting whales. Japan would not join with other countries protecting them. I hope whales are finally protected when you read this.

Also in the news, the price of oil is at its highest. It is thirty-two dollars a barrel, and gasoline at the pump is expected to reach over two dollars a gallon this summer. Our Westfalia Volkswagen pop-top camper gets twenty miles to the gallon. Although our yellow bus is sixteen years old and its kind is seldom seen on the highway anymore, it runs great. It is our home away from home when we are camping

Tomorrow, Donna and I are driving to New Mexico to visit the place I was born. We plan to camp along the Mimbres River in the Gila Wilderness area, north of Silver City. If you ever visit there, I wonder what image you will have?

I am sure that the great open pit copper mine of Santa Rita will be a visitors' site, as well as the Gila Cliff Dwellings. However, the ranch of the G.O.S. Cattle Company, where I came back one summer to work as a cowboy, is already gone. There is little private land left along the Mimbres River. Cattle, in the past, were grazed on U.S. Forest Service land. Anyway, Donna and I will be looking for the possibility of another home site here in the lower forty-eight while we are camping there. Wish us luck!

Can that be done from the future?

But as I said, today is the fourth of July. It will be celebrated here in Pleasant Valley at a community barbecue with baked beans, beer, dancing to a country band and extravagant fireworks after dark. This show and feed has been put on for more than twenty years as a gift to the community by Charles Sherrill, an absentee resident who has a small ranch in our valley.

Years ago, my trail crossed Chuck Sherrill's when I was a student at Phoenix Union High School. Chuck's dad was a physician in Phoenix. Chuck did not follow his father's profession, but speculated in land very successfully. Now, we in Pleasant Valley all benefit each year on "The Fourth," when he has permission from the Forest Service to fill the night with a display of rockets, colorful flares and sky bombs.

When I was a kid, it was not necessary to have a permit to explode fireworks of any kind. We kids were out early in the morning of the fourth, creating a din with various explosions and the poppity-pop of "lady fingers" strung together along a common fuse. Before the huge, giant firecrackers were made illegal, a neighbor, who operated a zinc mine, would set off sticks of dynamite that shook the neighborhood. He gave us kids dynamite caps to explode. My schoolmate Henry lost three fingers to a dynamite cap.

Today, about the only fireworks kids can set off legally in the United States are hand-held sparklers.

This is not the case in Mexico. When we drive to Rocky Point, on the Sea of Cortez, venders sell fireworks right on the beach where it is "Fourth of July" any day or night of the year. I wonder about you. Can you at least burn sparklers?

I am sure that public fireworks make even greater displays where you are than are made today. But it is hard for me to imagine anything more dramatic than those of the millennium celebration displays shown round the world on television last January. Anyway, I'd like to share a fireworks celebration with you. What I can share is a Fourth of July I experienced not far from here.

I was eighteen years old. It was a summer job with a survey crew in the Sierra Ancha Mountains south of the Mogollon Rim. Because the land was so rugged, townships and sections had never been surveyed by The United States General Land Office. By 1938, no land in Arizona was considered unsurveyable. Our camp was packed in among the rock cliffs on mules. From these camp centers, we went out each day to cut Manzanita and oak brush. Then we would set up our tripod with its transit scope and the Rodman would set a target for us to measure by dragging a steel tape called a chain. With today's electronics, this technique is outmoded.

Anyway, the Fourth of July was a non-working government holiday. Our campsite, with its three canvas tents, was on a bluff above a narrow canyon that cut down to Cherry Creek, a thousand feet below. As I sat munching my breakfast, I became aware that rocks in the cliff across the canyon seemed to be in too regular an order. I went into the tent and brought out the transit telescope. There was no doubt about it. I could see it was the facing of a mud and rock wall built into a rocky cleft of the canyon. It was obviously part of an ancient Indian cliff dwelling. Fortunately, it was the fourth of

July so the day was mine.

Johnny McCue, my surveying partner, was as excited as I was. It took us three hours to descend and scramble up the steep, brushy canyon slope. And sure enough, it was an ancient cliff dwelling far beyond our expectations. There were three rooms built into the rock cleft, and one was a second story. There was a large packrat nest filling the back of the lower room. I scratched out an ancient sandal of woven yucca to bring back to camp. Its wearer had disappeared over eight hundred years ago. The foot that had once had it on was smaller than mine. As I stood there with the sandal in my hand, I felt so connected to its owner that I would not have been surprised if he (or she) had stepped through the cliff dwelling door. Johnny and I felt that we were the first to step inside the cliff house since it had been abandoned more than eight centuries before.

Fortunately, since then this area has been designated as the Sierra Anchas Wilderness to protect it. Other cliff dwellings have been discovered and recorded since. The area is as rugged as ever. Cherry Creek had a four-wheel drive road bulldozed down it to a mining operation during World War II, but it washed out a few years ago. However, no place seems isolated anymore, not even Mars, to which an expedition is already being planned. You probably know more about Mars than I did about Alaska when I first hiked into the Brooks Range seeking Robert Marshall's tree plantings north of timberline.

Anyway, discovering that cliff house years ago made that Fourth of July one I will never forget. I have to quit writing now and get ready to go to the Pleasant Valley barbecue and celebration. Wish you could be here to go with us.

Have a great Fourth of July, wherever you are.

Your Great-Great-Granddad, Sam.

NINETEENTH

Dear Great-Great-Granddaughters and Sons,

Humor has always intrigued me. What is funny to one person is deadly serious to another. I am afraid I see humor in just about everything. This can be a disadvantage if your calling is considered a very serious one.

Anyway, when I was minister of the Marin Congregation of Unitarians in the San Francisco Bay area, I recall a particular situation that stands out above many others. It was not really a funeral. But it really was a funeral if a funeral has to do with a death and the ceremony that deals with it.

The dead man was very heavy. He had no known relatives. Marin County had the responsibility of burying him in the rural Olema Cemetery.

In ankle-deep mud, the mortician and I jostled the wooden casket onto a collapsible dolly. Rain ran down our necks in spite of our hooded ponchos.

I knew the undertaker only from a striped bass fishing trip. He was a friend of a parishioner with whom I had occasionally fished. The three of us had once spent a day together on San Francisco Bay. From that I knew he was a mortician and he knew I was a clergyman. We talked about fish and fishing. He knew little about the liberal faith I represented.

On this dreary Saturday morning my phone rang, and he said, "Sam, fishing with you, I know you are an O.K. guy. I figured you would bury or marry anyone who needed it. Would you lend me a hand before this storm washes out the grave site we had dug yesterday?"

Rain had begun its drenching downpour during the night. Somehow this phone call sounded like an adventure. I said, without hesitation, I'd be waiting for him to pick me up with the hearse.

The Olema Cemetery was on a hilltop. The open grave was just below the crest. I pulled. He pushed. It was slow maneuvering. The small wheels of the dolly dug into the mud, and the side tipping of the heavy coffin didn't help. As I reached the open grave, I carefully stepped backward just as the mortician gave the casket a final shove. My left foot slipped out from under me. I was briefly poised on the edge. I grabbed at the wet coffin and plummeted backward into the grave with the heavy casket and its contents pinning me on my back on the bottom of the hole in several inches of mud and water.

I remember looking up into the gray sky with its falling rain. There, peering at me over the other end of the coffin was the undertaker. His face was a blur in his poncho. He fitted all the images I had ever seen representing death. He could have been a horseman of the apocalypse minus his scythe.

It was then that this crazy quote ran through my mind: "Death where is thy sting, grave where is thy victory?" I burst out laughing. After a pause, the apparition joined in.

After wallowing and heaving in the mud to haul me out, my companion became very somber, as if this had been no laughing matter.

We finally settled the coffin down in its muddy bed and shoveled enough soil on top so it would not float if the rain continued. As we started down the hill, the mortician stopped and said, "Don't you think you ought to say something over the deceased, Reverend?"

This was the first I had heard him use a term like "Reverend" and I could see he was quite serious. What could I say? I nearly repeated, "Death where is thy sting?" when I remembered lines from an old revivalist hymn. So, as seriously as I could, I said, "Be not dismayed what e'er betide." Then after a pause, "Amen." He nodded with solemn satisfaction.

Sliding down the cemetery hill in the mud, I wondered with whom I could share the hilarity of this very grave experience. I guess it is you.

I'm enclosing a copy of an essay I once wrote on humor so you can have a sense of my perspective.

Your Great-Great-Granddad, Sam

LIFE'S SAVING GRACE

The Mirror of Reality – An essay by Sam Wright

What is life's saving grace? That quality which helps in moments of monumental stress? In the presence of mortal peril? When we stand confronted with the world's multiple miseries and mountainous evils? When the torment of life's tragedy rises within us to confound and demoralize us? When terror or tyranny looms over us to enslave or destroy us? What makes life worth living?

Someone once offered a prize for the best answer to this question and it was won by the novelist Rafael Sabatini. He won it with this epigram: "To be born with the gift of laughter and a sense that the world is mad."

Somehow this epigram found its way to a place over the portals of the hall of graduate studies at Yale University under the impression that it was a quotation from the classics.

It was found that the architect John Tuttle put it there. When he was contacted later, he wrote: "A type of architecture that had been designed expressly to enable yeomen to pour molten lead through slots on their enemies below. As a propitiatory gift to my gods," he wrote, "and to make them forget by appealing to their sense of humor, I carved the inscription over the door."

The place of humor in the human heart has for the most part never been appreciated by philosophy or religion. In fact, religion has often taken a gloomy view of life. It is nearly a truism that laughing has been considered by theologians and philosophers to be some kind of crime. Perhaps this is because philosophers and theologians cannot afford to be laughed at. Laughter frees people from fear. And on the day that human beings began to laugh at hell, the gates of hell started to crumble.

In the introduction to his book, "Oriental Humor," R.H. Blyth writes that, "What the Buddha and Christ thought of humor is not recorded. Some suppose that Christ founded his church upon a pun in Aramaic. (In

Aramaic, the word Peter means rock. Jesus is to have said, 'On this rock I will build my church'). The Buddha seems to have used fables and parables for easier teaching; but neither strikes us as conspicuously a humorist.

"As far as the Buddha is concerned," Blyth wrote, "his disciples, like those of Christ, and indeed all disciples, were deficient in humor, and Asvaghosa, the great Buddhist of the end of the first century A.D. tells the story of Buddha-life in the Buddacanta like this: 'How foolish is the man who sees his neighbor grow sick, and old, and dead, and yet remains of good cheer; nor is shattered by fear, as when a tree bare of flower or fruit falls, or is broken, the trees around are heedless of its fate.'

"This is the very antithesis of humor," writes Blyth, "humor, which teaches us to laugh at sickness, at old age and death...most of all the last. To know one's fate, yet be heedless of it is to overcome the world."

What is this strange, spontaneous, curiously creative experience that we call laughter, that blessed saving quality known as "a sense of humor?" Researchers tell us that of all the creatures that dwell on earth, only human beings have this gift.

Not all people know how to laugh, that is, to really laugh inside. Many of them go through the motions of laughter, but a genuine sense of humor is lacking without which laughter is just an emotional reflex, primarily a learned reflex. The evidence of this is overwhelming whenever a competent stand-up comic performs.

When I was a youngster, I went with a friend whose father was an actor in a live radio show. Behind the performers stood a person with several large signs that he held up at appropriate moments. I remember two of them, there may have been more. One read, "Applause," the other "Laughter." Today, our operant conditioning is such that an audience doesn't need the signs. They can read the performer's verbal and gesture clues.

There is little doubt about laughter being an emotional reflex and that humor, as a form of release from fear, is evident in jokes and cartoons relating to death. I recall a cartoon by David Langdon that showed two tombstones side by side. One of them inscribed "HERS," the other "HIS."

Most people are afraid of death, and by laughing at it we make it less terrifying. If we could think up a really good joke about the absurdity of nuclear and chemical missiles and international posing, we might do more to cure humankind of its present jitters than all the conferences and comings and goings of diplomats combined.

The problem with humor, however, is that there is no sharp standard. What seems uproariously funny to one person can seem devastatingly unfunny to another. What is humorous to me, or tragic (personally, I often find it impossible to separate these two) is that it is impossible to convince an unbeliever that something is humorous by argument. The outward visible manifestations of my own amusement are no help either. I find it very hard to learn that when someone is not amused, like Queen Victoria, "She is NOT amused!" And to see this itself as funny (which sometimes really fractures me) is not the best personality trait if one is a clergyman.

In exploring life's saving graces, I have observed that down through the ages there have been basic humorous situations. Take, for instance, fat people. In all ages and in most civilizations they have been considered funny. Or take sex, which through the ages, in one form or another, has kept people amused.

I suggest that we laugh at a fat person because we see ourselves. We see ourselves in the image of the ludicrousness of life in the flesh. In laughing at the fat man who endeavors to leap on his horse to rescue the fair lady but can't quite make it, we are in fact laughing at ourselves, at the human situation as such.

In particular, this applies to jokes about sex. It seems to me that there is no more perfect representation of the disparity between human aspiration and human performance than in the curious means whereby we reproduce ourselves. Particularly with all of its emotions, conventions and theatricals. Sex is hilariously serious. It has made the actress Madonna a star.

Malcolm Muggeridge, who for years was the editor of PUNCH, the sophisticated British publication known for its cartoons, said, "I often used to wonder about those strange little grinning gargoyles with which the builders of Europe's medieval cathedrals decorated, seemingly so inconsequentially, their sublime edifices. Now I think I see what they signified. The gargoyles were cartoons. They, no less than the steeple or tower, expressed a sense of the briefness of time in relation to eternity, of the inadequacy of the flesh as a dwelling place for the soul, of the inherent inability of the works of man, however exaltedly conceived, to convey man's illimitable destiny. Moreover, again, like a cartoon, they were reassuring. They savored the disconcerting fragility of mortality with the salt of laughter, and introduced an earthly chuckle even into divine ecstasy."

I believe it was Muggeridge who said that, "Perhaps what the serpent really whispered into Eve's ear, inducing her to eat of the forbidden fruit was the first joke ever made on earth. And, that when the earth comes to an end (whether through the ministrations of politicians, biologists, or nuclear scientists, or by some other means) the last joke is likely to be along the same general lines as the first.

Something I have noticed in vehicles of humor, like the New Yorker magazine, is the treatment of myth as if it were reality. The Near Eastern clothed person riding on his magic carpet is the form in which we see this cliché most often. But others are Adam and Eve, the apple and the serpent, discussing the future of humans in the Garden of Eden; or the Southwestern Native American doing a rain dance to get himself a glass of water to drink. These point out something that is intriguing to me. The frequency of myth taken as reality cartoons in sophisticated magazines raises a question in my mind. What is it that intrigues the editors and readers in a cartoon that has no other point than treating a myth as if it recounted actual events? Or the shaggy dog story, a related phenomenon that has puzzled a good many people. Like the Arab floating on his rug, it depends for its point on an assumption we know to be false. In the case of the shaggy dog story, the assumption is that animals talk and act like humans.

Is it possible that this kind of joke reveals a deep-seated though largely suppressed desire on the part of people to rid themselves of myths? Is it possible that through such jokes we can see ourselves revealed in the mirror of reality as men and women haunted by myths of which we would rid ourselves if we could? To see ourselves "in the mirror of reality" – is there a more profound experience than this?

Here we are on this grain of dust among the stars, lost in the cold immensity of space, wounded by pain, confounded by frustration, beset by wars and rumors of wars and troubles of every description; yet we humans struggle onward, dare to smile, chuckle with our neighbor, and occasionally fling into the teeth of the universe's darkness a great gargantuan laughter.

Humor is the token of our innate confidence that no matter how dark and dismal things may appear, all is well at the heart of things. That even upon its worst terms, life can still be good and our spirit remains unconquered and un-subdued by fate. What is more a mark and symbol of confidence than our sense of humor?

An American submarine under attack in World War II was taken down to the bottom of the ocean while depth charges exploded all around. The men waited tensely, sweating it out, death in every depth charge. Suddenly, a croaking voice from an upper bunk said, "Anybody want to buy a good watch?" A roar of laughter followed. The danger of hysteria was gone. In a way, we could say that laughter had conquered the fear of death.

In this vein I think of the pathetic gentleman at the optometrist's who came to be fitted for glasses. He says to the receptionist, "I'm here because I would like to see things less clearly, please."

I remember a tempest in a teapot over a cartoon drawn for a church bulletin board at Christmas time. Three royally clad gentlemen in turbans were getting into a taxicab in front of a lone service station out on a barren desert. The last one to get in was dramatically pointing at the horizon, saying, "Follow that star!"

Which reminds me of the large sign in gothic letters in front of a church at a turn onto a freeway entrance. It read: "Last Chance To Pray." Or the bumper sticker I saw last week: "Nuke a godless, secular-humanist baby seal for Christ."

Humor is a pin to prick the balloons of pomposity, a hand to pluck the feathers of pride. It is a knife to cut out cancers of stupidity and to strip away the sticky solemnity that has no reverence in it.

Laughter is the challenge to all that remains unresolved and unmastered. Laughter is a weapon to cut tyranny down to size and make totalitarians uneasy on their thrones, for they can withstand every other weapon, but cannot endure to be laughed at. Laughter is a drill to bore into and reveal the hollow inner core of the idols we make, and are so quick to set up and serve, forgetting that they are creatures of our own fancies.

Humor is the courage of the cheerful heart, the cheerful heart that smiles when it feels like crying, looks at the flower among life's weeds, notices the beauty behind the ugly face, and the astonishment of stars shining through the darkest night. It is life's saving grace, for by it we glimpse ourselves in the mirror of reality, knowing that at the heart of things, confidence dwells. Confidence, strong enough to laugh. Confidence that knows itself invincible, confidence that is courage of the world's new morning vanishing forever the receding dark.

-S.W.

TWENTIETH

Dear Great-Great-Granddaughters and Sons,

When I wrote you about the "grave" incident at the Olema cemetery in Marin County I was reminded of how active I was at that time in the San Francisco Bay area.

Before I was called as the first minister to the newly formed Unitarian Church of Marin, we were living in Wellesley Hills, Massachusetts. From there I commuted to my office at 25 Beacon Street in Boston. I was serving as the national Director of Liberal Religious Youth. This was the newly formed college and high-school youth organization, which combined both Universalist and Unitarian young people throughout the United States and Canada.

In Marin County our family increased. There, Patricia, Roberta and Chip acquired a new brother, William (Billy), whom we now call Bill. He was born twelve years after his sisters and brother, Chip. Today, Bill is living with his wife, Mary, near Sebastopol, California.

Back then, we were living in a new subdivision north of San Rafael. We were surrounded by open hills. There, the dairy cows grazed and chewed their cud in the shade of scattered oaks. Most of our neighbors commuted across the Golden Gate to San Francisco or took a ferry to the East Bay.

I took on the task of growing our new congregation by immersing myself in the Bay Area Community. I was soon elected President of the Bay Area Community Council. The Council represented health and welfare organizations of the five Bay Area Counties that were funded by the Community Chest. The term "community chest" is not often used today. Back then, it was a fundraiser for many organizations, from the YMCA to health and welfare clinics such as Planned Parenthood. I wonder if Planned Parenthood is still active where you are now? I hope so.

I was also President of the Bay Area Funeral Society and served on the Board of Trustees of Starr King School for the Ministry in Berkeley. As I said, I was a busy guy, but it was fun.

During that time we started construction of our new church building. It was on a hilltop overlooking the new Frank Lloyd Wright Marin County Center. To keep sane and physically fit, I also dug a swimming pool with pick and shovel beside the patio of our home. As I write this letter, it is hard for me to believe I had time to compose sermons and participate in state politics as I did.

When Senator John Kennedy of Massachusetts was trying to be nominated by the Democratic Party as its candidate for President, I was invited to give the invocation at a fund raising dinner in San Francisco in honor of Governor Pat Brown. At that time we were encouraging Adlai Stevenson to run again. Adlai was defeated for the presidency by Dwight Eisenhower. I had supported Stevenson, whom I felt was uniquely qualified for the position. He was also an active Unitarian. However, Stevenson was reluctant to run again.

That night in the banquet hall, we ate at separate round tables. At our table, I was seated across from Governor Pat Brown and Senator Kennedy. After my invocation, Senator Kennedy asked me what denomination I was. When I said "Unitarian," he said, "I thought so. My speechwriter, Ted Sorensen, is a Unitarian. Do you know him?"

Then Pat Brown asked if I was minister in San Francisco? When I said no, he said, "My mother went there. When I was a kid I roamed all through that famous church. Isn't it interesting that Jack and I are Catholics, and have this Unitarian connection?"

It was following this dinner that the Marin County Democratic Committee person, Elizabeth Smith, who was a member of my congregation, phoned Governor Stevenson in the presence of others, to inquire if he was an active candidate. The report was neither yes nor no. That evening, the northern California Democrats left Stevenson to give their support to Senator John Kennedy of Massachusetts for President. The rest is history that you know about.

Elizabeth Smith was appointed United States Treasurer during the Kennedy Administration. And as for me, I found it amazing and adventuresome to have been in a time and place where future history was in the making and I somehow knew it.

Another time I felt fortunate to be where history was being made was in Washington D.C. when Martin Luther King Jr. gave his "I Have a Dream" address in front of the Lincoln Memorial.

I was leading a workshop at a church conference on the Monterey peninsula at Asilomar. I volunteered to go, and a collection was taken up to pay my way to represent the conference at "The March on Washington." I caught the next plane east. It was a privilege to have been there in person. Call me "Lucky Sam."

Another trip I took to Washington was to visit the United States Pardon Attorney, Mr. Reed Cozart, and the U.S. Attorney General on behalf of Morton Sobell who was imprisoned in Alcatraz as part of the anti-Communist witch hunt of the time. I was not so lucky on Sobell's behalf, but I did have a private conversation with the U.S. Attorney General in the hotel bathroom.

While I occupied a private stall during the hearing recess, I was asked by a voice from the adjacent stall about my opinion of what was going on. I expressed my views, and in our conversation felt the other shared my perspective. He seemed intrigued that I was from California, and, as he put it, "did not seem to be like those radicals out there."

I was surprised when it was the Attorney General who came over to the sink where I was washing my hands, and thanked me for my opinions.

When I returned to Marin County I gave a sermon on the Sobell case. It was printed in the denominational magazine under the title "When Conscience Speaks" and had wide distribution.

You have probably never heard of Sobell or the Rosenburgs. The Rosenburgs were executed for subversion. They were important symbols at a time in our country when I felt that individual freedom and freedom of speech were very much in jeopardy.

Today people are pretty complacent about everything. It is hard for me to imagine how uptight we were fifty years ago when I was the new minister of the First Unitarian Church in Stockton, California. At that time, the development of a hydrogen bomb was prominent in the news. I was as uptight as everyone else. A copy of a sermon I gave on Sunday morning May 21, 1950, titled, "The Hydrogen Bomb" was sent to Mrs. Roosevelt and I received a personal supportive letter from her.

This morning, while writing you, I remembered that I had a copy of that sermon in an old file. I dug it out. After reading it, I again became as concerned as before. As you know, the hydrogen bomb became a tested reality and will not go away. The questions it raised for me will not go away either. That twenty-minute sermon is too long to incorporate in this letter, but I'd like you to have it. I'll incorporate it as an attachment. It may give you a sense of the nineteen fifties.

Here in Pleasant Valley, on this beautiful mid-July morning in the year 2000, a pair of brown and white striped lizards are sunning themselves on the flagstone of our patio. The hummingbirds are enjoying the feeder hung from the branching juniper tree above. Last night, a family of elk again chewed up the newly fresh sprouting leaves on our apple trees. This is not their first visit. This is the fourth time they have waited until the new leaves re-sprouted before leaping the barbed wire fence in the night and enjoying themselves. We hope they will move up to the Mogollon Rim, now that the rains have arrived.

I'll stop now and get the attachment ready. My love to you,

Your Great-Great-Granddad, Sam

THE HYDROGEN BOMB

A Sunday morning address, May 21, 1950
First Unitarian Church; Stockton, California
Samuel A. Wright, Jr. Minister

*Of one thing beware, O man; see what is the price at which
you sell your will. If you do nothing else, do not sell your will cheap. –Epictetus*

There is a cartoon in the Colliers magazine dated the twentieth of this month, which pictures a man and his wife at their evening pastime –she at her knitting, and he reading his evening paper. The headline on the paper shows the word "H-bomb." Her remark is, "Now you see how silly it was to worry about the A-bomb."

I was in New Mexico in secret war work when the first large atomic bomb was released at Alamogordo, and had the opportunity (if you would call it that) to see the first pictures of the bombing of Hiroshima and Nagasaki when they were returned to show the physicists how well they had done their job. (The experience played no small part in my entering this profession).

The night before the Alamogordo bomb was exploded on a steel scaffolding, there were interesting conversations among us who were expecting we knew not what. It was among these young physicists that I first heard of hydrogen in the destructive terms of which we read in the newspapers today. In talking about the atom bomb, the conversation went like this: "If that amount of energy is released, hydrogen could easily be involved in the reaction and... Poof, the earth goes like an exploding star!"

This was a continual theme. And so, when in the early morning before a now historic occasion, the conversation of so-called cold, atomic physicists involved more than more than mathematical speculation, it involved families and friends... race relations and questions of good and evil.

When I was first released from my duties with OSRD, the Office of Scientific Research and Development, many groups were interested in the opinions of those who were connected with the Manhattan Project in any form. We were in demand for addresses before service clubs and church groups. It was only a short time later that the public attitude could be expressed in the words of a woman who came up to me after I had spoken before a church forum. "We all know about the bomb, and I for one have heard all I want to about it. It seems to me that we can hear something pleasant for a change."

There are some facts, or what surely seem to be facts, for us to face as men and women who behold the possibility of worldwide atomic war. I am sure that we would all like to put our heads in the sand or pull the covers over our head and say it is just a bad dream. But as those who call themselves Unitarian, we must without hysteria, or fatalism, do some serious thinking – not only as individuals, but also as a religious institution. H-bomb warfare so utterly repudiates our convictions as free men and women with moral values that we abdicate reason and conscience if we surrender to those who plan and defend this planet-wide Armageddon.

There are those who say we who protest the H-bomb exaggerate and feed the fires of hysteria. I assure you this morning that I hope to appeal to reason; this is no time for hysteria. As William Lloyd Garrison, the great abolitionist said, "To speak of atrocious crimes in mild language is treason to virtue." And certainly the crime is atrocious when humanity itself is at stake.

In the face of such an issue, one's personal convictions on planned economy, or on the limits of individual freedom in a modern state, or the amount of recognition one must have to feel contented are relegated to their places of lesser importance. I am a minister in a Unitarian Church because I am convinced that the imperatives of ethical religion must be asserted as paramount. Men operated the jet planes which roared over our city yesterday. Young men, whose job is to follow orders even if they come from a subhuman primitive savage who can only express himself in our terms so he may hold an office of responsibility.

Our emergency committee of atomic scientists drew up this statement several years ago, which seems to be forgotten in our present world reaction.

1. Atomic bombs can now be made cheaply and in large numbers. They are and can be made more and more destructive.
2. There is no military defense against atomic bombs and none is to be expected.
3. Other nations can rediscover our secret processes by themselves.
4. Preparedness against atomic war is futile, and if attempted, will ruin the structure of our social order. (This process has begun.)
5. If war breaks out, our atomic bombs will be used, and they will surely destroy our civilization.
6. There is no solution to this problem except international control of atomic energy and ultimately, the elimination of war.

From this it is clearly seen that the intelligences who discovered atomic fission and then manufactured the bomb see no hope for the survival of the present civilization unless effective international control of atomic energy is realized; which means, the yielding of large areas of national sovereignty to an effective world government for the abolishment of world war.

This pulpit is one dedicated to the wisdom of every faith and creed and prophet; no voice of truth or love is alien to it. As I have the privilege to speak the truth as I see it, so you have the right to judge. I make no apology for my uncompromising statements this morning. If they are not pleasing to your ears, perhaps I am doing my job better than I realize. For a person who is content in today's world has lost all sense of moral obligation.

Those of you who read Pat Frank's book "Mr. Adam," recall how he makes fun of our insane power madness in the face of imminent death. Other writers have been doing the same, leaving the question of whether or not mankind is worth saving. For myself, I have no such cynical doubts. Civilization is worth saving. And, I might add, that in no time in human history have people had a greater right to hope for betterment and a greater incentive to work for improvement.

Let's look at the picture on the positive side. Our work is clearly cut out for us. As far as each of us is concerned, our getting along or living in the world as part of a society to be saved is to create a world government, world law, world court, world police force, outlawing atomic energy for human destruction, abolishing war and controlling atomic energy for human creative use in all the world. Here is a practical program. Practical because it is necessary for survival. And anything less is the most impractical idealism. Right now! At least once in history, radical idealism, which has always been called impractical, is the practice necessary for survival. The alternative is a falling rain of atomic bombs. (And if what I hear of the possibility of using hydrogen is halfway accurate, a rain of bombs would be superfluous.)

There is no substitute, as I see it, for the practical necessities I have outlined. Oratorical trickery will not prevent bombs exploding. Propaganda won't do it and may (as it seems at present) hasten it. The biggest army won't stop the bomb, the armed forces show we saw this weekend, implying the need for more planes, tanks, guns and battleships or a two-ocean navy may bring the fall sooner rather than later.

Treaties between nations – Atlantic pact, or what-have-you, will not stop atomic bombing. Only world government with teeth in it will furnish world law and the outlawing of the destructive use of atomic energy. World government is the positive, practical goal of all peoples of intelligence and courage and good will. Good will should be the aim of everyone who bears the name Christian or Jew or who accepts the principles of ethical religion. Yet – for all our work to have it otherwise, the hydrogen bomb may be built, and it may fall. Many worked for years to prevent the last war's destructive bombing; and yet it came. And so it may be with the hydrogen bomb.

If that statement disturbs you, if you are annoyed to hear me say aloud what may very possibly be the future; I can only say that I'd rather, in the name of vital realistic religion, have you now prepared against possible failure than to have you shocked into surprised neuroticism which is already doing its job of ruining lives.

People are talking and thinking about when the bomb falls. One of the real estate advertisements in the Bay Area, to persuade persons to move to Walnut Creek, tells prospective buyers to consider when the bomb falls. I know many people are already minor neurotics, worrying about when the bomb falls.

The bomb has already fallen.

It has fallen on Nagasaki and Hiroshima and on America. In Japan, one atomic bomb killed almost forty thousand persons in two square miles. Twenty thousand people to the square mile! That was Nagasaki. And in America – for imaginative and informed minds, the bomb has fallen with a sickening, prolonged explosion in their hearts. That is why people who are looking back on their life efforts are asking: "Was it worthwhile?" That is why there are distracted faces and haunted eyes over barroom tables. That is why millions are now looking seriously for a savior in the form of a Second Coming of Christ. That is the reason the attitude among so many young people is: "What is the use?" Or – in the words of a recently popular song: "Enjoy yourself, it's later than you think."

We have all asked the question whether clearly or not: What about us? What about me? Suppose the goal of world peace controlled by international law was too high a goal and the time to achieve it too short? Suppose it falls on our families, our friends, and destroys our civilization? How shall we act if it is really to happen? How shall we act now? Between now and then? Not two or five or thirty years from now, but now?

I am asking you to stare death in the face this morning. To face the end of civilization. How shall we act in the meantime?

You may think this is a sordid question, or one which is shockingly new, raised by the discovery of atomic fission. But let me assure you it is an old, old question. Plato's dialogues abound with the question. And, of course, bombs caused no human death in his day.

Plato might have put the question: "What will you do with your life?" And Aristotle asked, "What ends are worthy a wise man?" And Marcus Aurelius and the Buddha and many more have suggested that a person has not started to live thoughtfully until he faces the fact that some day he will not live at all. Jesus asked of what avail it was to gain the whole world and lose one's own significance.

Even if we achieve a world order and outlaw the hydrogen bomb and it never falls on you or on anybody, old age will make its claim, or disease, or an accident. The hydrogen bomb or old age – it is the identical question that foresighted people face. Our children will sooner or later die, and so will our civilization. How to live before one dies is an old, old question.

As I said last Sunday, the way I think one should live between now and eventual death is to realize that we all possess a treasure, and that treasure is life itself. Our life, given to love, to dream, to contemplate, to be a part of other lives. Life is the gift. Life is the miracle. And if you have it in you to appreciate the gift and to wonder heartily in your heart at the miracle of life, you will not find it difficult to accept the fact of death, hydrogen bomb or old age. Life is the miracle, death the fact. And to use that miracle for all it is worth of loving, striving, understanding, studying and playing, trying and searching.... and in the whole process to enjoy the moments of creativity as they flit by, is to be worthy of the miracle of life.

I think we should live as if life were sacred, as if life were a responsibility, as if life were a constant attempt to change fearing into trusting, hating into loving. We should live striving to change a warring world into a peaceful world. Our joy in life ought to come to us not because we succeed or fail. Creative joy in life is the accompaniment of trying to reach goals we set for ourselves.

Atom bomb, hydrogen bomb, or whatever may result, I am going to have fun.

I am going to have fun trying to see what my little brain and these feeble hands can do to turn this instrument of destruction that I helped to create into a creative use for all. I will sweat and complain, maybe; gripe sometimes; I shall have the pain, pleasure and thrill of creativity, in trying to change world chaos into world government.

This sermon in a sense has been in vain if no one here writes or telegraphs the White House their protest of the cold war. I urge you, irrespective of your political or economic faith, to write or wire Dean Acheson, or the President, demanding an end to this catastrophic arms race.

As far as I can understand it at the moment, the pain, pleasure and thrill of trying anything you think as the highest worth is the best way of honoring the miracle of your own breathing organism. Death or the hydrogen bomb is not the important thing. The most important thing is your life. Interrelated and somehow in some real sense inseparable from other lives. Try to make it creative for all it is worth. Try because you ought to try. And when you are tired with the thrill of trying, enjoy a meal, read a good book, play a game, go fishing, talk with your friend, make love to your mate, play with the children, lie in the sun, dream of another angle for tomorrow's trying. But for the sake of the godliness that is in you, don't lie in your bed at night stiff and tense doubting your own personal ability to create a world government in time to prevent a hydrogen bomb from dropping. The world of living, of life and death has not changed. It is the same as it was in Jesus' day, when facing the same question he said "And as ye would that men should do unto you, do ye also unto them likewise."

Living creatively is a matter of conscience; a matter of relationship between you and your conscience. Theodore Parker, Unitarian minister and reformer in the early 1800's said, "I think lightly of what is called treason against a government. That may be your duty today, or mine. Certainly it was our father's duty not long ago. Now it is our boast and their title to honor. But treason against the people, against mankind, against God is a sin not lightly to be spoken of." Amen.

Sam Wright

TWENTY-FIRST

Dear Great-Great-Grandsons and Daughters,

When I was about eight years old I had my first ride in an airplane.

It was a World War I biplane with two open cockpits. The pilot sat in one and we two kids were strapped in the other. We were too short to see out when the plane was on the ground.

There was no airstrip. The landing field was open range along the railroad tracks on which a coal burning steam engine pulled cars of copper ore from the mill in Hurley to the smelters on the Mexican border in El Paso.

My friend, Oren Wingfield, and I were being given this ride for passing out leaflets through the town offering an air show on Sunday, with acrobatics and a parachute jump. Following the show, passengers would be taken into the sky for $2.00 a piece.

It was early morning as I was finishing breakfast when the roar overhead brought us running outside. People all over town rushed out for the rare sight of these two double-winged aircraft that droned low over their houses before landing west of town.

It was Saturday. No school. Oren and I were among the first to arrive where the two pilots were checking the engines of their aircraft. We hung around all morning asking questions and becoming friends with the barnstorming aviators. This is how we got the job of passing out leaflets for the promise of a free ride.

I'll never forget that first flight. Since then I've spent many hours in small planes in Alaska and have a rating as a sailplane pilot. But that Saturday afternoon, strapped in an open cockpit, could never be equaled.

I vividly remember holding my breath as the pilot of the other plane pulled the propeller in an attempt to start the engine. Our pilot would yell, "Contact!" The other would answer, "Contact," and pull the propeller. Nothing happened. I let out my breath. We could not see out very well, mostly the sky overhead.

Then, on the third try, the engine caught and we were engulfed in sound and vibration. As we taxied across the rough ground for the take off, I was so excited I nearly peed my pants. I found out later that Oren did, but not at take off.

When we lifted off, and the pilot banked us over the town, tears streamed down my cheeks as I looked down on people out in their yards waving at us. There was my yard and my parents waving beneath us.

The other thing I remember about that ride was rolling upside down with our shoulder harness holding us in. It was scary. This is when Oren said he peed his pants. I recall little of the maneuvers in the sky that afternoon, but I was hooked. Someday I would be a flyer.

On Sunday afternoon, when the crowd had gathered, cars were lined up on the flat across the railroad tracks. I am sure the whole town of Hurley was there and also the mining town of Santa Rita. I felt like I was a part of the show. I had passed out leaflets, flown over the town, and the aviators called me Sam. Up until that time my parents and other kids called me Sammy. I have been Sam ever since.

I wonder if you ever changed your name to one you liked? I've known a lot of people who have, but not until they were grown up. Our daughter, Roberta Anne, changed her name to Bobbianne when she was an adult. Since our oldest son had my name, which was the same as my dad's, we called him Chip, ("off the old block.") We still do, and so does he.

Anyway, the air show began with the pilots circling each other in a mock air battle. The loser tipped over on one wing, spiraling down in a tailspin so close to the ground everyone held his breath until he pulled up. Then the other bi-plane roared head high toward the crowd and the line of cars. It pulled up and over at the last moment. They did other dives and rolls before landing to prepare for the climax. This was to be the parachute jump.

It was not a jump. Today, people do jump from the open side door of aircraft as a sport. Their parachutes are in a pack strapped to them. In 1928, the parachute I saw was a big, white bundle shoved into the front open cockpit. Mike, the parachutist, crawled in with it after cranking the propeller for the take off.

After they were airborne, circling above us, we could see Mike crawl out on a lower wing with the white bundle bunched against him. The plane circled higher and higher as we all watched.

Dr. Hanks had a pair of field glasses, which he passed around. With them I could see Mike with that bundle of parachute held between his stomach and the wing strut.

After what seemed an eternity of circling and climbing, a cry came from the crowd. A great white parachute billowed out behind the wing. It appeared to pull the stunt man off as the plane moved ahead. Then the parachutist rocked to and fro beneath the great white canopy, and everybody clapped and hollered and honked their horns.

Today, parachutes are of a different design, and people parachute jump for fun. Paragliding is popular at the Girdwood ski resort, west of Anchorage in Alaska, where our young family and friends work. They can take off from a mountaintop and catch an updraft, keeping them aloft to soar like an eagle.

It was soaring that intrigued me as far back as I can remember. Hiking into the cliffs above the mill town of Hurley, and lying on our stomachs on the edge of a bluff, we kids could look down on the back and outspread wings of a great turkey vulture as it circled below us, tipping from side to side to keep in the updraft. When I was young, I used to have dreams in which I was soaring. I wonder if you also have such dreams. I had one last night, which ticked off this letter to you.

When I was a teenager, my dad drove me out to the open desert north of Phoenix to see a glider launched. It was from Germany and had been promoted in the local paper. Its German pilot was there to demonstrate it. With its long tapered wings and a black swastika symbol on the tail rudder, the white fuselage was in sharp contrast to the somber green of creosote bushes that surrounded us.

With no engine, I was entranced when a long elastic cable attached to the back of a pickup truck, with a winch on its bed, launched the glider. The glider caught a thermal lift and soared above us. Again I was hooked. Someday I would soar.

I was then unaware that the swastika on this glider would soon represent evil after Hitler's Germany went to war. Before the Nazi regime, this was a southwestern good luck sign, adapted from early Native Americans who broadcast it on their pottery, blankets and artifacts.

Anyway, years later, when I was a professor in the Graduate Theological Seminary in Berkeley, California, I became a serious sailplane addict. Soaring above San Francisco's East Bay helped keep me sane during the Vietnam War with its protest marches, student unrest, innumerable meetings and academic concerns. At least once a week I would drive to the glider field and hook up to a tow plane. At fifteen hundred feet I would release below Mission Peak and soar with the eagles who nested there. It produced the following, which was published in the Soaring Magazine:

Watch the birds, they know the updrafts

Taut went the towline, we were airborne toward the ridge.

> At eighteen hundred feet, a pull on the release
> and I soar free in the rising air climbing
> to three thousand feet in the surging lift.

Above:

> The clean lines of a white sailplane
> passing its shadow across the sun.

Below:

> A golden eagle slides across my path
> as I sail along the ridge toward its peak
> where jagged rocks stand sheer against the wind.

Back and forth along the cliffs, soaring in rising air over the canyon below.

The bottom drops out, the air sinks!

Pushing the nose down to gain more flying speed in the steep turn my wing tip skims within a few feet of rocks and trees.

A gust of air lifts us over the canyon edge into open space.

There is the Eagle turning with me.

We tip toward each other. He banks away.

And I, smiling, turn on a wing and soar home.

More another time,
Your Great-Great-Granddad, Sam

TWENTY-SECOND

Dear Great-Great-Granddaughters and Sons,

Yesterday we had our neighbors over for Mogollon drinks and dinner. They are older people with grandchildren like us.

Oh yes, a "Mogollon" is a drink we make with tequila. It includes grapefruit juice and a sparkling lime beverage served ice cold in a salt-rimmed tumbler. Mogollon Rim is the name of the seven thousand foot high escarpment above our Pleasant Valley that extends east into New Mexico

Our neighbors have a grandson in prison for his association with a crime. They needed to talk about it. In the conversation, they asked me, "Have you ever been in jail? Do you know what it is like?"

My response was, "Not here in Arizona." Then I told them of my three days in a Juarez jail in Mexico when I was an older teenager. It had none of the amenities of jail in the United States. I thought you great-great-grandsons and daughters might be interested in my experience, so here goes.

That summer, I had hitchhiked from Phoenix to Hurley, New Mexico. It was to visit with a couple of friends I had known in grammar school. One was the doctor's son, Fred Hanks, and the other, Jack Jones. Jack's dad was an assayer in the copper company. We thought of ourselves as cool guys of the world and decided to visit a girl and her family who had a ranch near Chihuahua in Mexico.

We hitchhiked (with a lot of it hiking) to El Paso, on the Texas, Mexico border. There, we crossed the Rio Grande River by paying a two-cent toll to pass over the bridge to Juarez. As a border town in the late nineteen-thirties, Juarez was where anything imaginable was possible, from smuggling guns to white slavery.

To help control venereal diseases that crossed the border from Mexico, the military at Fort Bliss, near El Paso, had constructed a section of brothels. These cubicles were rented at a reasonable rate to the girls with the provision that they be medically checked and free from venereal disease.

From the number of service men in the bars in Juarez at that time, I suspect this effort at disease control was minimal. There were no effective vaccines then. At that time, AIDS or HIV were unknown. Syphilis and gonorrhea were the problem.

Today, in this year 2000, AIDS has been compared to the bubonic plagues of the past. With no known cure, it is sweeping the world. A news broadcast this morning reported that fifty percent of the population of South Africa was HIV positive. I hope and assume that when you read this letter, that particular disease is history. Anyway, Fred, Jack and I decided to become hobos. We decided to ride a freight train to Chihuahua, about three hundred miles south. We hiked to the railroad yards. There, an empty cattle car was slowly pulling out. We clambered aboard.

I remember little of the ride south across the desert that night. Sometime before dawn, the train stopped at a water tank and corrals. We got off and wandered a short distance down a wash where we built a fire and opened our bedrolls under the Mexican stars. We talked about our adventure, and then fell asleep.

The sun was shining brightly in my eyes when I was awakened by a voice in Spanish ordering us to get up. "What are you doing here? Where is your passport?"

Jack had better Spanish than I did. He said, in an authoritarian tone, "We don't need passports!"

The four or five Federales who accosted us in the wash were very impressive. They had rifles, cross belts of ammunition over their shoulders, and aggressive gestures of authority. They took us on a passenger train back north to Juarez.

Our wallets, and what few dollars we had in them, had been taken from us. Without any judgment or hearing, we were put in the Juarez jail. In those days, it was called "the tank."

The only amenity in the tank was a seat-less toilet. There was a faucet from which you could bend over and get a drink. Whenever someone was picked up by the police in Juarez for any reason, he was thrown in the tank. Our days in the tank were experiences I never again want to repeat. But what an education!

Drunks that had literally been hauled into the tank slumped on the floor in their own vomit and filth. I remember one guy who was shoved through the iron barred door. He tried to smile at us. He was bleeding profusely from his mouth. A tooth pierced his lower lip. "Buenos Noches," he said, and collapsed on one of the bare beds where he did not move until morning.

In the morning, a guard washed out the cement floor with a hose attached to our drinking faucet. This did little to change the odor of urine and excrement.

Jack, our Spanish-speaking representative, was not much help. He was belligerent from the first. He threatened the Federales, guards and police with what would happen to them when his father found out about this. He kept repeating that his dad was an important man with much authority and would call the Governor. Jack's threats were usually greeted with a satirical "Si, si, hombre."

On the third miserable day, we were given our wallets with all the money and identification gone. With much persuasion from Jack, we were given the few centavos needed to cross the Rio Grande Bridge into the United States.

Jack and Fred went immediately to the El Paso Copper Company office where arrangements were made for their return home. Although I was penniless, I wanted to make my own way back to Phoenix. With the assurance of youth, I felt I could get a job in El Paso and make my way home independently. After a good meal with Jack and Fred, they loaned me a dollar and we said good-bye.

I headed to a construction site across the street and asked about employment. The foreman laughed at me. "Son," he said, "I can hire ten Mexicans who know what they are doing at less than a dollar a day. However, I heard they are looking for an elevator operator at the department store across the street. My wife works there. Why don't you check it out?"

At the store manager's office I was asked if I had experience operating a public elevator. I said, 'Yes." I had watched operators pull the "up and down" handle to stop the car at different floors. I was sure I could catch on quickly.

"What was the name of the elevator you operated?" I was asked. I said I didn't remember. The manager walked me across the hall to the elevator and pointed to the iron threshold in front of the door where, OTIS ELEVATOR CO., had to be stepped over to enter. He said, "Sorry, son. I need someone with a better memory."

I did get a job that evening. It was on Alameda Avenue in a cafe called Molino Rojo, the Red Mill.

I went into the restaurant for a tamale and drink. Just before I was ready to leave, there was a confrontation between the owner and dishwasher, who stomped out swearing in Spanish. The owner told me his troubles. I asked for the job, and became the dishwasher at a dollar a day. Also included were my meals and a bunk bed in a back room of the restaurant.

I learned a lot about smuggling and underground dealing, during the next few weeks at the Molino Rojo. It was not my world. And it was with relief that I left on a bus for Phoenix. I swore to myself that I would never again return to El Paso. I thought of it, and Juarez, as a hellhole.

Years later, after World War II, I returned and learned to like El Paso. The circumstances were different. I was a faculty member of the College of Mines and Metallurgy and owned and operated a diaper supply service.

Today, babies' diapers are disposable, with names like "Pampers." When I was a baby, people bought diapers by the dozen and folded and washed their own. When we moved to El Paso from Albuquerque, I met a returned veteran who sold me his large supply of diapers with which he had planned to start a business. He could not acquire washing machines. They were scarce following the war. Jean and I were fortunate in locating two new machines and a large used dryer. With these, we started the A1 Diaper Supply Service. It was the first one in El Paso. We were so successful we had to contract with the El Paso Laundry to keep up with the demand.

When the University (The College of Mines is now called University of Texas in El Paso) added a Guidance and Counseling Service Center for returning veterans, I was appointed its Director. This was in addition to my teaching role in the biology department. We sold the diaper service for what we had invested in it.

It was at this time in El Paso that I was active in the Junior Chamber of Commerce, became a Third Degree Mason, discovered liberal religion and the Unitarian faith. But more about that some other time.

With affection, Your Great-Great-Granddad, Sam

TWENTY-THIRD

Dear Great-Great-Grandsons and Daughters,

Scientists recently announced they have unlocked secrets of the human genetic code.

Genetics was the area in which I was accepted for a doctoral program at the University of California in Berkeley over a half century ago. At that time I would have been working in genetic modification of tomatoes for uniformity in size, form, and resistance to spoilage when the autumn semester began.

We had moved from El Paso to the small community of Cloverdale, California north of San Francisco in the redwoods country. I had been called as summer minister of the community's Congregational Church. The brown, redwood shingled church building was in the middle of the village on Highway 101.

I wonder if the highway still continues north through Oregon and Washington when you read this?

Anyway, the large parsonage, next to the church, gave all the space we needed for the five of us. The baby in the family was Chip. He was born in El Paso.

Last week's announcement that genome researchers have mapped the genetic code is, to me, the most significant happening at the beginning of this twenty-first century. It implies that disease might become a thing of the past. It could mean the elimination of birth defects and stop the aging process, even manipulate intelligence.

Back in the autumn of 1948, as I drove south through Petaluma and San Rafael to catch the ferry across San Francisco Bay to attend the university, the unknown genetic code was much on my mind. Also, the meaning of life.

Life's meaning had taken on new dimensions for me following World War II, and the birth of the atomic age. I had enrolled as a graduate student, studying for the ministry at the Pacific School of Religion. This was to justify my role as minister of the Cloverdale Church. As a theological student, this also gave me a dormitory room next to the university.

In Cloverdale, I preached on Sunday, and carried out my professional duties. Then, early on Monday I left for Berkeley. In Berkeley I attended classes, did my library study and laboratory work before driving home at the end of the week to enjoy my family. The end of the week also included calling on parishioners, committee meetings, and preparing Sunday's sermon-address.

Before fall classes began at Pacific School of Religion and the University of California, it had been a wonderful summer break, exploring the redwood country between Cloverdale and the Pacific Coast.

Harley Grove, a young father and member of the church, was the State Game Warden. His territory covered the many square miles of rivers, creeks and uninhabited coast. There we fished and dived for tasty abalone together.

Harley was born in Cloverdale and his father had been the Game Warden before him. He knew the best places to angle for sea going, steelhead trout. He took me where the deer were fattest and tastiest. He was delighted to have me accompany him on his patrol rounds. I gave our time together high priority.

I also gave high priority to the newly created Starr King School for the Ministry in Berkeley. The former Unitarian West Coast Seminary ceased during the Second World War years, and was being recreated with a new name and a radical program for its time.

Having been Director of Guidance and Counseling for the Veterans Administration at the College of Mines and Metallurgy in El Paso, I shared in the structuring of the new program for Starr King. A decade later I became a permanent professor on its faculty. It became a model for other graduate schools. I was its first graduate in its new program, along with my class-mate, Jack Kent, in 1950. More than fifty years ago seems a long time to me. I cannot imagine how long ago it seems to you.

Anyway, I dropped my doctoral program in biology at the University of California for a new one being created under the departments of Psychology, Sociology and Anthropology. I also officially registered as a Starr King stu-dent in our new graduate program and continued my graduate studies at Pa-cific School of Religion. In 1949 I was a full-time student in three graduate school programs as well as minister, serving the Congregational Church of Cloverdale, where I had a wife and three children awaiting me on weekends.

From here in Pleasant Valley, fifty years later, I cannot imagine running at that pace. It does astonish me when I look back. I did not feel rushed then. It was all adventure.

That sense of adventure, seeing for the first time, or seeing the old in a new way, is for me what gives life its zest. As I write to you, I hope what I am trying to share can somehow be sensed as a kind of adventure.

Today that sense of adventure still intrigues me. It is why I am writing you. I guess I really wish you were writing to me telling me what I can only dimly imagine might be in your time and in your life.

Anyway, after graduating from Starr King, I was called by the First Uni-tarian Church of Stockton, California and was ordained as its minister. I continued to serve as Chairman of the Admissions Committee of Starr King School in Berkeley, and was Regional Vice President of the Unitarian Fellow-ship for Social Justice. This was a tense roll at the time as I was teaching a night class in the Junior College.

At this time, both in Stockton and the State of California, the fear of communism had created such paranoia that the state legislature had passed what was called a loyalty oath. It was a requirement of all teachers, employed by the state, to sign a form that they were not and had not been a member of the Communist Party. If you did not sign the oath, you would lose your job. There were a number of teachers in our church including the Superinten-dent of Education. In the climate of the times, there was great resentment in having to publicly deny being a member of a political party to which you might belong.

One politically naive member of the Communist Party, who taught art in night class, lost his position, as he could not sign the oath that he was not a member of the Communist Party. All other teachers in the district signed it. I refused to sign it, but continued as an unofficial, unpaid volunteer to continue my Great Books Class. You would not believe the letters I received directly and otherwise from those who said this proved my un-Americanism, and that I should be deported to Russia.

It all sounds silly today, but it was very serious at the time. I hope this is as much past history for you as it is for me.

Tonight the crickets are chirping in the moonlight, and coyotes are singing songs on the hill beyond. It is after ten and we must get up early to pack for our trip north to Koviashuvik in Alaska. So I'll say goodnight and write more at another time.

My warmest to you.

Your Great-Great-Granddad, Sam

TWENTY-FOURTH

Dear Great-Great-Granddaughters and Sons,

I'm writing you this morning in mid-July while sitting on a bench in front of the Safeway grocery in Payson, Arizona. Payson is our shopping center, over sixty miles from Pleasant Valley. Thirty miles of it is uphill on a rough dirt road before it connects with major highway two-sixty.

Across the huge, busy parking lot from where I sit, the highway traffic is dominated by motor homes, cars, and pick-ups pulling boats and trailers on their way to lakes and resorts.

When I was a kid, living in the Phoenix area, Payson was a small, isolated mountain village. Today it is a vacation boomtown where the local Indian tribe has built a gambling casino on the main highway to relieve tourists of surplus income.

In the early nineteen sixties, when I visited my Navajo friend in central Arizona, Indian reservations were recognized by old, abandoned cars and rutted dirt roads. They are now recognized by new casinos with flashing neon signs and crowded, paved parking lots.

My Navajo friend was a member of the large, extended Begay family. We were in the University of New Mexico together where he earned a PH.D. in anthropology. Following the Second World War, our paths crossed again when I read a paper he had written in a scientific journal. I tried to get in touch with him and found that he "had gone native," moved back to the reservation.

As I said, it was in the early nineteen sixties when I drove my Jeep from Berkeley to Kayenta, Arizona on the Navajo Reservation, trying to find my friend. In Kayenta, I was given general directions over the many dirt roads to Begay's hogan. It was nearly dark. After miles of branching dirt tracks, I pulled up to a corral of sheep and goats next to a dark, round hogan. It was Begay's.

He introduced me to his Navajo wife, who nodded with a shy smile and returned to the loom where she had obviously been working on a half-finished, classical red, black and gray rug.

However, it is the conversation we had that night that I want to tell you about. We talked into the early hours of the morning about his return to a primitive life style in Navajo land.

I told him that I had heard he'd gone native, and that former colleagues questioned his mental health. Why had he left his hard earned faculty position to return to a dirt floored hogan without electricity or running water?

He said he had nothing against electricity and modern plumbing. He said, "I had a nice home near the campus, but these were not what I spent a quarter of my life to acquire."

I asked what he wanted to acquire?

He told me that when he was given an academic scholarship, he saw it as a chance to become someone people respected; that he felt it an honor to be accepted in the white academic world as an equal. He said, "I was told many times that I was an example of achievement for my people. Not just the Dinneh (Navajo) but all native Americans."

During that late night conversation in the lantern lit hogan, I remember asking why he had chosen anthropology for his doctorate study? He took a long drag on his cigarette and watched the blue smoke float up to the juniper poles of the ceiling. After a long pause, he said, "I guess I didn't choose it. It chose me. In my academic field, I learned that what I was seeking was not indoor plumbing or academic honors. It was something much more subtle and meaningful. I guess you could call it a way of life."

He looked past me to where the colorful rug hung on its loom.

"It's the kind of life that gives a person a sense of wonder, so that each activity is not a task but an opportunity."

We both sat in silence for a while, and then he said, "As a student of life styles and people throughout history around the world, I kept coming back to that question you asked. 'What is it you want to acquire?' Well, I acquired all those things that the commercials and others say are success: Enough money to live well and status in my field. However, the question that kept bugging me was where is the good life?"

He stood up and walked to the open door of the hogan where I could see the stars glittering on the horizon beyond him. He turned around to me and said, "Sam, I guess what happened is that I discovered that meaning was richest in the life I knew here among these red sandstone hills. Do you remember the question people have asked from earliest times? 'Where is the good life?' For me, it is here in the beauty of my familiar world."

Since that evening in Begay's hogan, I have often thought of that phrase, "In the beauty of my familiar world."

In the silence that followed, I thought of the sandstone towers of Monument Valley and billowing clouds with summer rains and the hushed silence beneath sparkling stars. I said, "I hear you loud and clear, Begay."

Where is the good life? I was reminded of this question and also that visit to my Navajo friend, when I looked up from my writing to you to see the car loads of vacationers heading out to acquire the good life this week-end. Where is the good life for you where you are at the time you read this? For me, like my Navajo friend, it is in the beauty of my familiar world. But I ask myself what I mean by "familiar."

According to my dictionary, "familiar is knowing intimately." By this definition, I guess the beauty that is most familiar to me, is not in this Safeway parking lot, or where the week-enders' highway leads beyond, but in a time and place of joy called Koviashuvik.

It is there that Donna and I will soon be in the beauty of familiar surroundings on a lake we know as intimately as ourselves. I will write you from there. In the meantime, I hope you are in the beauty of you own familiar world where you are.

My love, Your Great-Great-Granddad, Sam

TWENTY-FIFTH

Dear Great-Great-Granddaughters and Sons,

I'm writing you this morning from our cabin on the shore of an arctic lake in Alaska. The air is wet from the cloud cover that dropped down to obscure the surrounding mountains. The floatplane bringing us in had to fly over eighty miles up the river valleys from Bettles airstrip. We flew a few hundred feet above tree level to reach our lake, which is deep in the mountains of the Brooks Range.

As I believe I have written to you before that we call our home in the Arctic Circle, "Koviashuvik," a place of joy. It is certainly that this morning here in our snug cabin. I wish you could be here to enjoy it with us.

However, it would be a bit crowded as there are four of us here. Besides Donna and me, my grandson, Rene Henery and his friend Bryce Mather, flew in with us. They are employed by a large Internet bookstore in Seattle, called Amazon.com. Because their time is limited, the bush pilot will fly back next week to pick them up.

I wonder if this dramatic range of mountains across northern Alaska will still have its wild mystery when you read this.

Yesterday, a grizzly bear ran up into the spruce forest as our boat approached the shore. Later, a lone caribou came within fifty yards of the cabin and a wolf sang a short song from across the lake.

Donna and I are delighted that these young men have had a first hand experience of a fast disappearing world. They caught three great northern pike and participated in their preparation before we cooked them for supper on the Yukon stove.

It was unusual for a caribou to be here this time of year. They migrate in herds over the mountains to their summer calving and breeding grounds near the Arctic Ocean. The wolves accompany them there. However, there are always a few stragglers left behind. Of course the grizzly is at home here, although he does wander about at this time of year seeking blueberries and lingonberries. We had blueberries in our sourdough pancakes at breakfast this morning.

People still speak of the Brooks Range as a wilderness. However, there is now a road called the Dalton Highway, which crosses the mountains west of us to the oil fields of Prudhoe Bay on the Arctic Ocean.

When I first hiked into this wilderness, there were no roads. The nearest pavement was hundreds of miles south in Fairbanks. I had to fly into this mountain vastness in a small bush plane that could set down on a small lake where I was abandoned with my companion, David Scheyer, a photographer and theological student at the seminary in Berkeley, California where I taught.

With our backpacks and rifle, we began more than a hundred mile hike and exploration of the range seeking Robert Marshall's tree planting plots. Thirty years earlier, Robert Marshall had planted seeds of white spruce beyond northern timberline.

This was my excuse for the hike into this wilderness. It was to locate these small tree-planting plots and ascertain whether or not they had grown. You can read about Bob Marshall's tree seed plantings in his journals, titled: ALASKA WILDERNESS, published by the University of California Press in 1970. I am mentioned in the introduction to this edition by his brother, George Marshall, who wrote:

"If the great wilderness of the Brooks Range and of the Upper Keokuk in particular are to be saved, many more individuals and organizations in and out of government must speak up now, and many have done so. One of them is Samuel A. Wright, biologist and former professor of social ecology at a graduate theological seminary. He and his wife are spending a second winter in an isolated cabin at Big Lake in the eastern Koyukuk Drainage. In his testimony on the proposed trans-Brooks Range pipeline and road at the Interior Department hearing at Fairbanks, August 26, 1969, he warned of the fate of the Brooks Range wilderness unless people speak out. He said: "We have chosen to live in this last great wilderness, disturbing it as little as possible and becoming a part of its ecology. One reason for this choice was the recognition that at this moment in history this great wilderness is doomed unless voices speak out in its behalf. And, certainly, a voice should come from the wilderness itself."

Bob Marshall, after whom the Robert Marshall Wilderness in Montana is named, died suddenly in his late thirties. He never followed up on his seed planting experiment in this wilderness. So, about thirty years later, in 1966, I hiked into the mountains near the top of the range to find his seed plantings. Using his journal notes as guide, we found his carefully marked plots. There was no sign that the seeds had ever sprouted.

Two years later, with my new wife and wilderness companion, Billie Rose, I back-packed one hundred white spruce seedlings into Bob Marshall's plot on Barrenland Creek where we planted them north of timberline to help confirm his theory that northern timberline, here in the Brooks Range, was determined primarily by the length of time the trees took returning north following the last ice age, rather than the severity of weather in this northern climate.

Twenty years later, after Billie's death, my new wife, Donna Lee, and I were flown by my friend Steve Lewis, in his floatplane, to a small lake on the summit of the range. From there, Donna and I hiked steep Dall sheep trails through mountain passes to Barrenland Creek where Billie and I had planted one hundred four-inch white spruce seedlings. We found five of them still alive, not much taller than the seedlings I had planted there in 1968, twenty years before.

I started this letter to you over a week ago. And as I write you today from our isolated log cabin, is does not seem that it was over thirty years ago that I resigned from my professional role, moved into these mountains, and built our log home on the shore of this sparkling lake. Little has changed here. At that time a floatplane left us with our supplies on the shore, then as a speck it disappeared into the blue over the mountains. Our nearest neighbor is still a two-day hike over the mountains, and grizzly bears are as much a concern as they were when I was first here. We still catch our summer meals of lake trout (char), great northern pike and grayling. When here for the winter, it is moose, caribou and ptarmigan. We bring flour, sugar and other staples in the floatplane with us.

So here Donna and I sit across the table from each other in our cabin. She is sewing pieces for a quilt and I am writing across the years to tell you how it is for us at home in the Brooks Range in this summer of the year two thousand.

Last night a grizzly bear cleaned up the char and pike fish remains we put out some distance from the cabin for ravens and gulls. When I say "night," I actually mean when we are asleep. It never gets dark north of the Arctic Circle at this time of year.

Anyway, the bear did not awaken us, but its tracks this morning told us to keep alert. We wish the bear had come to visit a couple of days ago before my grandson was flown out by the bush plane that brought us in earlier. Rene had only a week's vacation from his position with Amazon.com. It was his fist opportunity to visit our remote home and he and his friend had a great time fishing and eating fresh great northern pike and lake trout. At least he had the opportunity to hear a chorus of wolves howl their song outside the cabin one night.

Donna and I expect to stay here at Koviashuvik until just before freezeup in mid-September. Today is the second of August, and our daily chores, both outside and in the cabin are now calling us. I'll write again later and keep you informed of what is taking place here. In the meantime, my warmest best,

Your Great-Great-Granddad, Sam

TWENTY-SIXTH

Dear Great-Great Grand Sons and Daughters,

Here at Koviashuvik the arctic terns swoop in front of our shore cabin in their effortless dips to scoop up insects from the surface of the lake.

My grandson, Rene, was fascinated to learn that these birds, who hatched here on our shore, would be dipping along the Beagle Channel of Terra del Fuego at the tip of South America a few months from now. We told him about our back-packing trip in the southern Andes mountains several years ago. Our key reason for that trip was to see where our terns had flown eleven thousand miles to avoid the winter cold and dark. Donna and I call them "birds of light." Not just because they follow the sunlight, but their whiteness when the sun shines through their wing and tail feathers as they hover is so light and beautiful.

It was fun having Rene here with us even if it was less than a week. He might even be your great-grandfather when you read this. He will be twenty-six years old in December of this year 2000. One of the first things he did on arrival was hook a great northern pike, which Donna cooked for supper. I remember the first fish he ever caught was at Haegler Creek when visiting me in Arizona. He was very young then. Since the excitement of that first small trout, he has become a skilled, ardent fisherman.

I remember when I caught my first fish. It was a catfish. I was five years old. We were on a picnic outing south of the mining camp in which I was born, Santa Rita, New Mexico. An arroyo had been dammed to catch the water from a natural hot spring, which formed a large pond surrounded by huge cottonwood trees. I remember my dad saying, "I'd be surprised if there isn't a fish or two in there."

We discussed the possibility of inventing some kind of fishing tackle. Mother had brought her sewing basket along. To keep her hands busy, she said. So, using a safety pin refashioned with a pair of pliers into a hook, and a length of mother's coarse thread attached to a willow wand for a pole, I was ready to fish. I used a piece of picnic hot dog for bait.

That eight inch catfish, which swallowed the hot dog baited pin, hooked me more than I hooked him. I have been a fisherman ever since. I still vividly remember the feel of that limber willow pole with a live fish whipping the line through the water as it swam left and right in an effort to escape.

That fish also gave me my first lesson in food preparation. With the pliers that fashioned a hook from the safety pin, I learned that catfish had to be skinned as well as eviscerated. Years later, as an Alaskan guide, I always carried pliers and still do. This was not to skin catfish, which do not live in Alaska, but because a pair of pliers is one of the most useful tools an outdoorsman can carry. I'll bet they are still useful for you.

One of the choicest fish Donna and I enjoy is the arctic grayling. This beautiful fish is rare outside Alaska and northern Canada. When I say "beautiful," it is hard to describe the colors of this iridescent fish with its large dorsal fin dotted with rows of orange spots and emerald green ones mixed between, edged with orange and red. When it flashes on the surface for a fly I have cast, a grayling is the essence of life itself. Its delicate, white meat can be compared with no other fish I know. Arctic grayling are sensitive to any kind of pollution. Lumbering, mining and petroleum waste are major reasons they are rare outside northern Canada and Alaska. I hope they are not extinct when you read this.

Another beautiful, tasty fish, which is a staple here at Koviashuvik, is our pink-fleshed char. The one Donna caught for supper last night probably weighed about six pounds. We do not keep any fish under eighteen inches and are annoyed when we hook one much larger. We like our fish fresh. A larger fish means leftovers for the next day.

Enough about fish for the time being. Our Yukon stove is hot enough for sourdough pancakes. We keep a crock-pot on a shelf above the stove where flour and water feed the wild yeasts that make our tasty blueberry flapjacks. Blueberries are ripe now, and a cup of them in the sourdough batter makes our breakfast sing along with the percolating coffee pot.

It is now after breakfast, with a contented stomach in which five blueberry sourdough hot cakes are tucked. I can now return to tell you more about our summer cabin on the shore.

I originally built our shore cabin thirty-two years ago in a cove of the lake two miles from here. I had staked a mining claim there at the end of the dogsled trail from the village of Wiseman. Wiseman is across two mountain passes on the Koyukuk River. It had six residents then. They were all "old sourdoughs," no women. A plane landed there once a week delivering mail.

After acquiring title to my Headquarters Site at the lakeshore, Donna and I decided to disassemble the old cabin and rebuild it in our homestead location with replaced logs. Printed above the door inside our rebuilt cabin: "This cabin – recycled – moved into and dedicated to joy on August 8, 1994 by Donna Lee and Sam Wright."

Its dimensions are twelve by sixteen feet. From it we look out the north window to Mount Truth's rocky spine. Our front porch and open door catch the morning sun as it is reflected from the sparkling surface of the lake.

About three quarters of a mile up the hill behind the shore cabin is our winter cabin on Last Chance Creek. Gold rush miners named the creek a century ago. We also use our winter cabin in the summer, but most of the time we like to be here on the shore with the Arctic terns, red-eyed loons and snowy gulls.

Oh yes, a pair of swans nested here by the cabin last summer. What a treat!

I have to stop now and replenish the wood stacked under the stove, but you will hear more from me again later.

My love to you,

Your Great-Great-Granddad, Sam

TWENTY-SEVENTH

Dear Great-Great-Granddaughters and Sons,

Since it is wet this morning here at Koviashuvik, I've decided to put off the cutting of turf for our winter cabin and write to you.

Our little battery operated radio reported its weekend edition from Fort Yukon's Public Radio broadcast that Governor George Bush of Texas and Senator Dick Cheney had been nominated at the Republican Convention to be their Presidential and Vice President candidates.

Apparently, it was a ho-hum convention from the way it was reported. I imagine it will be the same at the Democratic Convention. Vice President Al Gore has chosen Senator Joseph Lieberman as his running mate. As liberals and conservationists, Donna and I will again support the Democratic Party platform. I wonder if liberal and conservative are political references in your time?

We have a concern for ANWAR, the Alaska National Wildlife Arctic Refuge in which petroleum interests wish to drill through the tundra for oil. Here we use the tundra for our roof.

Tundra is the name of the six to ten inches of moss, roots and plants growing above the frozen ground, called permafrost. It is this turf I had planned to cut and peel from the frozen ground to add to the roof of our winter cabin. All our cabins have this living tundra, which protects us from the weather. I guess we have the only tundra roofs in the Arctic today. When I first came north, thirty-four years ago, many cabins in Arctic Village and the Eskimo village in Anaktuvuk Pass had turf roofs with their growing green moss.

When we disassembled and moved our shore cabin here, the turf roof had several twelve inch spruce trees growing on it. We used its tundra roof to cover the scar left where the cabin stood. Today it is hard to tell that there was ever a log cabin there.

Years ago, when I built our adobe home outside El Paso, Texas, it was not turf that I dug up for a roof. It was clay soil that I mixed with water and straw to make mud bricks for the walls. After they were dried in the sun, the adobe bricks were substantial enough to support our roof of galvanized iron.

Here in the Arctic, what soil there is has little clay to hold it together. Our walls are logs, chinked with moss and covered inside with corrugated cardboard from flattened cartons in which we flew in our basic food supplies. Because glass is heavy to fly in, I made our windows of clear plastic sheets with an inch and a half of dead air space between them to keep winter's sub-zero cold at bay. They work well in our winter cabin and do not moisten up.

I imagine that in your time, houses are primarily pre-manufactured as are mobile homes today. When I was young, doors and windows were pre-manufactured, but nearly all other home construction was at the building site by carpenters, brick layers, cabinetmakers, electricians and plumbers.

Here at Koviashuvik, we enjoy making our home out of the materials at hand. An example is our summer refrigerator. With a hammer and chisel, I cut the top from a fifty gallon steel fuel drum that had been sledded in years ago. Then I dug a hole for it in the permafrost beneath our storage cache. It keeps supplies at refrigeration temperatures in the permafrost all summer long.

Perhaps I should tell you that the storage cache is a small log house built on poles eight to ten feet above the tundra and reached by a ladder to protect supplies from grizzly bears and wolves. In the winter it is nature's freezer.

I remember the first home freezer my parents bought in Arizona in 1929. I should say, "refrigerator", but it did freeze ice cubes. We had moved into our new parsonage south of Phoenix. It was a General Electric refrigerator with a large, round crown of white heat dispersing tubes on top. To me it was a marvel. It made its own ice cubes. Until then, ice, in the form of a big block weighing twenty-five or more pounds, was delivered once or twice a week. It was placed in the top of the refrigerator, and we chipped pieces from it to make cold drinks. It was not very effective at keeping things cold. At least they were cool and the butter didn't melt.

There was a new product at that time called oleomargarine. It was packaged in a one pound, slick cardboard box like butter but was white like lard. A little package of coloring came with it so it could be mixed into the oleo making it look like butter. At that time the dairy industry made it illegal for the oleomargarine manufacturer to color their butter substitute, so the color came separate.

Where I lived in the country south of the Salt River near Phoenix in Arizona, many families made their own butter from their milk cows' cream. Today, kids and most adults don't know that the buttermilk they drink was left over whey after churning the butter out of the milk. When I was a kid I didn't like buttermilk the way adults did. I guess I am an adult because I like it now.

Here at Koviashuvik, we bring in a butter substitute called Shedd's Spread-Country Crock in a three-pound container. It looks and tastes like butter but is forty-eight percent soybean oil. The container says, "One third fewer calories than margarine." Today not many kids know what real butter tastes like. I wonder if you do?

When I was a kid we used melted butter to flavor our popcorn. Here at Koviashuvik we use olive oil to pop our corn in a kettle on a small gasoline pressure stove. In our rock hogan in Pleasant Valley, Arizona, where we have electricity, we pop our pre-packaged popcorn in a microwave oven. Our kettle popped corn here in Alaska's Brooks Range tastes much better. Wish I could share it with you.

Will write more later.

Your Great-Great-Granddad, Sam

TWENTY-EIGHTH

Dear Great-Great-Grandsons and Daughters,

When I first moved to Alaska, an Anchorage developer by the name of Wallace Hickel was running for governor. Our trails crossed in the small Inuit village of Anaktuvuk Pass on the top of the Brooks Range.

He flew in for a couple of hours while I was there in order to campaign for votes. I am sure that he picked up very little support. As the two villagers, Jack Ahgook, and Simon Paneak, told me later, "He's just another talking bag of wind who cares nothing for the villages," said Jack.

"He just wants votes," Simon, the Village Chief, told me, and made a downward motion with his thumb.

In the short time we spent together, I found "Wally" glib, likeable, opinionated and ambitious. He later became the Governor of Alaska and selected a member of my Anchorage Unitarian Universalist congregation for Alaska's State Attorney General. Because of Hickel's right wing development views, President Nixon selected him as United States Secretary of the Interior, which produced so much dissention that he had to leave and returned to Alaska after a short time in Washington D.C.

I had been called as the first minister of the Anchorage Unitarian Universalist Fellowship during my second winter. It was there that I became a dissenting voice when petroleum development on the North Slope of the Brooks Range was being promoted with a proposed pipeline across the state from the Arctic Ocean to Valdez on the southern coast of Alaska.

In the winter of 1968, from our isolated cabin, I initiated what I called "a journal of human ecology." It was titled "View From the Top of the World." I was able to reproduce twenty copies on solidified gelatin in a tin plate, as well as seven of the following eleven issues. The smeared master copies were used to start fires in the Yukon stove. Today, Xerox copies of the twelve issues are in the archives of the library of the University of Alaska in Fairbanks and available to research students.

To give you some idea of my wilderness concern at the time, I'm enclosing a copy of a piece I sent out in issue #8 of View From The Top Of The World, titled "Voice From The Wilderness." It was when Wallace Hickel was U.S. Secretary of the Interior. Since then, the Trans-Alaska-Pipeline has been built, and the Hickel Haul Road was redesigned as the Dalton Highway which now crosses the Yukon River and Brooks Range to the oil fields at Prudhoe Bay on the Arctic Ocean. Wally Hickel is presently retired but is still promoting development and living in Anchorage.

I wonder if any of these concerns, which seemed to us so important for the future, are a concern for you who are the future?

This summer morning, I'm writing to you thirty years later from the same cabin that "Voice From The Wilderness" came.

Life here at Koviashuvik is much as it was. The Arctic terns have returned from the other end of the earth to nest on our shore. A grizzly bear ate the remains of fish we had caught and put out yards beyond our cabin for scavengers.

However, Fairbanks is now a busy city with commuter traffic and the Dalton Highway to Prudhoe Bay carries overnight buses where tourists can cross the Yukon River, the Arctic Circle and over Atigun Pass of the Brooks Range. Where, if lucky, they might glimpse a moose or caribou.

As for us, there are fewer small planes on floats today and no place here to land an airplane with wheels. Koviashuvik is much as it was.

Will write you more later,

Your Great-Great-Granddad, Sam

VOICE FROM THE WILDERNESS

Last spring I wrote a "Letter from the Arctic" as a great caravan of heavily laden trucks were growling over a new winter road across the Brooks Range and down the north slope to the great oil strike near Prudhoe Bay on the coast of the Arctic Ocean. I wrote that, "This great wilderness of the Brooks Range is doomed... doomed unless we act to save it now."

My letter was read aloud by Mrs. Olaus Murie at the Eleventh Wilderness Conference in San Francisco, and was printed in the spring issue of the Wilderness Society's quarterly, THE LIVING WILDERNESS. Among the letters I received were statements from across the country affirming the need to preserve this great wilderness. Many of these were from people in conservation organizations, such as Sierra Club members, who emphasized that the Sierra Club led the fight to preserve the coastal redwoods, the Grand Canyon, the North Cascades and have at present a central concern for Alaska. I was delighted and joined with my small support.

It is now a year later, and not only are the trucks in greater numbers than ever grinding over the mountains on the "Hickel Haul Road," which was first bulldozed through last winter, but another is being cut through the mountains fifty miles to the east. This new "all-weather" oil pipeline road is already in heavy use. Caravans of trailers and heavy equipment are being hauled up the Dietrich River into the wilderness of the Brooks Range.

Across the range, another contractor is constructing a road for the pipeline route. Daily, great Hercules aircraft fly over our small, isolated cabin in the wilderness to Galbraith Lake on the north slope of the range. This is a staging arena for "the assault over the pass," in the construction of the road and oil pipeline south to the Dietrich River.

As I write this, Governor Miller of Alaska has just stated on a radio interview that permission for construction of the oil pipeline has not yet been given by the Secretary of the Interior, Walter Hickel, but he expects the permit go ahead by April 15.

If the present bulldozing, construction camps, airfields and traffic can exist without the Secretary of the Interior's permission, I wonder what more will happen to the wilderness if the go head is given? The answer of course is, "more!"

To those who live elsewhere, this last great wilderness in northern Alaska may seem a far-away and distant concern compared to oil on beaches, dirty air and debris in the city's back yard. But this wilderness is the heritage of all of us, and all of us should have a say as to whether or not it should be desecrated or destroyed. This should not be the choice of oil companies, contractors and a few officials.

One definition of wilderness is that very few people inhabit it. Therefore, there are few voices within to speak on its behalf. As a resident in the Brooks Range, I feel it not only my privilege, but duty to speak for those whose voice might never be heard if I did not represent them.

Who are the voiceless? They are manifold. They are the caribou who have called this their home for thousands of years. They are the wolf, the lynx, the fox, the wolverine. They are the majestic Dall sheep, the grizzly bear, the gyrfalcon and the arctic tern, who yearly flies eleven thousand miles from Antarctica to nest in the lakes of this wilderness.

Who will speak for those spruce which struggle up the Dietrich River, moving timberline north... trees whose diameter is seldom more than eight inches, but which were seedlings when George Washington was inaugurated President? Who will speak for solitude... where the ancient sounds of life can be heard without the whine of gears or the drone of an airplane? Who will speak for this last great wilderness? I have no choice. I am not voiceless, and this is my home.

For myself, and the voiceless that I have taken the prerogative to represent, I say that all the oil in the State of Alaska is not worth the loss of this last great wilderness which is the heritage of us all. Since it is the heritage of us all, we should all be heard. I cannot speak for you. You have a voice of your own. But for myself and my voiceless neighbors, "HELP!"

Sam Wright
Brooks Range
Via Bettles Field, Alaska 99726
March 21, 1970

"Let us keep our silent sanctuaries,
for in them the eternal perspectives are preserved."
– Senancour

TWENTY-NINTH

Dear Great-Great-Granddaughters and Sons,

Yesterday I was cleaning out spruce cones, dried moss and mushrooms (litter that squirrels had packed into a box of old papers I had stored in our winter cabin on Last Chance Creek).

As I shook out squirrel droppings from folders of my past writings, I found a carbon copy of a letter I sent to several colleagues from Fairbanks in the autumn of 1968. I thought it might be of interest to you since I recall writing you about tree planting on Robert Marshall's plots on Barrenland Creek.

This is a note to those of you who may be interested in learning that I planted 100 four-year-old white spruce seedlings north of the Arctic Circle in the Brooks Range. This planting is part of the scientific method of testing a theory. But more than this, if these trees survive and continue to grow, they will be a living memorial to Bob Marshall who mapped and named many of the tributaries and mountains of the Koyukuk drainage over thirty years ago.

Robert Marshall had a theory that northern timberline in Alaska is not the result of unfavorable environment for tree growth, but that there has not been time since the last ice sheet receded for the forest to migrate farther north. (See Arctic Wilderness by Robert Marshall, Univ. of Cal. Press, 1956, pg. 47). Increment borings of white spruce near timberline on the North Fork of the Koyukuk River in the Brooks Range indicate this by the growth of the most northerly trees.

In my study of tree growth at timberline I found no record that anyone had followed up Bob Marshall's experiment to test his theory, in which he planted white spruce seeds on Barrenland and Kinnorutin creeks north of timberline just four months before his death in 1939. I confirmed this with his brother, George Marshall, who was then President of the Sierra Club, a board member of the Wilderness Society and active in many conservation concerns.

So in August of 1966, accompanied by a student in the seminary where I was teaching, I hiked from Chimney Pass Lake, where a bush pilot could drop us, over the mountains and up the Hammond River to Kinnorutin Creek. Here Bob Marshall had planted white spruce seeds in the summer of 1939, but I could find no evidence that they had either sprouted or grown. The same was true of his plots on Barrenland Creek, which was over two passes and north of the confluence of the North Fork of the Koyukuk River and Alignment Creek.

Marshall wrote in his journal in July, 1939:

We stopped for lunch at the edge of foaming white water dropping from a bright green basin entirely devoid of any sort of tree growth. While Jesse and Nutirwick were making tea, Harvey and I followed that tributary up a stream a couple of miles to a point where we could see the entire head of this valley. It was fascinating in its barrenness, so we called it Barrenland Creek.

After lunch I repeated the experiment which I had tried with negative results nine years before–the experiment to test my theory that lack of time, not unfavorable climatic conditions had prevented the further progress of northern timberline. I had brought with me this time some white spruce seeds which the Lakes States Forest Experiment Station had provided.

I marked two square plots on a flat about ten feet above the creek. On a larger one, 12 by 12 feet, I sowed the seeds directly among the sphagnum moss, Dryas octopetala, and dwarf willow. On the other plot which was 8 by 8 feet, I scraped away the vegetation and sowed the seeds on mineral soil." (Arctic Wilderness, page 154)]

Although there was no evidence that Bob Marshall's seeds had sprouted, I still felt his theory valid and planned to return in the future to replant in his original site on Barrenland Creek.

The opportunity came in 1968 when I included in my Sabbatical Study in Human Ecology, the Eskimo village in Anaktuvuk Pass, which lies in the center of the Brooks Range in northern Alaska.

My plan was to hike the forty or fifty miles along the top of the range to Barrenland Creek from Anaktuvuk Pass, going south far enough to gather seedlings for planting north of timberline. However, I was fortunate to be given one hundred four-year-old white spruce seedlings from the Forestry Sciences Laboratory at the University of Alaska by a research ecologist named Leslie Vierek. I also found that a bush pilot and big game outfitter could drop me on a small lake at the headwaters of the North Fork of the Koyukuk and Itkillick rivers so that the hike to and from the planting would be no more than twenty steep mountain miles.

With this good luck, on August 4th, and with one hundred rooted seedlings tied to my pack, I took off. On August 5th, 1968 I wrote in my Journal:

"By seven p.m., rimming up Barenland Creek's north side, I looked down on the tree planting site where Bob Marshall's stakes still mark his plot after nearly thirty years of arctic freeze-up and break-up."

The next morning was spent planting the white spruce seedlings within the markers of Bob's earlier plot. I made four rock corners around three foot tall willow stakes, leaving Marshall's as they were found. One of his plots had washed out, with only one of his original corner stakes remaining. I took his weathered stake with me, a symbol of continuity, to take to his brother, George Marshall. Then, inside a tobacco can and a peanut can, I placed papers with the following inscription:

Note: Within these markers are planted four-year-old white spruce seedlings from the Forestry Sciences Laboratory, University of Alaska, gift of Leslie Vierek. Planted August 6, 1968 by Sam Wright on site of planting of seeds 29 years earlier by Robert Marshall. Old markers of willow – Robert Marshall's original site markers – This planting, a continuing test of Bob Marshall's theory of northern limit of spruce growth. Please do not disturb and report to Sam Wright, c/o 2441 Le Conte, Berkeley, California 9470.

Since returning to Fairbanks, I have shared this site location and the 16mm film with several competent observers who may find themselves in the wilderness area of the upper North Fork of the Koyukuk. In the future I too shall return to check the results and continue my arctic research."

Samuel A. Wright 1968

A few weeks after writing this letter, I resigned from my professional position at the Seminary in Berkeley, California and with my spouse, Billie, moved here, into the wilderness of the Brooks Range.

As I wrote you a couple of weeks ago, Donna and I returned 20 years later to discover five of the white spruce I had planted were still alive. Barrenland Creek is now within the Gates of the Arctic National Monument.

I wonder if those five white spruce, that had survived when Donna and I visited the plot, are still alive when you read this?

My love to you from Koviashuvik.

Your Great-Great-Granddad, Sam

THIRTIETH

Dear Great, Great Grandsons and Daughters,

Years ago, when I met the late Dr. Albert Schweitzer, I thought at the time I would remember something he said that I considered very wise. Today all I recall is how impressed I was by his small physical stature and we could look each other in the eye.

I also remember the twinkle in his eyes above his walrus-drooping mustache when I asked if he ate meat in his equatorial hospital in Africa.

We had been discussing his "reverence for life ethic" in President Frederick May Eliott's office at 25 Beacon Street in Boston. This was headquarters of the American Unitarian Association. I was then Director of American Unitarian Youth, the national organization of our denomination's college and high school young people. Dr. Schweitzer had received an honorary membership in the Unitarian Church of the Larger Fellowship along with a contribution to his medical mission in the Congo.

Was Albert Schweitzer a vegetarian? I should know. I posed the question to him directly and have no memory of what he said.

Today, vegetarianism is no longer considered a fad, as it was when I was a kid. It appears to have little to do with reverence for life. According to private and public health advocates, personal health and longevity would appear to be guaranteed if people were vegetarians.

When I was a kid, finicky eaters were those who would not eat broccoli, lima beans or rutabagas. Beef, pork, lamb or fish were not in the finicky realm. The reason I am writing you about this subject is because I wonder what advocated diets there are in your time? It is also because I am writing to you from our northern wilderness home where our summer staple is fresh fish. When I was trapping here in the winter, it was caribou and moose. I could not conceive living on a vegetarian diet in those active winters in these mountains.

On the other hand, I doubt that I would enjoy fat caribou in the summer heat of Phoenix, even in the best air-conditioned restaurant.

I am sure you are getting my point. Diet was once determined by the place people lived, including the food supply and custom. Today it appears to be primarily custom, determined by promoters of their products, from tofu to beer. The word "natural" appears on every food container in our cabin, even salt.

I guess I am telling you this because I wonder where it may lead in the future? That old French saying, "There is no accounting for taste," may no longer be true when you read this. I know that tastemakers have taught me to like green olives, unsweetened hot coffee, hot chili and expensive beer, but not lima beans. They are now working on me to dislike fresh meat, bacon and gravy. I wonder how your taste has been trained when you read this?

Of course taste is not just in the mouth. The sweet smell of our frying bacon on the Yukon stove added to the aroma of sourdough pancakes with blueberries in them popping with fragrance, is a large part of its savoryness. Even the soft gray of cloud cover shrouding the mountains, and the flat stillness of the lake where a loon glides by, is part of the taste of this mid-August morning in the year two thousand.

I am reminded that taste, smell, sound, sight, feel – the temperature and barometric pressure – time of day or night – remembrance of the past – prospects for the future – all make up an accounting for taste.

Since I am writing from the past, I'm sending along an essay I mailed out in twenty copies of View From The Top Of The World in December of 1969. In re-reading it, I was acutely aware that a revolution has taken place since then. Women are no longer considered second class. Although I would say that, "I never thought of women that way," I was shaken to read my own use of the term "man." Of course I would have argued that I was including women in the generic term "man." So, why do I want to re-edit "A Time for Human Ecology" before sending it along to you? Well, I won't! Here it is in what would be called an attachment if I could send it to you by e-mail.

My warmest to you from Koviashuvik,

Your Great-Great-Granddad, Sam

☙ A TIME FOR HUMAN ECOLOGY

Old values are in disintegration. The established institutions developed over the past two centuries are decaying. A new social mobility, a restless, almost gypsy-like yearning for change pervades our western world.

This is a time in history when thought has exceptional opportunity to break out of old molds. More than this, it is being forced to do so. The dangers and opportunities of our age take on a focus with parallels between the present and the Renaissance.

The Renaissance

Our age closely resembles the Renaissance. Some four centuries ago the breakdown of feudal society produced an indefinable period, an intermediate social zone, when old institutions were clearly in decline and new ones had not yet arisen. The human mind, freed from the burden of traditional thought, roamed freely and spontaneously over the entire realm of experience producing astonishing visions, often far transcending the material limitations of the time. Entire sciences and schools of philosophy were founded in the sweep of an essay or pamphlet. It was a time when new potentialities replaced the old actualities. The burdensome particulars of feudal society were broken through when man, stripped of his traditional fetters, turned from a transfixed creature into a vital, searching being. In time, a new society crystallized out of this flux, bringing with it an entirely new body of institutions, classes, values and problems to replace feudal civilization.

The Parallel

The parallel is that for a time the western world was loosening its shackles. It sought a destiny that was far less defined than we suppose today with our retrospective historical attitude. Today this world haunts us like an unforgettable dawn, richly tinted, ineffably beautiful, laden with the promise of birth.

In this latter part of the twentieth century, we too are living in a period of social disintegration. Like our Renaissance forebears, we live in a period of potentialities where we are searching, seeking a direction from the first lights on the horizon. It is no longer the right question to ask that institutions merely free themselves from nineteenth-century letters and update their theories to the twentieth century. We must look ahead. We cannot be extravagant enough in releasing the imagination of man. To this end I propose that the new thinking must embody a revolutionary kind of wholeness as its goal, involving a more inclusive study of nature than social thinkers of the past have considered either practicable or necessary. I see an expanded use of the science of ecology answering this need.

Ecology and Progress

Since the interrelationships between life and environment are the peculiar business of ecology, a few words on that branch of study are in order.

Beginning in 1859, with a landmark in man's intellectual progress, Darwin's Origin of Species by Natural Selection was published. Darwin had at hand two powerful intellectual tools, one borrowed from geology, and the other from political economy. The first was the principle of uniformity, which assumed that in nature events of the past have been determined by those forces seen in operation today. The second was the idea that living beings have a far greater capacity to reproduce than to survive. Somehow their numbers, through generations, are kept in balance with the space and means of subsistence available. Many are born that do not mature, or if you prefer to be scriptural, many are called but few are chosen.

Fortunately Darwin was a naturalist, trained to observe nature in all her aspects. He noted, although he could not explain, the tendency of plants and animals to vary, and showed that not all variations were equally well fitted to particular environments. And so he concluded that environment tends to eliminate the less fit while favoring their more suitable competitors.

Thus the seeds of two other studies were planted... genetics to deal with variation and inheritance, and ecology to investigate the interrelation between life and environment. Curiously, a generation was to pass before either gained much headway and when they did genetics raced ahead much faster. Toward the close of the 19th century, the pioneer work in ecology filtered across the Atlantic to receive its warmest welcome at two youthful universities in the mid-west, Chicago and Nebraska. First to be developed was plant ecology, later came animal ecology, and their combination, bio-ecology. Human ecology, our present concern, is still in a tentative stage, but the ultimate goal is a general ecology, embracing all forms.

Ecology is above all a source of perspective in time and space and a means of understanding the great processes of which we are a part. We must keep in mind that our essential business is to study process, and in particular the process wherein life and environment interact. We must understand both living organisms and their environment...a task complicated by the fact that living organisms are themselves a part of the environment of other living things.

The hunter knows, like the naturalist, that plants and animals occur in characteristic communities or groups. To speak of jackrabbits or prairie dogs is to suggest grassland. We would expect to see a squirrel in a woodland of oak and a ptarmigan in the beautiful flowered alpine meadows above timberline, a polar bear in the arctic. Even insects and microscopic forms of life may be known by the company they keep. Thus one can read climate, soil and even quality and their history by observing living communities.

Man

This was once true of man. Reach up to chin yourself and note the articulation of your shoulder joint and the ability of your hands to grasp a bar (or branch) strong enough to sustain your weight. Then ask yourself what kind of community... desert, grassland or forest, did early man, your own ancestors, probably come from? We are equipped with a remarkably versatile vocal system capable of reproducing an infinite variety of sound combinations. It is thus possible to have spoken symbols enough to communicate our thoughts and experiences to others. Knowledge could be exchanged and accumulated, and handed down through generations. The upshot was a biological revolution, the birth of culture, carrying with it its awful gift of conscious responsibility.

We are a Novelty

We were able to do what no other organism could do without changing its original character. Culture change was, for the first time, substituted for biological evolution as a means of adapting an organism to new habitats in the widening range that eventually came to include the whole earth and probably soon our solar system.

The human record becomes less vague, more continuous and clear, following the invention of agriculture and cities. It is not enough, however, to know the record. We need to know its meaning as well. Until very recently history told us much about man but very little about environment and practically nothing about interrelationship. In other words, moral history was a thing completely apart from natural history.

Establishing Perspective

The ecological viewpoint implies that man ought not be too self-centered, that instead of emphasizing the taking advantage of his surroundings, he might do well to spend more effort in getting his bearings. Science and technology are still being applied to competitive and exploitive ends in far greater measure than they are to establishing perspective. The prolonging of life, and the increase of food supply through science and technology seem to raise as many questions as solved.

The critical perspective of ecology has been much in the news: the creation of deserts out of once fertile lands, the poisoning of the air, the pollution of water, and the destruction of wilderness. Not so obviously ecological, has been the imbalance of the social structure in the relation of man with man; the ills of urbanization; the reproductive manipulative devices of mass management and control of human beings; the half-calculated, half-unexpected results of acquisitive enterprise, so devastating in effect on both the quality of man's life and his environment; also the uncontrolled birth and death rate; war...The list could go on.

Reversal of Organic Evolution

Ecology derives its critical edge not only from the fact that it presents this awesome message to humanity, but because it also presents this message in a new social dimension.

From an ecological viewpoint, we are in trouble because we have reversed organic evolution. Instead of contributing to the endlessly differentiating and individualizing process of which evolution consists, our methods of social organization, environment formation and production tend toward a crude uniformity... toward a tasteless leveling with normative values and controls arrived at by quantitative measures. The standardized, the regulated, and the pressure of the mass circumscribe all that is spontaneous, creative and individual.

Evolution for man should mean greater individuation, the strengthening of independence, balance, private judgment, resourcefulness, and self-reliant decision. The processes of efficiencies upon which we seem more and more to depend frustrate such qualities.

Again, from an ecological viewpoint, the reversal of organic evolution is the result of contradictions between mass manufacture and craftsmanship... centralism and regionalism... town and country... state and community... the bureaucratic scale and the human scale.

The massive technology of the Industrial Revolution with its assembly-line systems of labor organization, the centralized nation-state with its bureaucratic apparatus have reached their limits. Whatever progressive or liberating role they have had has already become regressive and oppressive.

Hidden Realities

It is important, however, to recognize that within all these mechanistic systems of control, organic life-processes still continue. They are the hidden realities of human relations and behavior... Hidden because they are difficult to define and almost totally ignored by ideological accounts of social organization. It is this neglect of human qualities of human beings which allows manipulative theory to gain so much unchallenged authority. It is this authority that in time generates in people everywhere a feeling of dependence upon those external rules and artificially derived conceptions of social identity. It is dependence upon this authority that produces the dehumanizing effect. We must not only close the gap between the humanities and the sciences, but also restudy human values with an eye to man's long evolutionary background and his growing role as a natural force. What environment does to him and what he in turn does to it is of far more significance than the loves of monarchs and quirks of generals. Conquests and migrations, campaigns and battles, creative arts and religious philosophies all take on a fuller meaning in the context of ecology.

A Human Ecology

Knowledge and data are meaningless unless they are organized around a central purpose or vision of the world. There are many individual causes and personal ideologies left over from the past, from Marxism and fundamentalist religion to worship of the scientific method. But like our Renaissance forebears, we live in a time when old causes are neither large enough nor coherent enough to bring together poetry, biology, atomic physics and highway engineering into relevance with each other and the lives of people.

At a time when man has more power, wealth and knowledge than any organism ever known, the future of the human race is in serious question. It does not take an ecologist to read the symptoms where 70 per cent of people are on 2 per cent of the land area in the richest nation on earth; where airports jam, road traffic clots, railroads disintegrate, air and water get dirtier, housing scarcer, prices higher, welfare rolls grow, ghettos erupt and a war no one wants drags on and on. But these are only outward symptoms of the inner illness brought about by the reversal of organic evolution.

The hidden realities, the organic processes, the life qualities of the human spirit are still there to be released. From the perspective of human ecology, an answer to the cry, "What must we do to be saved?" seems self-evident. It is recognition and acceptance of the ancient primordial ethic of survival and knowing that survival is not static, but requires innovation, diversification and change. But more than survival, this ethic carries within it the central purpose and cohesion around which a new vision is already forming, bringing together all our resources and disciplines.

The implications of an ecological approach are revolutionary in our western thought-patterns. Ecology is not only an integrative and constructive perspective, but also intrinsically a critical point of view on a scale that the most radical systems of political economy fail to attain. It is the essence of morality. This aspect of ecology, carried through to its implications, leads directly to the idealized areas of social thought carried in the great religious traditions.

Finally, we are faced with a question of value. If we are to survive and grow into the new era of possibilities, which haunt us like the dreams of childhood, it is a time for human ecology. The choice is life or death.

Samuel A. Wright, December 10, 1969
Koviashuvik, Brooks Range, Alaska

THIRTY-FIRST

Dear Great-Great-Granddaughters and Sons,

Here at Koviashuvik, the past few days have been particularly interesting and exciting. The misty, rainy weather blew out following a storm from the north over the range. It left the air crystal clear and ice on a bucket of water on the porch of our cabin. The thermometer registered twenty-four degrees Fahrenheit. This is not usual for the fifteenth of August.

The lake was like a giant mirror. We boated across to an area where, several years before, Donna had found a black Alaska jade spear point in the shallows of the shore. It was obviously a very ancient artifact. We presumed it had been in an animal that had later died. It was in perfect condition, far too valuable for an ancient hunter to lose.

We had searched the shore again for signs of ancient humans, and today, half a decade later, Donna retrieved another four-inch black Alaska jade spear point!

Shortly after we returned to the cabin for lunch, a floatplane circled over us and dropped to the lake's sunny surface. After the aircraft cut its engine at the shore, there was my son Chip and his spouse Lisa, who stepped out on the float. We knew there was a possibility of a visit, but for the past week the weather had been non-flyable into these mountains. We had expected them this month, but assumed circumstances might have changed their plans. But here they were on a beautiful day and Donna had a treasured artifact to show them.

After the bush plane roared off down the lake and we sorted the supplies they brought in with them, we took Chip and Lisa to again walk the eastern shore looking for artifacts with interested excitement but without success.

Chip may be your great-grandfather when you read this. His two sons, Joaquin and Tao are now living in California. At the moment, Chip is my fifty-two-year-old namesake who is minister of the Unitarian Universalist

Church in Yakima, Washington. I tell him that now, at age fifty-two, he is a full deck.

Anyway, that spear point was found three days ago. Today, the August mist and rain have returned and Lisa and Chip donned rainwear and rowed out into the lake to fish for grayling. We had seen them schooling off shore. Their fishing was not successful. The fish ignored their lures.

However, in the shallows, they spotted a strangely shaped object. They retrieved it with a fishnet and found it to be the cranial cap of a human skull. They marked the site for our return in better weather.

The bone is stained black and brown from the tannin and minerals in mud and water. It appears to be a mature adult. Based on caribou and moose bones left over seventy years ago from native fish camps, this skull could be at least a century old, or a good many more. Hairy Mammoth bones and tusks have been retrieved from the permafrost here since the miners arrived following the gold rush of 1898. The cold and tannins from the tundra are also effective preservatives.

Needless to say, Chip and Lisa were intrigued and excited to bring us this human skullcap, which is now sitting on the cabin table along with the black jade spear point. Donna and I are also intrigued with it and share their wonder. Who was this? When did he or she die? How? Is there a relationship with the spear points found?

Thirteen years before, I had retrieved a black jade skinning knife and ulu in the shallows about a mile away along the same shore. And now we are waiting for the weather to clear. Hopefully, it will later today or tomorrow so we can return to the site and see if more remains. Yes, I'll keep you posted on what we find. But for now I'll have to quit writing and split wood for the stove.

NEXT DAY

All four of us have just returned from gathering more of the ancient human remains from where the skull was found in the shallows yesterday. We now have a lower mandible (no teeth), two thigh bones (femurs), a right tibia and a few other small pieces.

What a story might be told by this ancient dweller, whose life ended a few hundred yards from our cabin on the shore, if only he or she could speak. Did he drown? Freeze on the lake ice in winter? Was he an Inuit (Eskimo)? Earlier? I speak of him as "he" based upon the shape of the femur and hipbones. It could have been "she." All indications point to a young, mature adult, based upon tooth sockets and skullcap.

Anyway, a breeze came down from the snow dusted rocky spire of Mount Truth and ruffled the water, so we left for a cove to cast for fish for supper. The fish appeared to ignore our efforts until a great northern pike selected Lisa's lure. It was the largest taken this summer. We took its picture, including Lisa. She provided our entree for supper.

Any day now, we expect to hear the ya-honk of geese as they pass over us in great vees on their way south. This afternoon a pair of snow geese swam in front of our cabin inspecting this strange anomaly on the shore. There is no doubt that they have stopped here on their way to winter elsewhere. It is the beginning of autumn. The alders are turning crimson and the birches and willows are spotted with gold. The higher mountains are now white capped and we put on our jackets before going out to enjoy the view from our privy.

From here it seems strange to hear from our little battery radio that Vice President Al Gore has accepted his party's nomination for President that he and Texas Governor George Bush, who is running against him, each repeat the phrase over and over again, "The American people want......!" I hope they know what the American people want.

I look at the skull on the oilcloth of our table in front of the north window that looks out on the craggy peak of Mount Truth, and wonder about the world its owner saw through these now empty sockets. Was he or she an American, centuries before Europeans made it across the Atlantic? What did she want? A great northern pike for supper?

Or like us, was there something more? I wonder if you ever ask yourself questions like these where you are?

Will write more later,

Great-Great-Granddad, Sam

THIRTY-SECOND

Dear Great-Great-Grandsons and Daughters,

As you know from my last letters I am writing you from northern Alaska. My son Chip and Lisa, his wife, are still with us and at present are out on the lake in a drizzling rain to fish for grayling. This has given me an opportunity to go back to sorting papers and clippings out of the past, which survived spruce squirrel nest-making.

Among other past things, I discovered a resume of mine printed the year I resigned my teaching role at Starr King seminary in Berkeley and moved into this northern wilderness. I'll include it as an attachment to this letter.

Chip brought a small tape recording machine with him, and last night asked if he could record my commentary as I recalled the time of merger between the youth organizations and then the Unitarian and Universalist denominations. I was the first official employee representing both of them as a Unitarian Universalist. I consented to comment, but pointed out that this was more than four decades ago when the context of that time in the United States was one of concern about communism, atomic war and economic instability.

The previous Director of American Unitarian Youth, the Reverend Stephen Fritchman, had become a controversial figure. He was labeled a Russian communist sympathizer in a widely touted book, "I Led Three Lives" by a Herbert Philbrick. Also at that time, the Editor of the Unitarian denomination's Beacon Press was convinced that Steve Fritchman was a subversive supporter of Marxist-Stalinist dictatorship. In the climate of those times, "Un-Americanism" was the term. There was even a congressional committee titled Un-American Activities Committee.

It was a time of suspicion and paranoia. The USSR had launched a satellite called Sputnik, and along with millions of others around the world, I stood with my family and watched it blink overhead across the dark sky. I think this was the first time it really hit home for many of us how vulnerable we all were in this new technology.

At that time, the word "computer" referred to a huge machine housed in a large structure, manipulated by skilled technicians. Today I am editing my handwritten letters to you on a notebook computer I can carry under my arm. I imagine even this computer sounds ancient to you.

However, this was the context in which I was chosen as Youth Director. I was a young, relatively unknown but effective minister in the small college town of Stockton, California, and my resume included experience in a secret wartime role and Director of a Veteran's Administration Guidance Center at a University where I taught. Following the call, I hitched up a small trailer to our new, yellow Nash sedan and drove across the United States to the environs of Boston, Massachusetts. With three small children and a Siamese cat, the eight-foot house trailer was crowded but homey. Our residence for the next three years was in Wellesley Hills, Massachusetts. From there I commuted to my office at 25 Beacon Street in Boston, next to the State Capitol.

It was during these three years, as Director of American Unitarian Youth, and then the newly created Liberal Religious Youth Inc., that Chip wanted my recall of the time. He was also interested in the talk of the time about a merger between Universalist and Unitarian denominations. This was back in the early nineteen fifties when Chip was graduating from kindergarten. At that time I was traveling about the country visiting churches, conferences, and participating in "Religious Emphasis Weeks" which were then in vogue on University campuses.

As I look back on that period, I realize how fortunate I was to be able to share perspectives with people whom I had only known through their writings or books. I learned that a great literary scholar or eminent scientist could be the dullest bore as a person. Also, that many charismatically articulate personalities have little to share beneath their entertaining public image. I imagine this has not changed in your time.

Here come Lisa and Chip dripping wet from their fishing expedition. Will finish this letter later.

LATER

It is now morning and yesterday's rain has turned to snow. Lisa and Chip had breakfast with us. Sitting on top of a twenty-foot white spruce, a northern hawk owl watched us through the window with bright yellow eyes. Shortly after we climbed into our sleeping bag last night, we heard the ya-honk of geese and rushed out to see two large, wavering vees of approximately one hundred Canadian geese, silhouetted just under the clouds on their way south.

Chip and Lisa have now hiked through the falling snowflakes up the hill to our winter cabin where they are bunking. Donna and I have put things back in order after we shared sourdough blueberry pancakes, coffee, and talk around the breakfast table.

We are delighted that we are having this August snow flurry. It will mean the end of the mosquito season and turn the birches golden. When the clouds lift, snow covered mountains will have us in a white fairyland. We know this snow will not remain but it is a foretaste of what will come a month from now after we have joined the geese flying south.

In a way, I am sorry we will be leaving before freeze-up. When staying through the winter, freeze-up is the most interesting and exciting time of the year. It is when we take our moose or caribou for winter meat and start snow shoeing trails for the trap-line. We make sure our teepees of wood supply are standing before the snow deepens.

The aurora then becomes a glorious part of our night sky and at freeze-up the lake snaps and groans as it echoes the songs of wolves beyond the shore. At freeze-up the crackle of wood in the Yukon stove seems to sing a different, more pleasing tune than at any other time. Even the lingonberries taste sweeter after freeze-up.

I'll probably write you again before we follow the geese south. So until then, I'm your great-great-granddad back in the year 2000.

Sam

P.S. I found this resume I'd prepared the year I left for Alaska. Thought it might be of interest to you. S.

Professor Samuel A. Wright

Resume – 1968

Professor Samuel A. Wright, Director of the Department of In-Service Education, Starr King School for the Ministry, Center for Religious leadership, Berkeley, Cal. 94709

From 1954 until his appointment in 1961 to the staff of Starr King School for the Ministry, Mr. Wright was minister of the Unitarian Universalist Church of Marin (Marin Fellowship of Unitarians). In the San Francisco Bay Area he served as President of the Marin Council of Community Services, as Vice President of the Bay Area Welfare Planning Federation, and as member of the board of the Marin Family Service Agency, Marin United Fund, Mental Health Society, and Child Guidance League. He served as Vice President of the Bay Area Funeral Society and is an incorporator and board member of the Society for Humane Abortion, and was on the Executive Board of Starr King School.

Denominationally, he served the Unitarian Universalist Association, as Regional Vice President of the Unitarian Fellowship for Social Justice, President of the Unitarian Universalist Pacific Coast Council, President of the Pacific Coast Unitarian Ministers Association, and is presently on the board of the Pacific Central District of the UUA, as well as having served on many local and national committees.

Mr. Wright came to the San Francisco Bay Area as first minister of the Unitarian Church of Marin from Boston, Massachusetts where he was Executive Director of American Unitarian Youth, Inc. and then the first Executive Director of Liberal Religious Youth, Inc. (created by the merger of the American Unitarian Youth and Universalist Youth Fellowship, college and high school groups of the U.S. and Canada).

He was formerly minister of the First Unitarian Church in Stockton, California and was minister of the First Congregational Church in Cloverdale, California while completing graduate work at Pacific School of Religion and the University of California. He was ordained in 1949, and received his theological degree from Starr King School in 1950.

Before entering Starr King School, Professor Wright was instructor in biology at Texas Western College in El Paso, Texas where he was also director and counselor for the vocational guidance program under the Veterans Administration. In El Paso he established and operated a successful commercial business. He has continued his interest in biology, presently working on the ecology of tree growth north of timberline, which took him to the Brooks Range in Alaska in 1966. He has done study on the "world's oldest living thing," the Bristlecone Pine. His last article on the subject appeared in Pacific Discovery, published by the California Academy of Sciences.

It is as Professor of Human Ecology that Mr. Wright sees himself in his teaching role at Starr King School. His involvement of students in field trips and direct experience encounters have ranged from the Haight Ashbury district of San Francisco to a Sierra Nevada wilderness, and from Anaktuvuk Pass, an Eskimo village in Alaska, to the deserts of the Southwest. Plans for his sabbatical year, 1968-69, propose an ecological study of value formation in communities of divergent cultural history and social structure, but all facing the same ethical value questions thrust upon them by a worldwide technology and communication. Seeing the most relevant frontier today as the realm of value, Mr. Wright finds the most relevant approach the ecological one. The relation of living things to their environment and to each other. Within these relationships man is a part -- but only one part of that total environment.

He is presently working on a manuscript under the general title "Theology of Nature." Among his publications and monographs are: "The Inner Meaning of Conservation," "Theology of Wilderness," "Letter from the Desert," "Eskimo Visit," "Nine Days in March," "Sierra Theology," and others. He is the publisher of The Modern Utopian, a magazine of social change, and Directory of Social Change.

The Rev. Mr. Wright is a graduate of the University of New Mexico where he was an instructor before entering personnel work during World War II for the Office of Scientific Research and Development.

He is married, in his forties, and is the father of four children between the ages of nine and twenty-seven.

THIRTY-THIRD

Dear Great-Great-Granddaughters and Sons,

Last night a big grizzly bear cleaned up the fish heads and entrails we had placed for scavenges several hundred feet from our shore cabin. We did not see him or her, but the immense pile of excrement full of crowberries and blueberries was left as a calling card.

Here at Koviashuvik, I've had a lot of interesting experiences with bears. One of the grizzlies we named "The Phantom." This was the bear I wrote about in the beginning of my book, KOVIASHUVIK. Another was a large grizzly that, like The Phantom, learned that cabins were a place to explore for food until he became the center dish for our Thanksgiving dinner.

Although black bears (which are often brown) are uncommon this far north in Alaska, a black one did make a mess of our cabin one summer when my spouse, Billie, and I were away serving as Native Counselors on the Trans-Alaska Pipeline Project. Fortunately, I was soon able to cross its trail and sent it to black bear heaven.

When a bear learns that a cabin is not something to avoid, the only choice we have is to eliminate the bear or suffer his continued mauling of everything. When I say "everything," there is little in a cabin that a bear will not explore with his teeth and claws, raking down shelves, turning over the Yukon stove, biting holes through aluminum pots and kettles as well as boots and bedding. Donna's stainless steel dishpan, which is still usable, is marked by dents of grizzly bear teeth.

Fortunately, bears in our isolated area are generally wary of the strange smells and activities of humans, as are the wolverine and wolves. They do scavenge our fish leavings, but over the years our relationships have generally been good.

Last summer a bear broke a ground level window in our winter cabin when we were out fishing. It did not enter. We assumed it had seen its reflection and had taken a swipe at it with its heavily clawed paw. Shortly after we discovered the broken window, the bear returned and we banged metal cups and pots together to frighten it. Instead of running away, the bear observed our shouting and pan clattering with what seemed to be amused curiosity.

I took my 30-06 rifle and fired a shot over him. He responded to the loud concussion, which echoed up the creek, with the same unperturbed curiosity. Then, giving us a last look of wonder, he turned away from us, and in a casual, rolling stride, left us never to return. Donna and I wondered what kind of tale he might tell another bear about those strange, noisy creatures he had never seen before.

However, bears that are familiar with people can be a problem. Some years ago, Billie and I were tenting in a public campground at Lake Teniya in the Sierra Nevada Mountains of California. I had built a breakfast fire by a large granite outcropping and put our food chest on the picnic table provided for campers.

Then I heard loud voices yelling, "Bear, bear, bear!" As I looked up, a large black bear with two cubs following appeared across the picnic table with the obvious intention of raiding our food chest.

It was then our contest began. I was determined that she not get into our food chest. She had determined otherwise. The bear rose up across the picnic table and I rushed threateningly at her from the other side. She dropped back on her four feet and moved behind her cubs who, with curiosity, had approached the table and me. With the cubs between the mother bear and me, she made a gruff sound and rushed back toward me around the table. Her cubs gave her license to charge around the table as a protective mother. I ran around the other side and picked up a stick of firewood. She rose up over the food chest as I defended it from my side. The cubs moved away from the table as the sow and I did a merry-go-round about it. While this feint-and-run-dance was going on, I called for Billie to light a roll of the newspapers we had from the campfire. She had been watching this charade from the door of our tent. As I made a circle around the tent side of the table, I grabbed the burning roll of newspaper from her and thrust it across the food box into the bear's face. She dropped away and loped off with the cubs following her beyond the huge house-size granite boulder next to which we were camped.

Then came a loud chorus of affirmative shouts, with hand clapping and whistles from above. I looked up to where half a dozen campers were standing atop the huge rock. They had been watching this drama below them.

I made an exaggerated stage bow and pointed to the food box, followed by a "thumbs up". The cheers continued as I placed the food chest by the fire and began taking out our breakfast stuff.

Here at Koviashuvik our grizzly bears are not so domesticated. However, with a highway from Fairbanks to the Prudhoe Bay oil fields on the Arctic Ocean just two mountain ridges beyond us, the inevitable domestication can be expected. I wonder if there is any place left in the world where bears are not semi-domesticated when you read this? I hope so.

One of my early meetings with *Ursus horribilis*, the grizzly bear, was during our first winter in the range. It was totally unexpected because it was mid-winter when bears are normally in hibernation.

I was following my trap-line trail in the dim winter light. When I left the cabin, the temperature was a normal ten degrees below zero on our Fahrenheit scale. I was caught up in the shush-shush rhythm of my snowshoes when I saw something large coming toward me on the trail. I quickly clambered, as best I could, up the nearest spruce tree with my snowshoes on!

The bear never looked at me. I could see that ice crystals had practically covered the hair around its eyes. The back of its hairy coat was also as white as the snow of the trail. I wondered why it had not denned up somewhere for the winter, but felt relieved as it passed without sensing me. The spruce tree, which I had hurriedly struggled to climb, was small. I was hanging precariously no more than six feet above my snow shoed trail.

Many times since, I have wondered if that grizzly survived the winter. I also recall how grateful I am that I was not the means of his survival if he did.

I have many bear stories, but this is enough for now, as I have to take our bucket out in the lake for water. At the shore cabin we get our drinking water from the lake. There are not many places left where water can be drunk without chemical treatment. I imagine that when you read this even our lake will not be safe for drinking.

Will write more later. Your Great-Great-Granddad, Sam

THIRTY-FOURTH

Dear Great-Great-Grandsons and Daughters,

Here in Alaska more people fly small planes than in any other state. Donna and I had just tucked ourselves into our sleeping bag when the whine of an engine raised us upright. An airplane burst over the mountain ridge above us. We could see it had floats, not wheels, and wondered who would be flying in here that we had not expected. Although it was after 10 p.m. it was still light at this time of year.

We were in our winter cabin, over a half-mile from the shore of the lake. We could see through our field glasses that the aircraft did not set down in front of our shore cabin. It disappeared behind a point of land leaving a track on the water. We wondered about who might have flown in, and then we dropped off to sleep.

Again, when a plane awakened us with its sudden arrival over the ridge, then landed behind the point, we were curious. I considered getting dressed and hiking down to the shore. But then the plane took off.

After the fourth landing and take-off, Donna and I assumed that Dall sheep hunters had stopped to unload supplies, fuel and extra weight so the plane could land and take off from a small lake higher in the mountains. I recalled that fish and game personnel had cached extra fuel with us during sheep hunting season.

Anyway, this was a mystery to be resolved in the morning. So we closed the window curtain for the fourth time to shut out the northern arctic light and fell asleep.

The next morning, with our small outboard motor, we glided across the lake's glassy surface and around the point to do our detective work. It was obvious that people and supplies had been shuttled in and out. The foot-prints and marks, where the airplane's floats had been pulled ashore verified what we had assumed.

To charter a bush plane and pilot for the short eighty-five miles from Bettles Field costs us over five hundred dollars. I have frequently been asked why we don't have our own aircraft on floats? I point out the cost of flying in fuel, maintenance, and the time and concern it would take to deal with the weather in summer and storage in Fairbanks in winter if it were not in use with skis. No matter how one tries to figure it, an airplane is a very expensive machine to maintain. Here in the Brooks Range, it would soon own us and dictate to us on its terms, not ours.

As I look back over the friends and acquaintances in Alaska who are no longer living, a great many owe their demise to aircraft. They would have denied this, saying that the problem was the pilot's or the mechanic's.

I remember my neighbor, Meader, who lived at Wild Lake, saying this before he stepped too far forward on a float and into the whirling propeller. He was trying to catch an anchor rope on the shore of the Koyukuk River at Bettles.

The body of my neighbor, Ackerman, who lived at Chandalar Lake, was not found until several years later. His plane was discovered in the lake's deep water. I joined in an aerial search one winter for the Bettles Air Field Manager, whose plane was later discovered where it had nosed into the mountains with him.

The remains of a plane on the hillside, a few hundred feet above us, recalls the summer that two people escaped death but were severely injured here at our lake. This also recalls the time our friend, Troy Thacker, and his son were flying over from Coldfoot to visit us and crash-landed on our frozen lake. Fortunately, they were not injured but had a harrowing experience hiking back over the mountains to the Trans-Alaska Pipeline haul road.

It would be ghoulish for me to continue listing, but I could easily add half a dozen more who were not so lucky.

Since I had written to you about my interest in flying when I was young, and of the many hours spent soaring in gliders when I was living in the San Francisco Bay area, I assumed you probably wondered about flying in Alaska. Here, we use commercial bush plane air taxis. And now you know why.

Even so, I recall several close encounters with disaster in bush taxis, but they are not so memorable as those having to do with winter cold. I suppose these winter experiences come to mind because the tundra is turning icy crisp underfoot right now, heralding the beginning of freeze-up.

I imagine that you have read Jack London's classic wintertime, fictional short story, "To Make A Fire." I say "fictional" because the experience was not his. His stories were created from tales he heard in Alaskan bar rooms. Any northern trapper would share my recognition of his fiction. But still, he is effective in pointing out that cold is dangerous. It doesn't have to be forty or more degrees below zero Fahrenheit, but it does seem more dramatic! The cold can be lethal if one is chilled for only a short time. This I learned one summer when our bush pilot, Paul Shannahan, stopped in our shore cabin for a cup of tea after bringing us our mail.

While we sat talking the wind shifted, and his aircraft, which was against the shore but untied, drifted out about twenty feet into the lake before we noticed it through the open door of the cabin. We scrambled outside. I kicked off my loose fitting rubber boots and pulled off my sweatshirt, before running out into the cold water to capture the drifting airplane. I was soon swimming, just a hand's reach from the pontoon float. However, the airplane was drifting fast enough to stay ahead of me. It was then that I became aware that I had put myself in jeopardy in the icy water. I knew I could not make it back to shore if I did not catch a cleat on top of the aluminum float. The cold water made every move slow motion. In a final surge, I caught hold of the tying cleat on top of the float.

By then I was so cold and exhausted I could not pull myself onto the float and out of the icy water. All I could do was desperately hang on while others pushed our rowboat from the shore to come to my rescue. I have never shaken more violently from chill as I did when being rowed to shore. It was an hour after being warmed that I ceased shuddering.

Another close call from the cold was a day that I foolishly went out to check my trap-line one winter. The thermometer outside the cabin window registered fifty degrees below zero Fahrenheit. At fifty below, one has to move slowly and breathe carefully through the wolverine ruff of his parka and facemask so as not to frostbite a windpipe or lung.

I had removed a frozen lynx from a trap near a collapsed miner's cabin and was delighted that a wolverine had not found it. When I tried to reset the trap, I foolishly took off one of my big mitts to reach in an inside pocket of my parka for pliers to cut a piece of wire, with which I'd fastened the trap to a small spruce tree. I had also taken off my snowshoes. And though I had on cotton under-gloves, I became aware that my hand had no feeling.

I immediately knew I was in trouble when I tried to replace the pliers with a numb hand. I had matches; wood shavings and a piece of candle in another pocket, but had to take my other hand outside of its big mitt to get them. I knew I needed to make a fire or my hands would be unable to get my snowshoes on. I remember fighting panic when I could not feel the matches. I tried to light them. They scattered in the snow. I had crawled into a hollow made by the downed roof of the old cabin. There, with careful deliberation, I finally lit the wick of my stub candle I carried for such purpose.

I am writing to you about this experience from our warm cabin this September morning, making it seem unreal. I hope it doesn't seem so to you. At that time, I knew my odds for survival were mighty slim. Under those tense circumstances, a sense of panic was as big an enemy as the cold.

With much fumbling by blistered fingers in burnt gloves, I got a warming fire blazing from the frozen, half rotted rafters of the downed cabin. I knew I had to feel warm enough before attempting my return. For over two hours I marched in standing position, turning myself around in front of a fire that I continually fed while suffering those terrible pains in hands that had suffered frostbite. When I felt up to it, I tied the frozen lynx on top of my backpack and with difficult deliberation strapped on my snowshoes.

It was dark when I felt able to leave my life saving fire. The aurora was already lighting the sky, reflecting my joy at finally seeing the distant kerosene lamplight in the cabin window that February night. I remember how good it felt to be alive.

It feels good to be alive this sparkling, blue-sky morning as I write you across the years. Even though frost has turned the tundra white, the red alders, yellow willows and golden birches have returned the sunshine captured during the past three months

Donna and I will begin chinking between the cabin logs with moss. And before we leave, we will bar windows and door to dissuade bears, wolves and wolverine from entering.

Flour, sugar and other foodstuff, which will remain through the winter, will be carried into our high cache and the ladder removed.

I'll try to write again before we leave Koviashuvik later this week.

With affection,

Your Great-Great-Granddad, Sam

◣ THIRTY-FIFTH

Dear Great-Great-Granddaughters and Sons,

On this Labor Day weekend Sunday, as Donna and I were returning across the lake after exploring a lingonberry patch on the island, we heard and saw a monstrous machine which appeared from the distance to be a bluish military tank approaching our shore cabin.

Through our field glasses, we could see it had an occupied cab with windshields that would fit an eighteen-wheel highway truck. Behind the cab, were two people in camouflage clothing, sharing the large truck bed with a steel fifty-gallon drum. The vehicle rolled over the tundra smashing down six to eight foot spruce trees with its huge tracks. I estimated them to be at least eight feet apart.

As we shared the field glasses, we wondered if we were being invaded by a foreign force. Actually, we were. It depends upon how you define "foreign" and "force." This huge device had obviously come into our home site across uninhabited country by way of the Bettles River north west of us. It was rolling over obstacles that would be a hindrance to anyone on foot.

As we watched from the lake, the machine stopped. Its occupants had apparently seen the roof of our high cache or cabin on the shore. Instead of continuing into our property it turned right, paralleling the shore about two hundred yards inland until it stopped above a beach across our bay where we often fish for great northern pike.

They had not invaded our personal property (our homestead here on the shore) but we certainly had a sense of invasion of our space. Here, the natural sounds and sights of our wilderness home have been a respite from the frenetic urban bedlam of the world outside for more than thirty years.

As I watched through the field glasses, a small four-wheel all-terrain vehicle, with its occupants, joined the other invaders on the beach and I could see they were having a discussion. After about an hour, the huge tractor-truck left, followed by the smaller four-wheeler. It returned along the same track it had made on its arrival. Donna and I speculated as to why they left at evening time. Normally they would be setting up camp. Here is the case we made, at least for ourselves:

This is the Labor Day weekend, a time to get away and fish before freeze-up. We assumed they also knew that we normally were gone by Labor Day. We assumed one or more of the invaders had been here in the past and that our boats, which we pulled up and turned over high on the shore, had been used when we were away. We assumed this was the goal of the tractor until its occupants spied us watching them from the lake with our field glasses.

Although we rowed in to our cabin on the shore, the invaders made no move to make contact. Nor did we. Their awareness of us being aware of them, when our presence was not expected, was an embarrassing situation. Instead of camping as they had planned; as they – as they might have put it – "got the hell out."

Anyway, this blot on our beautiful Labor Day Sunday raised many value questions. What is privacy and in what context is it defined? We are the only private landowners on our lake or near it for miles. Why do I say "our lake"? The lake belongs to all U.S. citizens, as do other navigable waters, National Parks, and public lands. I would be within my legal rights to defend my property, which is poorly marked by blazed trees. What about the sound of an all-terrain tractor, or the smell of its exhaust that crosses our legal property line? And why is it that people congregate where others are? Even here, where we are not on any track or trail? For privacy, Donna and I moved and rebuilt our shore cabin here after twenty-five years of residence on the Lake Creek Bay.

I recognize that people are innately gregarious. Every city is an ant den of busy interaction. It is all the more reason for places apart and a time not to be caught up in the whirl of the crowd. If anyone questions that ours is an ant den society today, all they need do is look at a highway map. I wonder if Alaska will by covered with highway systems like other states when you read this? Already, the Trans-Alaska-Pipeline haul road has been upgraded for year-round travel to Prudhoe Bay and the oil fields north of the range. The Dalton Highway (as it is now called) has made this fragile wilderness accessible to all-terrain vehicles, which, with their summer use, have torn up the old winter dogsled trails, making them un-walkable quagmires. I hope that the Alaska I have known will be much the same for you. It is one of the reasons I so strongly supported setting aside the Gates of the Arctic National Park and the Alaska National Wildlife Refuge. Even so, I am aware that there is always a public demand for "use." And beyond that a demand for "the comforts of home," meaning showers, transportation, restaurants and everything a city can offer.

I feel I should apologize for venting these concerns of my time and place on you. But in a way, they are also a part of your time and place, your inheritance. I try to imagine what your world is like based upon my dramatically changing one. I feel fortunate to be alive at a time when the future seems more unpredictable than ever in the past. However, people seem to be pretty much biologically and psychologically the same as then. If so, it makes me wonder more than ever about you and your time. I wish you could write me back, but time's arrow points only one way. At least it does where I am at present.

Tomorrow we begin putting things in order to leave. This is the week we told our bush pilot to pick us up for the daily flight to Fairbanks from Bettles Field. Donna has just gone out to climb the ladder into the high cache. There she will inventory supplies, which will be kept safe and frozen through the winter. And now I have to split and stack firewood for our return after break-up next year.

So, until you hear from me again, my affection to you.

Your Great-Great-Granddad, Sam

THIRTY-SIXTH

Dear Great-Great-Grandsons and daughters,

It is the sixth of September and this is my last letter to you from Koviashuvik in the Brooks Range in the year 2000.

Back in July, when we were flown in, I told our Bettles Field bush pilot, Lance Carey, to pick us up September seventh, weather permitting. It is always "weather permitting" here in the mountains north of the Arctic Circle. This morning dense fog has blotted out the mountains down to the surface of the lake. We hope it will lift as the day progresses and that tomorrow will be a flyable one for Lance to pick us up. In the meantime we shall be busy closing up for the coming winter.

Closing up means storing any foodstuffs for the future in the cache away from animals, drying sourdough in the pot for our return, barring windows and door to discourage grizzlies, hauling the boat high above the shoving ice which comes at spring break-up and dealing with all the details of inventory so necessary when we return next year.

Believe it or not, our biggest worry when we return is damage from spruce squirrels. It is impossible to keep them out of cabins (they can always find or make a hole) and being rodents they have to gnaw and they do this on anything chewable. They make their nests in anything nest-able and pull out hair from our moose skin rugs to do so. Here they cannot be trapped with bait as they only eat spruce seeds, which they shuck from the cones they store. Their only control is to have hungry ermine about. Last winter we were fortunate to have little squirrel damage. From ermine scat and squirrel remains, it was evident that white ermine (which we call weasels when brown in summer) had found our cabin a great restaurant serving spruce squirrels. We cannot expect to be so fortunate as to have resident ermine again this winter.

The fog has lifted and the sky is blue above the peaks. And since this is our last day here, we shall take time out to catch our last of the season fish for supper. Donna suggested a great northern pike, so we shall take the boat to Pike Bay (guess why we call it that?) and try our luck. Will write more when we return.

LATER

It is now noon and the pike were apparently aware of our coming and made themselves scarce. Not a one made a run at our lures. However, a fat lake trout char apparently did not get the word. He got hauled into the boat for supper.

It is spawning time for the char, so his colors are brilliant with bright red pectoral fins edged in white, much like the red alders on the mountain-side that are edged by the white snow below the peaks. This char will make a tasty meal with lingonberries tonight. I will write more later but we must be ready to leave by tomorrow when the bush plane arrives, so again I'll set this letter aside until evening.

AFTER SUPPER

The beautiful char was delicious. Donna poached it in milk (we bring in powdered milk with our supplies as well as dried fruits and vegetables). Donna has it figured close. We are now at the end of our larder and ready to leave. I hope tomorrow's weather is like today's so the plane can fly in as scheduled.

I remember the time some years ago when the bush pilot was to arrive with supplies just before freeze-up. We were staying for the winter. When he did not arrive and there was still open water for floats, I assumed he would be in after freeze-up on skis. In the meantime I had taken a moose for our winter meat. However, we were short of about everything else – flour, sugar, coffee, tea and tobacco. At that time, my wife, Billie, was a chain cigarette smoker and I shared her habit along with my pipe.

We began to ration what we had, but the tobacco was soon gone and the lake not yet frozen. It would be two to three weeks before the ice would be thick enough to land a plane on skis. We began to explore substitutes for tobacco. First we tried Labrador tealeaves, and then dried poplar and alder leaves. They were terrible. We even explored lingonberry leaves and spruce needles. Dried willow leaves were best, but I think we thought so because we assumed they contained aspirin as it was from willow that aspirin originated.

Anyway, Billie felt desperate. She had also run out of cigarette papers but that was not my concern with my pipe. My concern was for her, as her addiction had never been tested before, and my sympathy did not help much. I never considered myself addicted to tobacco, although I had smoked since before my teens with others. I became aware that I had never smoked alone. My smoking addiction was what the Japanese called "the weed of friend-ship." It was sharing a smoke that was my addiction. I became aware that sharing things together was my addiction. Whether eating, drinking, playing cribbage or sharing philosophical perspectives, sharing was my addiction. Not the weed, it was the activity, the game, the sharing, and the doing together.

Anyway, Billie had also run out of cigarette papers as well as tobacco. She was cutting the margins from her journal for a substitute when we heard the whine of an aircraft. We could see it had wheels as it buzzed over us. We then recognized our bush pilot, Daryl Morris, as he made another turn and waved. We thought he just wanted us to know we were not forgotten because the plane continued across the lake. Then it turned and again flew low over us. As it did so, an object dropped with a streaming yellow surveyor's ribbon attached. It was a package containing a large can of tobacco and papers with a note attached, saying in effect, "I understand your predicament. I went over your grocery list. Will bring in groceries after freeze-up."

This kind of concern and friendship seems rare today. Back when we were more isolated from human contact it was common.

This is now the day we are to be picked up and flown out to Bettles and to catch our commercial flight to Fairbanks. This morning is clear and the thermometer registers 25.

Last night, when I got up and stepped outside to pee, there were northern lights sweeping across the sky in violet and rosy streamers. They should be called southern lights here because we look south as well as overhead to see the aurora. It is now dark enough at this time of year for this great display, which we accepted as a goodbye gift.

Another goodbye gift was a chorus of howls from a pack of wolves across the lake this morning as I was putting up our protective window covers for the winter. As always, we hate to abandon this bit of paradise, but we shall now leave it to the wolves, moose and caribou as the lake groans and cracks while it freezes. Soon the snows of winter will spread their white blanket over all, and the grizzlies will have snuggled into their dens awaiting the sun's return.

LATER

It is now five o'clock and beginning to rain. After waiting all day, listening for Lance to fly in for our pick-up, we became chilled. I went through the process of removing bear protection covers so we could at least make a fire in the Yukon stove and keep dry. We had made pick-up arrangements so we could meet our flight out of Bettles because we were to be picked up by a friend in Fairbanks. However, at this late hour we are wondering if we are on anyone's schedule at Bettles Field? My concern is that we planned our supplies through breakfast this morning. If the plane does not arrive before dark, do we wait another day, hoping we are not forgotten? Or do we start the long journey on foot over two passes to the pipeline haul road, there hoping to catch a ride?

The nighttime temperatures are now below freezing and there is snow on the surrounding mountains. A two-day hike with heavy packs is not a welcome prospect.

I hear an airplane but its sound is not the Beaver we expect. It sounds like a Cessna. Donna has just confirmed that it has floats and is dropping its flaps to set down. Hooray!

Will write more later,

Your Great-Great-Granddad, Sam

THIRTY-SEVENTH

Dear Great-Great-Granddaughters and Sons,

Donna and I flew out of Koviashuvik to Bettles yesterday evening. We soared between mountains that were scarlet with alder, and yellow gold with birches, willows and aspen.

At the Bettles float pond (a small lake where we landed a few miles from the lodge and village) it was raining and our pilot, Lance Carey, had four hunters and their gear waiting for him. He was to fly them out in another aircraft, so we left him there and drove ourselves in the transport vehicle to Bettles Lodge. There, we were lucky to get a room for the night.

We could have pitched our tent in the willows by the Koyukuk River, which we have done in the past. However, it was raining, and after six weeks in the range it was great to sip a beer, take a hot water shower and collapse between sheets in a queen size bed.

I am writing to you this morning from a booth where we are having breakfast in the Lodge's dining area. This dining area and the kitchen that was later built as an extension of the Lodge did not exist when I was first here thirty-four years ago. The Lodge was then owned by Wien Airlines, which had a weekly flight from Fairbanks and was operated by their pilot, Paul Haggland. Paul had an employee who made beds and cleaned the few upstairs rooms. She was also the cook who prepared meals for guests, which at that time were primarily hunters.

Paul made weekly scheduled flights to the Eskimo village in Anaktuvuk Pass at the top of the Brooks Range. It was he who flew me and my student companion from there to Bettles Field after we had hiked the many miles through the mountains seeking Robert Marshall's seed planting plots of white spruce back in nineteen sixty-six.

Since then, much has happened in Bettles. It is now the entry Head-quarters of the Gates Of The Arctic National Monument, and Bettles Lodge has had a number of other ownerships and management.

About thirty years ago, our friend and bush pilot, Daryl Morris, created the Bettles Light and Power Company here by hauling in two huge diesel generators across the snow packed tundra and frozen rivers.

One winter, my wife, Billie, and I spent a month overseeing the electric generating system while Daryl and his family took their first long-needed vacation to a warm climate. At that time we became an intimate part of this small community while our home at Koviashuvik was isolated in the mountains over eighty-five air miles away.

Today there are very few people who were here at that time. Jeannie Stevens, who was Postmaster then, is still filling that role. Her son, Bret, is baggage handler for our flight today. Bret, who told me he is now thirty-one years old, came into the world the year we were living here.

I will have to write more later as Donna and I have just been informed that our plane is ready to take off.

LATER

What a treat we had flying out from Bettles. Instead of returning directly south to Fairbanks, there were weather delays and problems with other flights. Therefore, we were rescheduled to fly down the Koyukuk River to the native village of Alakaket and from there to the Eskimo village in Anaktuvuk Pass at the top of the range before returning to Fairbanks.

We flew to Alakaket but could not land as the airstrip was fogged in. We returned to Bettles Field. At Bettles we picked up two other passengers, Dave Peterson and his dog, Chicha. Chicha climbed up on the seat facing me, but on take-off she dropped down on the toe of my boot and against my shins where she felt protected during our take-off vibration from the gravel airstrip. Then we climbed between snow-covered peaks up the John River to the Eskimo village in Anaktuvuk Pass.

I would not have recognized the village in this wind-swept mountain pass into which I had hiked thirty-four years ago. We landed on a black macadam runway and parked in front of a modern building while freight that we were carrying was unloaded. We were only briefly on the ground so I did not leave the aircraft. The village beyond the airstrip was visibly not the community I had known in the past with its scattered tents and sod houses.

What I saw as we flew in reminded me of the subdivisions that are everywhere in the lower forty-eight. The large metal buildings by the runway were reminiscent of the warehouses in Fairbanks. This dramatic change has taken place with money from the oil bonanza on the north slope of the Brooks Range. There is still no road into Anaktuvuk, and as we flew out across the snowy peaks and looked down into the deep valleys, I was again caught up in the stark beauty of where I had once hiked over trail-less terrain into the pass.

I wrote a monograph to share with my colleagues when I returned to the San Francisco bay area, titled ESKIMO VISIT. If I can find a copy of it in my files, I'll send it along with this letter. It will give you a description of the village as I found it thirty-four years ago last month. Sorry, could not find it.

Donna and I expect to be in Alaska for another week with her son Keinan and daughter Melea and their friends, so will write you more later.

Keep kovianak-tok (happy)!

Your Great-Great-Granddad, Sam

⤷ THIRTY-EIGHTH

Dear Great-Great-Grandsons and Daughters,

This morning I am writing to you from Girdwood, Alaska. It is a ski and resort community in the Chugach Mountains about fifty miles from Anchorage. Donna and I have been here this past week with son, Kienan, and daughter, Melea, who, with several other young people, are working this summer in these resort facilities. They rent a large Chalet house in which "the tribe" includes Melea's partner, Thomas Roed, and four others. Donna and I have our sleeping bags on the floor with our backpacks in Melea and Thomas' room.

Actually, "the tribe" includes four or five more, all under the age of thirty. All have living quarters elsewhere here in Girdwood. Donna and I feel it a privilege to be included in the group as the two older members of this tribe.

We came here on our way back to Arizona from Koviashuvik. We are here to visit thirty-four acres of land that nine of us have purchased in the Talkeetna Mountains near Chickaloon, Alaska. We hope in the future to construct individual homes on our community held property. At present it has one small sixteen by sixteen foot cabin. This past week we spent several days walking the land and sharing sleeping bag space on the floor of the cabin. We new owners are delighted with our setting on a wooded mesa above fast-flowing Chickaloon River and below the craggy cliffs of Castle Mountain.

Our thirty-four acres are heavily wooded with aspen, birch and spruce trees. A bark beetle infestation several years ago left large standing-dead evergreen trees whose wood, now air cured, will provided many board feet of lumber for future cabin building.

The nine of us new landowners are Donna's son, Kienan, Jesse Gesten,

Jeremy Kimmel, Donna and me, and two other couples. They are Melea (Donna's daughter) and Thomas Roed, and Bianca Flores and Jeffery Whaley. The Jeff/Bianca couple, along with Thomas/Melea, are planning their weddings in Hawaii in April, where our extended family will gather to celebrate.

The last celebration in which Donna and I participated was the wedding of her niece, Sara Whaley, and Jacob Gold. This was the day before we left for Kovaishuvik. I conducted the ceremony of union and their exchange of vows outdoors at the Wrigley Mansion, overlooking the glittering city lights of Phoenix on July twenty-second. The summer heat was stifling but inside the air-conditioned ballroom we celebrated and danced well into the night. The next day, we flew out of Phoenix for Fairbanks, Alaska on our way to Koviashuvik.

I have written you about our summer at Koviashuvik. Now we are on our way back to our hogan in Pleasant Valley, Arizona. We will fly to Seattle where my son Chip will pick us up and drive us over the Cascade Range to Yakima. There, he and Lisa are anxious to show us their new home and apple orchard in the small town of Tieton. I mention all these people to you because you may find you are related when you read this letter.

This contrast between our summer in the northern Alaskan wilderness and the busy world in which we are now becoming immersed is dramatic. I feel bombarded by the busyness, commitments and news from which we have had a brief pause. As I write you, I wonder what news will be of significance to you when you read this?

One interesting news item to me is that a spacecraft, launched four years ago, is now sending data about the asteroid Eros. It is the first asteroid to be studied close up. The craft, called NEAR (Near Earth Asteroid Rendezvous), is scheduled to end its mission in February when it drops to the twenty-one mile long rock, which passes close to Earth but never crosses its orbit. Asteroids are in the news as there is speculation that an unknown one might cross into Earth's orbit and the catastrophe it could cause.

When I was a kid, "Doomsday" was speculated to come from outer space in the form of aliens, usually from the planet Mars. With the creation of atomic chain reaction, "Doomsday" speculations came closer to home. Now the speculation is again returning to outer space. What seems never to change is the belief in "Doomsday."

Whether in the form of an asteroid, atmospheric warming, aliens or plague, I try to imagine what form "Doomsday" has taken when you read this letter. I'll bet it is still around.

Also, I'll bet the issue of church and state is still around. President Clinton just signed a bill that prevents municipalities from using zoning laws to keep out churches or temples they don't want inside their city limits. Cities and towns have tried to use zoning laws to stop new churches or temples from moving into their area. Having been involved as a minister in the building of new churches I find this significant legislation.

Here in Alaska, where the opening up of ANWR (Arctic National Wild-life Refuge) to oil drilling is a national legislative possibility, I hope President Clinton will declare it a National Monument before he leaves office as a legacy to you.

A legacy I would like to leave for you since I have mentioned "Doomsday," is the right to die in the manner you choose. Here in Alaska a suit is being brought contesting the criminal status of assisted death. Albert Wagstaff filed in the state Superior Court, arguing that the terminally ill Alaskans have the right to choose to end their lives with medication given to them by doctors. At present anyone who assists a person in death is guilty of a felony, no matter if the person assisting is a doctor, family member or friend.

Only in the State of Oregon have residents made it legal to end their lives with physician-assisted death.

When my former wife, Billie, was terminally ill in Arizona, she chose to end her life with self-induced medication. Being an illegal act, it had to be carried out in secrecy without physician assistance.

Here, in the city of Anchorage, a former parishoner of mine, an attorney, Sylvia Short, has made public this short letter to her doctor:

"If my medical condition becomes hopeless and death is the only predictable outcome, I would prefer not to suffer but to die in a humane and dignified manner. I therefore request that my physician help with all options for a gentle death including medications that I can self administer to help my death be as peaceful and timely as possible."

Assisted death, like she describes in her letter, is not legal in Alaska or in any other state, with the exception of Oregon. I hope this is not the case when you read this letter. In the present I will work for and hope that when you do read this letter you will have the right to make your own decision about this "grave" subject.

I will probably not write you again until we are back home in Arizona. Until then I hope all is well with you in your time and place wherever you are.

Keep Koviashuktok.

Your Great-Great-Granddad, Sam

THIRTY-NINTH

Dear Great-Great-Granddaughters and Sons,

I am writing you today from Puerto Penasco (Rocky Point) on the shore of the Sea of Cortez in northern Mexico.

A line of pelicans skims just above the wave tips. They flap their huge wings, and then glide in turn before again catching the air with lazy strokes. We are here because it is October and the moon is full.

Every year at this Halloween time, a group of families take this weekend break from work and school on this Mexican beach. It is a time to snorkel, sit and watch the shore birds, to read and write. So I am writing to you, as you have not heard from me since I wrote you from Alaska.

Several of us are sitting in folding chairs or stretched out on the sand beneath a palm frond covered palapa. This permanent palapa is much larger than a beach umbrella, which it imitates. It provides shade from the brilliant sub-tropical sun. In southern Mexico, where the Alaskan "tribe" which I wrote you about, gathers on the Pacific shore in the village of Mazunte, Oaxaca, palapas are the permanent housing for shelter from sun and rain. In Mazunte a house is called a palapa when it has a palm-thatched roof.

A couple of years ago, Donna and I helped Kienan in the construction of a permanent palapa for Juan Vargas, an indigenous Aztecan Indian in Mazunte. He can rent it as income for his family and it is housing for us (the tribe) in the off-season. Mazunte is where sea turtles climb up the sandy beach beneath palm trees to dig holes and lay their eggs.

A few years ago the turtles were in danger of extinction. Today, conservationists are trying to protect the sea turtles from commercial exploitation by egg gatherers. I hope that when you read this the Mazunte sea turtles will be thriving.

One reason for the palapa construction was to provide a source of income for the Vargas family instead of their exploiting the turtles and their eggs. When I was teaching comparative zoology, we used turtles in the laboratory to represent the cold-blooded reptile family. Along with their dry land relative, the tortoise, their life span seems amazing compared to us mammals. I suppose they in part intrigued me because I once had a desert tortoise as a pet when I was a kid living south of Phoenix.

The Sonoran desert began across the irrigation canal from where we lived. It was there I found Petunia, the tortoise. Petunia got her name because she preferred Petunia blossoms in her diet. I was not sure that Petunia was a she, but at that time, with her choice of diet, it seemed logical that she was.

Petunia was estimated to be about fifty years old according to my biology teacher. From today's information, I'm sure she was much older. To a tortoise, a hundred years is nothing to brag about. From the few one hundred-year-old people I have known, and many who still have a while to go there, they may have something to brag about. However, from the shape most of them are in, the tortoise comes out way ahead.

As I watch the line of pelicans skim above the surface, I imagine them as pterodactyls or ancient flying reptiles that preceded birds, mammals and us, eons ago. This reminds me of how short a time it is that I preceded you. Yet, based upon changes I have seen, I cannot imagine what your world is really like. Of course some things are the same, or change very slowly. Like the flight of these pelicans and the sea turtles' moonlight rendezvous on a tropical beach of southern Mexico.

A person who brought to our beach a morning paper, the *Arizona Daily Star* from Tucson, has interrupted me in my writing to you. It has the headline: "Mideast Peace in Ashes: Israeli helicopter gunships rocketed Ramallah and Gaza City after a Palestinian mob stabbed and stomped to death three Israeli reserve soldiers and then paraded a mutilated body through town."

This illustrates the shifts that can happen overnight, changing the future dramatically. As you are a part of that future, what is happening now and how it is handled will affect you in ways I cannot comprehend.

Another report in the paper is about a meteorite, estimated to weigh about 220 tons when it smashed into the atmosphere spraying bits of space rock over a frozen lake in Canada's British Columbia. A Canadian, driving on the ice of Tagish Lake, spotted bits of the meteorite. Working in minus twenty-degree temperatures, he collected about two pounds of the black charcoal-like fragments in a plastic bag and stored them in a freezer. Preliminary tests of this primitive material found it loaded with organic molecules, which could have been the original raw materials for the formation of life on earth.

For me, I find this a unique experience to be sitting here on this Mexican beach writing to you who are not yet born; while at the same time writing about a five and a half billion-year-old meteorite and my pet tortoise, Petunia.

Someone once spoke of human awareness as a "time binder." I guess that is what I am this morning as I watch the pelicans glide from here to there and from there to here.

I hope your time is as full of wonder as mine, and you can say "Isn't it wonderful just being alive?"

Your Great-Great-Granddad, Sam

FORTIETH

Dear Great-Great-Grandsons and Daughters,

When I last wrote you from the sunny beach at Puerto Penasco in northern Mexico, I told you about a five and a half billion-year-old meteorite. You can see that I'm intrigued with the idea of life or its possibility not being confined to our planet Earth.

An interesting discovery just reported by a couple of environmental biologists, Russell Vreeland and William Rosenzweig, revived a spore that was locked inside a salt crystal believed to have survived in suspended animation two hundred and fifty million years ago. If so, it could be evidence that life forms can live long enough to drift from planet to planet. The salt crystal was taken from a shaft eighteen hundred and fifty feet below the ground at the U.S. Energy Departments Waste Isolation Plant thirty miles east of Carlsbad, New Mexico. I wonder if such life forms in suspended animation might survive in ancient subterranean salt deposits on Mars?

By the time you read this letter you probably can answer my question. But for me now, stuck back here at the beginning of the twenty-first century, I can only speculate about what you already know as fact.

I am reminded of this when I recall the announcement of the creation of ENIAC, the Electronic Numerical Integrator And Calculator, back in 1946. I was with OSRD, the Office of Scientific Research and Development during World War II at the time. This thirty-ton computer had eighteen thousand vacuum tubes. At that time, IBM was making a larger, more powerful one. Also, at that time, I could only speculate about computers by the ton.

However, only two years later in 1948, Bell Laboratories soldered a germanium crystal onto a metal face, which replaced the vacuum tube by what is now called a transistor. Today instead of three tons, I have a notebook computer on my lap with which I edit my handwritten letters to you. I could never have made such a speculation in 1948.

Speaking of speculation, it was in 1948 when I was visiting my parents in Mentone, California that I drove through San Bernardino where a hamburger stand had a large sign, "Buy 'em By the Bag!" At fifteen cents each, I bought a bag of these pre-wrapped hamburgers for our lunch. It never occurred to me to speculate that I next might see this "Buy 'em By the Bag," called "Chef Speedee," in Phoenix, Arizona in 1953, and being advertised by two yellow sheet metal arches which became the symbol of MacDonald's fast foods. Today, those golden arches and hamburgers, which I first ate in San Bernardino, can be found in every major city on earth.

It was in the nineteen fifties that crew cuts, flat tops and duck tails were cool. Even as a clergyman, I kept my crew cut through the next decade until I moved into the wilderness of northern Alaska. It was in the nineteen fifties that the minimum wage was boosted from seventy-five cents to a dollar an hour, and "under God" was added to the pledge of allegiance. It was the time of the War in Korea, and the United States detonated a hydrogen bomb in the Marshall Islands, "To show the world."At that time, Senator McCarthy was branding people communist sympathizers. The Rosenbergs were executed as subversives, and Margaret Chase Smith from Maine was the first woman elected to the United States Senate.

As I look back, while writing you today, I remember that the way it was for me at that time seemed pretty weird. I acquired a theological degree and became an ordained minister in Stockton, California. From Stockton I was called to become Director of American Unitarian Youth of the U.S. and Canada, with headquarters at 25 Beacon Street next to the Capitol (called State House) in Boston. From my second story office window I looked down on the Capitol's lawn and statuary. It was at 25 Beacon Street that I met Senator Adlai Stevenson, a Unitarian and the Democratic Party's candidate for the Presidency. And it was at a rally across the street on the Boston Common that I shook hands with General Dwight Eisenhower who defeated Stevenson for the Presidency.

It was at this "weird" time in my life that I learned that the FBI (Federal Bureau of Investigation) had a file on me as a possible subversive communist sympathizer. In Stockton I had publicly spoken out against the California State Loyalty Oath and had refused to sign it as a state employee teaching a night class in a Great Books program. An FBI agent had visited me at the time and cautioned me about my perspective in those times of tension.

Here in Pleasant Valley, Arizona this autumn, we are delighted that our dry spell has been broken by three days of rain. It has washed the junipers and pines so they glisten in the sunshine. Donna is working on a quilt and I am writing you while our satellite dish is picking up the world news to tell us about the European economic relationships with China and the possibility of peace talks between the Israelis and Palestinians. Here in the U.S. the news is dominated by the coming presidential election in which the Republican and Democratic Party arguments sound much the same. The Green party candidate, Ralph Nader, stands no chance to be elected, but Donna and I hope his platform will affect others.

Back in 1965 Ralph Nader, at age thirty-one, wrote a book about auto safety titled: "Unsafe at Any Speed." Since then he has been a voice for safety and environmental concerns. Now, thirty-five years later, he is a third party candidate for President. I wonder if the Green Party will be around when you read this?

I am very much aware that much of what I'm writing to you must seem irrelevant to you in your time. I try to imagine what I would like to hear from my great-great-granddad if he had written to me about his life in his time. What would interest me today might not be anything he would think of mentioning. This is why you get such a hodgepodge from me. I know that half of what I write you may be meaningless but I write so the other half may reach you. All I can do is tell you the way it was and is for me.

So I send you this letter with my love,

Your Great-Great-Granddad, Sam

FORTY-FIRST

Dear Great-Great-Granddaughters and Sons,

I have mentioned our hogan here in Pleasant Valley from where I am writing you today. We call our house a hogan because it is circular (actually six-sided) and has an east-facing door, as do the traditional homes of the Navajo whose hogans dot the high plateau northeast of us. Our hogan is on a knoll along Mail Trail Road.

Mail Trail got its name before I was born. It was the end of a trail that packhorses used to bring the mail to Ola Beth Young's house here in Pleasant Valley. Her home became the Post Office. This is why our community appears today on maps as Young, Arizona.

The year I graduated from Phoenix Union High School I had a summer job surveying here in the Sierra Ancha Mountains for the United States General Land Office. It was 1938. I celebrated my eighteenth birthday with an eight-member survey crew, which had been packed into this rugged country on horseback to make the first general survey. We marked Townships and Section corners in a terrain that had been declared unsurveyable when Arizona became a state in 1912.

To me at age eighteen in the year 1938, the year 1912 seemed very old and ancient. It was way back before paved roads, telephones and refrigerators. Twenty-six years is a long time when you are eighteen. Anyway, as I recall the mournful, eerie cry of a mountain lion beneath Aztec Peak and the dry clatter of a rattlesnake under a Manzanita bush, that summer seems as if it were this past one.

Isn't it interesting that the time before we were born seems like it was a long time ago; yet what we remember can seem like only yesterday? I wonder if this is the same for you?

Today, the jagged terrain of the Sierra Anchas is much as it was sixty-two years ago when, on a Fourth of July, I climbed over sharp boulders to explore an ancient Indian cliff dwelling. If you recall, I wrote you about that exciting find some time ago.

When I came back from Alaska, I returned to this area, which had caught my sense of adventure. Here in Pleasant Valley I constructed our hogan home of rocks and logs of ponderosa pine. And again, this reminds me of how different time can seem. That was a short twenty-two years ago!

I say "short," but since then I have served eight interim ministries in Unitarian Universalist churches, from San Antonio, Texas to Reno, Nevada and acquired a new family and published two books. When I look back, that time seems short. When I try to look ahead, time is still like it was when I was a kid, a long road ahead toward where you are in a time that is impossible to imagine.

I don't think it was that way for people who were born and grew up in the same community in which their great-great grandparents had been born. When I first walked into the Inuit Village in Anaktuvuk Pass, the friends I made there were in many ways still living as did their great-great-grandparents, dependent on caribou, and at home in a familiar environment.

Today that has all changed. They watch the same television shows and news broadcasts I receive on my satellite dish here in Pleasant Valley. They can no more imagine what the future will bring than I can. As they look back to the comfort of the sod hut where their parents sliced caribou ribs for supper, which was for the Paniak and Agook kids just a short time ago, they now sit on a Governing Board of their Native Corporation trying to fathom the future and come up with the best investments for their Corporation's funds.

What is permanent and what is transient? This question is as old as written history. Today in my time, little seems to be permanent. Even the patterns of biological evolution can now be manipulated in the laboratory. It is possible that biological death may be under human control by the time you read this. I doubt it but who knows?

As an epistemologist, this kind of question intrigues me. It may be that what is most permanent is our questioning. What do you think? I wish I could hear from you since I'm sure a lot has happened which might answer many of my questions when you read this. I know that today many people are annoyed by this kind of speculation, called "philosophical." As a friend of mine said, "I want answers, not questions."

Because you live in a time of answers to many of today's questions, I would like to hear from you. But since I can't, I will assume that with many of the answers I seek, you still have just as many questions in your time.

One question we may share could be related to weather. Not just rain, snow, heat or cold, but the psychological weather, which is sometimes called the context of the times. Today is a third, gray, rainy day, which is not common here in central Arizona. I am aware that it affects my perspective and helps define my attitude. So does the economic, social and political news, which bombards us this election year affecting the climate of this time.

I wonder about your climate when you read this? My immediate concern is the condition of our thirty-mile dirt road up to the paved highway on the Mogollon Rim. It may be slick with mud and I have a commitment to fill the pulpit of the Unitarian Universalist Fellowship in Prescott this weekend.

I may write you a bit more before we take off, but if not, my best wishes for a good climate of all kinds. And I'll write more later.

Your Great-Great-Granddad, Sam

FORTY-SECOND

Dear Great-Great-Grandsons and Daughters,

The road was muddy and it snowed on our way to Prescott. The congregation to which I spoke was full of gray heads. Prescott has become a retirement community for those who moved west to seek the sun while avoiding the heat of the desert.

We stayed with Bobbi Root, a long time friend of Donna's, who is building her retirement condominium with others in a communal village called Manzanita. It's on a hill overlooking the city. I talked to the congregation about the question of what is transient and permanent since this question came up while writing to you last week.

Isn't it interesting that you, who have not been born, were there? You were there because I told them you were the reason I was considering the philosophical question of the transient and the permanent. So they now know about you. And when you read this, you will know of them. I guess this could be called time binding.

We are all time binders as we put together the events of our experiences. Also, when we share them with others, the way I am in writing you about mine. As I have said, I'd give anything to hear from you but the nature of time won't allow it. So I'll write what I think may be of interest to you as it comes to mind.

Since this is a presidential election year and next Tuesday people will vote, I recall the election year back in 1960 when John F. Kennedy, whom I was supporting, won by less than half of one percent of the votes cast. Today, few remember that he was not a popular candidate. It reminds me of how important a vote can be. It was also in 1960 that the birth control pill was approved after much objection on so-called religious grounds. In that year the census listed 180 million Americans. Today it is over 276 million.

In the nineteen sixties, when I was living in the San Francisco Bay area, I was Professor at the Starr King Seminary in Berkeley. At that time the world appeared to be coming apart. President Kennedy was assassinated. The country was caught in the tragic Vietnam War and the campus of the University of California was in turmoil with sit-ins. A student by the name of Mario Savio had caught national attention as a voice of dissent, and I too was caught up in the Free Speech Movement and was asked to head up the creation of a separate voice newspaper called The Berkeley Citizen. This was the period of the sixties that the famous march to Montgomery, Alabama with Martin Luther King took place and where my friend and colleague, the Rev. James Reeb was clubbed to death. It was at this time, after twenty-seven years together, that I separated from my wife, Jean.

The Berkeley Citizen never was launched. I had visited the Brooks Range in northern Alaska seeking the results of Robert Marshall's white spruce tree planting experiment. And as I have written you, the next year I resigned my professorship and moved into the Alaskan wilderness.

My friends and family considered me a dropout, a term coined by Tim Leary, who had been a psychologist with the seminary where I taught. Later he acquired notoriety as a promoter of the psychedelic drug experience.As for me, I did not see myself as a dropout. Mine was a move into the search for a more meaningful life than the frenetic one that currently dominates urban American society. In many ways I found it in our un-stressful life on the shore of an arctic lake. There I had the time to step back and ask questions about worth and meaning in a way that could never be done in the context of the lifestyle I left.

I did not remain there in the subsistence style of hunter, trapper and guide, but I did learn, and am still learning, how to bring those wilderness values into the context of today's go-go world.

I wonder if your world is as other-directed as today's? When I say "other-directed," I mean all those things that demand our attention, giving us little or no time to do what we would like for ourselves. What I learned was that our wilderness life gave us a sense of personal time even though we were other-directed by the stove, which required wood, the fish to be caught, meals to be prepared and the usual maintenance of our environment and ourselves.

At Koviashuvik we were not being run by the telephone, automobile, commuting schedule or the thousands of daily demands which we did not choose, but which more and more demanded our attention and time. As I look at the pace of our time today, I cannot imagine your time.

I remember how I looked forward to vacation time, when school would be out and time would be more mine than the scheduled patterns that were set for me by others. Today it is considered irresponsible not to have one's time filled by the demands of others or other things, whether it is the lawn to be mowed, car washed or the job schedule to be met. If these were personal choices I would say "Fine." If not, "Make a change. Don't just gripe!"

This is what I said to myself back in the sixties when I "dropped out" and moved into Koviashuvik, a time and place of joy in the present moment. Since then I have been trying to find ways to bring Koviashuvik into the context of the time in which most of us have to live. I try to imagine how, in your time, you can find a perspective that is less other-directed than mine.

I imagine this has been done, or your world is more an ant den than the human communities ever envisioned in the past. For you, I hope this is not your world, and wish you could write back and give me clues as to what has taken place. All I can do is tell you the way it is and was for me and hope it will be helpful.

I'll have to put down my pen, as I am being other-directed by the fire that is dying in the fireplace. I must bring in wood if we are to keep warm, so will write more later.

My love to you. Your Great-Great-Granddad, Sam

FORTY-THIRD

Dear Great-Great-Granddaughters and Sons,

When I started writing to you I began by telling you what I first remembered.

From there, I went on to share with you the way it was in my time as I remembered it. I have tried to choose what I imagine might be of interest to you. For this reason, events have not been in chronological order.

Today I am writing to you from a specific time and place. It is in the Wal-Mart shopping center parking lot in Payson, Arizona. I am sitting in the sun's warmth in the front seat of our car listening to the radio. Yesterday's national election is being contested. The votes were too close to give a victory to either Vice President Al Gore or Governor George W. Bush. The news report is that a recount of the State of Florida's votes has already begun and absentee ballots from Americans overseas could affect the outcome either way.

Of course this will be past history to you when you read this. After staying up until after midnight, the news report gave victory to Governor Bush. We went to bed with a deep sense of disappointment.

Yesterday morning, after stopping at the Young Public Library that is our voting center, Donna and I drove up the snowy road to Payson where I had an appointment with my dentist to have a tooth filled. We then had supper with our Payson friends, Bob and Betty Poynter, with whom we watched the election returns on television and spent the night. The after-effect of my tooth filling did not help my spirits as I watched the electoral votes pile up until the news media declared a Republican victory for Governor Bush.

This morning, we learned that Vice President Gore has not conceded defeat and has a majority of the popular vote. This is why I am listening to the news while writing to you here in the parking lot as Donna shops for next week's groceries.

I recall the first presidential election I can remember. The contest was between Al Smith and Herbert Hoover. I remember hearing adults say that if Al Smith was elected, the United States might be taken by the Church of Rome because he was a New York Catholic. The only Catholics I knew were the Spanish speaking laborers in Mexican town. I knew my Mexican friends called themselves Roman Catholics but I wondered what New York had to do with it.

My young ears also heard that if Al Smith were elected he would make whiskey available to everyone and cause terrible trouble by repealing the 18th amendment. I knew my parents had strong feelings about drunkenness and were therefore strong supporters of Herbert Hoover. On Election Day, my dad worked at the polls in the mining town, counting votes until after supper. I remember him returning with a big smile, saying, "Well, Herbert Hoover and the Republicans carried the day here!"

Four years later, my parents voted against Hoover, supporting Franklin Delano Roosevelt for President. They became members of the Democratic Party. They never did feel comfortable about the repeal of the 18th amendment but I did. At age fifteen I had a driver's license in Arizona and could buy a bottle of beer.

At that time I felt that the voting age should be sixteen or possibly eighteen, not an ancient twenty-one. Looking back, I suspect I was pretty intense in verbally expressing my views. I still am. And now that the voting age is eighteen, I feel I might have had some role in the change.

I am continually amazed at how strongly people resist change of any kind. I remember a railroad engineer telling me, "You can't beat steam, Sam."

This was when diesel engines were being seriously considered. Our trails crossed some years later and he had become a railroad diesel engineer. I asked him what he thought of his new engine and he said, "They are great! You can't beat a diesel."

I guess we humans have a biological resistance to change that protects us from being too venturesome. But I still believe "You've got to jump off cliffs all the time and build your wings on the way down."

A phone call a couple of days ago reminded me that my letters to you could come abruptly to an end. It was a call to tell me about a long-time friend who had a stroke and is now unable to speak or write. He is my age so this caught my attention. But then, he could also have been a passenger on the Singapore Airline plane that crashed on take off for Los Angeles that same night with many Americans among the others who can now no longer read or write.

This morning's sun recalls a beautiful sunny day in Seven Mile Canyon south of Pleasant Valley. It was there that I was sharply reminded of that narrow margin between life and death, being alert, and just a little careless. In that brief instant my foot slipped, and the professional chain saw I was using changed my life experience and put me on crutches for several weeks. It was a reminder of that narrow margin in eons of time in which each of us is given the gift of life.

This unusual narrow margin in yesterday's election reminded me again of you, who are only in my imagination, as I write you. You have not yet been given the gift of life, but when you read this you will be a unique reality and no part of my imagined creation.

Whoops, back to my reality! I see Donna pushing a grocery cart, full of plastic bags, so I'll finish this when we get home.

Here I am back two days later:

The news is full of election results. A recount in Florida has narrowed the margin. Governor Bush is only three hundred and sixty votes ahead of Vice President Gore. However, the absentee ballots from overseas will take another week to process.

The other time in our history that this kind of close race happened was way back in 1876. Rutherford B. Hays was elected President over Samuel J. Tilden by one vote. When I say "way back," I am reminded that what I am writing in the present is "way back" to you. I knew nothing about Hays and Tilden except that Hays was to me an obscure President of the past. I'd never heard of Samuel Jones Tilden, the Democrat who ran against him, until today, when the news presented these data.

Again, I wish I'd had a great-great-grandparent who had written to me and shared his or her perspective. In a way I feel cheated. It's one of the reasons I have been writing to you.

I will keep you posted on this historic presidential race even though it will be way back in the past to you. Somehow I feel that what is taking place will have significance in your time.

However, at the moment in our time, Donna and I need to take our 29-year-old Ford pickup and gather wood for our fireplace before this expected storm moves in with its rain, sleet and snow. The weather map on the television screen has given us a prediction we cannot ignore.

Again, my love to you.

Your Great-Great-Granddad, Sam

FORTY-FOURTH

Dear Great-Great-Grandsons and Daughters,

In my last letter I mentioned my twenty-nine year old pick-up truck with which we gather the wood we cut in the Tonto National Forest for our fireplace. That Ford truck has carried me over the Alcan Highway to Alaska several times in both summer and winter. At that time, much of the road was unpaved. The truck had a self-contained camper on its bed.

After many miles, I traded a professional chain saw (the one that nearly did me in) for a newer engine. It was taken from a truck that slid off on a turn on our mountain road. All the rocks, concrete, timber and building materials with which I built our log hogan have been hauled in it. It has become a special pet.

The first car I ever owned was also a special pet. It was a 1928 Model A Ford roadster. I was seventeen years old and the car was seven. It had a rumble seat in back that opened up for two passengers. The windshield would lie down over the gas tank that was in front behind the dashboard. When I wanted to, I could drive with the wind in my face. I paid forty dollars for it.

Then I overhauled the engine, replacing pistons and rings. I also replaced its rear end. The rear end did not actually need replacing, but the 1927 Model A had a faster differential and I had seen a discarded wreck among the cottonwood trees in the Salt River Wash south of Phoenix. Using a block-and-tackle hoist, attached to the overhanging limb of an ancient cottonwood, my friend, Johnny McCue, and I hoisted up the back end and I made a replacement.

After that I painted the roadster a canary yellow. With a red trim and purple wheels, it was "one of a kind." I ultimately paid for its cost with a small charge to classmates whom I drove into Phoenix Union High School in the city.

I've owned, repaired and rebuilt many vehicles over the past sixty-five years, among them, five Volkswagen campers. Today, with the computer controls and sealed ignition, people do not do their own repairs as we did in the past. My twenty-nine-year-old pick-up truck is an antique.

When Donna and I drive on the East-West Interstate Highway 40, with its huge trucks and traffic, we try to imagine what the world of the automobile might be in your time. As I look back to the simple traffic at the time of my Model A Ford roadster, I wouldn't even make a guess.

I am writing to you today as I sit beside the swimming pool of Donna's brother, John, and his wife, Sandy. Their southwestern style home, here in the Pinnacle Peak area of Scottsdale, Arizona, is similar to others in the many subdivisions in this desert north of Phoenix. It doesn't seem possible that we were stuck in snow on our way here yesterday.

The thirty-mile dirt road to the paved highway was still in process of being plowed when we left Pleasant Valley. We tried to creep around the grader on a steep hill and slipped into a drift where we were stuck. Our elevation was nearly seven thousand feet above sea level and the snow over a foot deep on the unplowed road ahead.

With the help of some men in another vehicle, and the plow operator, we shoved our car out behind the blade of the grader. Fortunately, our small car has front wheel drive and we carefully crawled behind the blade for ten or fifteen miles to the major paved highway, "Two-Sixty." I wonder if our highways are numbered the same when you read this?

I remember when Highway 66 (which was famous in stories and song) was replaced by Interstate 40 across northern Arizona. Every fifty to one hundred miles on 66, you could buy Indian curios, something to eat, and most important, fill the tank with enough gasoline to take you to the next stopping place. Automobiles needed refueling more frequently then. Today, in most cars, you can drive over three hundred miles without stopping for gas.

While sitting here in the sun without a shirt and with bare feet, I remember how tough our feet became after a summer of going barefoot. Today I find it uncomfortable walking on the pebbly concrete around this pool. When I was a kid, I found it hard to wait until school was out in May, so I could shed my shoes and start toughening up the soles of my feet for summer. Today, nearly all kids wear sandals or canvas tennis shoes. I wonder what the footwear is in your time?

Anyway, here we are in the Valley of the Sun this November weekend where visiting "Snow Birds" are pouring in by the thousands to escape the snow and cold in the East. Donna and I have noticed that nearly every third license plate is from another State. Most are from the mid-west and north-east. We are also aware that most of these winter visitors have gray hair and push their shopping carts slowly and with caution.

Our hair is also gray, but we do not identify with this populace that is filling the Sun Belt. Each year we are made aware of our difference on the downhill ski slopes. There we find ourselves a respected minority.

I wonder if by the time you read this, gray hair will be common on the winter ski lifts? Somehow I doubt it, but it will be their loss, which I find sad. Donna and I are expectantly awaiting the opening of Sunrise Ski Resort on the Apache Indian Reservation in the White Mountains. The storm that gave us a problem yesterday will have left its contribution to a solid base for winter skiing.

We expect to be on the slope before Thanksgiving, and there I will imagine you on skis, (or a snowboard) high on a mountain like ours, and sharing that tingle of expectation before pushing off. Isn't it interesting that shared experience is another kind of time binding?

I'm feeling a bit sunburned, so will say "adios" until I write again.
My warmest best to you,

Your Great-Great-Granddad, Sam

FORTY-FIFTH

Dear Great-Great-Granddaughters and Sons,

Here in Pleasant Valley Donna and I toss food scraps and unburnables down the bank of a dry wash that runs behind our hogan. There, birds and coyotes pick over our leavings.

Just before I sat down to write you I glanced out the window and there was a large javalina chomping on grapefruit rinds and apple cores. He looked up at me with glistening black eyes, but his jaws, with their exposed curled teeth, never stopped moving until I gave him a wave. He whirled around and disappeared down the wash.

These native wild pigs that root for acorns under the scrub oaks are a problem for gardeners in our valley. However, the major concern this year is the elk. These huge deer easily leap over normal fences and strip leaves and bark from our apple trees. My neighbor strung lights and had a radio blaring all night in his orchard to discourage them. I asked him if it worked. He said he had decided that the light and sound attracted them. He now has a ten-foot high fencing around his orchard.

Since Election Day, the top news story is the unprecedented close race for the Presidency. All last week, a recount of ballots in Florida has been getting world attention.

With our satellite dish we watch international news reports in English from the German broadcast in Berlin. Besides our too-close-to-call Presidential election, our State of Arizona was a top story in the news because of a case before the World Court at The Hague in the Netherlands.

This case highlights the sharp division over capital punishment between Europe and the United States. Angered by Arizona's execution of the brothers Walter and Karl La Grand, who were German citizens, this first case was brought before the World Court dealing with capital punishment. As one who has publicly opposed capital punishment, I am glad to see this world attention.

The only pause in executions during my lifetime was between nineteen sixty-seven and January of nineteen seventy-seven, when Gary Gilmore was legally executed by a firing squad in Utah.

The first legal execution that I remember was a German by the name of Bruno Hauptmann. He was convicted of the kidnapping and murder of Charles Lindberg's baby. I was thirteen years old and had been a follower of Lindberg's career ever since that personal contact I wrote you about when I was a young kid living in New Mexico.

The Lindberg baby's body was found in the woods near their home. I remember the talk between my parents about circumstantial evidence. They questioned the death penalty. I guess I've questioned capital punishment ever since.

I hope, along with physical torture and slavery, capital punishment will be ancient history when you read this letter.

Writing to you on this cloudless November morning, I am reminded that north of the Arctic Circle the sun disappeared behind Mount Truth this month. It will not shine again on our shore cabin at Koviashuvik until February. It is strange that I find a few days without sunshine here in these Arizona mountains a bit gloomy while two months of sunless days in the arctic winters were not. I suspect it is the quality of light. To me, winters in the Brooks Range were not gloomy. Also, I never felt confined in our small cabin. It was great to warm up in it and also to snuggle between flannel sheets in the winter dark.

Here, in this valley, there is a feeling of being confined when days are gray. It is a sense of openness and light that lifts my spirit. Bright yellow is my favorite color. I wonder what yours is?

I have friends who love the gray days. They prefer them in contrast to what they call too much sun and glare. I'll bet their favorite color is a dark blue or purple. Anyway, there is a saying today: "Different strokes for different folks." I assume it is the same in your day.

Speaking of "strokes," I put my pen down and went out in the sunshine to our woodpile. There, I spent several hours splitting dry juniper and oak we had collected for the winter. I find physical exercise akin to that quality of light that adds an after-glow to the experience.

When I came inside, I found this farewell from Gabriel Garcia Marquez. It was posted on my internet mail from dear friends Judith Ashley and Howard Reed. Gabriel Garcia Marquez was awarded the Nobel Prize for Literature in 1982 for his novel "One Hundred Years of Solitude," the story of several generations of a Colombian family as his grandmother might have told it. He has cancer of the lymph nodes that has been getting worse and has sent this farewell letter to his friends. I want you to know of it:

"If for an instant God were to forget that I am rag doll and gifted me with a piece of life, possibly I wouldn't say all that I think, but rather I would think of all that I say.

"I would value things, not for their worth but for what they mean.

I would sleep little, dream more, understanding that for each minute we close our eyes we lose sixty seconds of light.

"I would walk when others hold back, I would wake when others sleep. I would listen when others talk, and how I would enjoy a good chocolate ice cream!

"If God were to give me a piece of life, I would dress simply, throw myself face first into the sun, baring not only my body but also my soul.

"My God, if I had a heart, I would write my hate on ice, and wait for the sun to show.

"Over the stars I would paint with a Van Gogh dream a Benedetti poem and a Sarrat song would be the serenade I'd offer to the moon.

"With my tears I would water roses, to feel the pain of their thorns, and the red kiss of their petals...

"My God, if I had a piece of life... I wouldn't let a single day pass without telling the people I love that I love them.

"I would convince each woman and each man that they are my favorites, and I would live in love with love.

"I would show men how very wrong they are to think that they cease to be in love when they grow old, not knowing that they grow old when they cease to be in love!

"To a child I shall give wings, but I shall let him learn to fly on his own.

"I would teach the old that death does not come with old age, but with forgetting.

"So much have I learned from you, oh men... I have learned that everyone wants to live on the peak of the mountain, without knowing that real happiness is in how it is scaled.

"I have learned that a man has the right to look down on another only when he has to help the other get to his feet.

"From you I have learned so many things, but in truth they won't be of much use, for when I keep them within this suitcase, unhappily shall I be dying."

Gabriel Garcia Marquez

This letter of Garcia Marquez comes from me to you with my love.

Your Great-Great-Granddad, Sam

FORTY-SIXTH

Dear Great-Great-Grandsons and Daughters,

Donna and I have just returned from a hike down Eight Mile Canyon. There, we had a picnic lunch and gathered ancient pottery shards left by Indians who dwelt there over a thousand years ago.

It was exciting for our guests, Dick and Liska Snyder, who were visiting us from Alaska. I had known them in the north for more than thirty years. Today they were thrilled to pick up artifacts of broken pots used long before Europeans even speculated about the earth being round or that another continent might exist across the sea to the West

As I have written you, I had worked with a government survey party here in the Sierra Ancha Mountains when I was first out of high school. I have an attachment to this isolated wildness.

Some years ago, Ray Manker, Minister of the First Unitarian Church in Phoenix, wrote to me at Koviashuvik in northern Alaska that this acreage, surrounded by National Forest, was for sale in the Sierra Ancha. He saw it as a possible retreat and conference area for our congregations. After spring break-up, Billie and I flew out to Arizona where I learned that the acreage in Eight Mile Canyon was no longer available. Ray was as disappointed as I was. Together, we explored other possible retreat sites.

Then, the Eight Mile property came back on the market and several of us pooled our resources to make a down payment in order to secure what is now known as SAWUURA Conference Grounds.

Today, while we were there with our Alaskan friends, Donna and I showed them the rock house I built among the pinon pines on a hill top There, Billie and I spent several winters as caretakers of this unique mountain area.

I wonder if SAWUURA is still a haven you can visit when you read this? I hope so. Therefore, I am enclosing the following excerpt from something I was asked to write as a brief, personal, historical sketch of the beginning of this mountain retreat more than twenty-five years ago.

THE DREAM OF SAWUURA

The dream of Sawuura, which became a mountain retreat for religious liberals, began for me in 1973. With my former late spouse, Billie, we were on tour throughout the United States promoting her award winning book, "Four Season's North."

While in Phoenix, we were guests of Ray and Gretchen Manker's family where we talked about possible retreat and conference areas in Arizona. Ray said that over the years, groups from the Phoenix church had visited various sites but that this ongoing concern of the few had never grown into a larger church interest.

We pursued maps of Arizona and, among others, talked about this area of the Sierra Ancha Mountains with which I was familiar. Years before, as a youth, I spent a summer with a survey crew in these mountains that were then considered one of the wildest areas in Arizona.

After Billie and I returned to our wilderness home in Alaska, we received a letter from Ray saying that he had seen an advertisement for 109 acres surrounded by National Forest in this area. He spoke of it with enthusiasm, as a unique find, but its cost was over a hundred thousand dollars. We shared ideas of how it might be acquired. The next letter from Ray said that the property had been sold.

In the meantime, Billie and I were seeking a site outside of Alaska to spend winters. We had moved to Northeastern Washington when Ray notified us that the property was again on the market.

Along with others, we invested in the dream in order to hold the land. And because we were able to do so, we moved to the wilderness site as volunteer caretakers.

The year 1978 was a crucial year for SAWUURA. Church members, Pat and Roger Weare loaned money for the initial down payment, but then soon called for its return. However, it was Ray Manker whose encouragement to all made the dream work. Here is a hand written note he sent us dated December 28, 1978:

Dear Billie and Sam,

Thanks for your continuing inspiration, strength and perspective and participation in securing for the church and our church families our beautiful Sierra Ancha property. That this lovely wilderness will forever be bringing joy and renewal to Unitarian Universalists for generations to come is a very satisfying thought. Your $3,000.00 gift is an important and essential part of making it all possible. As you know we will need your gift by January 15, 1979 to allow me to meet our initial commitment. We have set Tuesday, January 16, for our next meeting – 8pm at the church. We hope to have a sample Article of Incorporation and By Laws for discussion and approval. I hope you will be there.

Love, Ray

PS. Enclosed is a sample of the letters of confirmation and thanks that I am sending out to each of our pledged donors. It is too "stilted" for you, I know. I hope it is not for the others. See you Monday (before you get this)! R.

It was at the January 16, 1979 meeting that SAWUURA was finally born. Being aware of the many tensions over the past year, I felt that some unifying vision or perspective was needed if we were to move ahead together. Before we formally began our meeting, I was asked to share my "Legend of Sawuura" (pronounced, sa-woo-rah).

THE LEGEND OF SAWUURA

Now it came to pass that many did hear of Sawuura as the stories of old did speak of Shangri-la and El Dorado, the fabled lands beyond.

Wherever the story was told, in the marketplace and in the temple, Sawuura did ring in the hearts of those who heard it.

Some said Sawuura existeth not, 'twas only a tale to be told of the ancients who once dwelt beneath the western sun and ground their maize and painted their pots among the pinon and ponderosa pines; yea, even as in a garden beneath the cedars of Lebanon.

Others did say that Sawuura hath a place and a time in the great southwest, albeit the name Sawuura had not been spoken to them. When they heard it spoken they asked not from whence it came.

Then one did inquire of him who seeketh the source of legends, "Whence cometh Sawuura?"

And he who seeketh the source of legends did ponder this question exceedingly. Then did he open his mouth and spake thus:

"Sawuura hath an ancient past. Even before the days of our fathers and mothers it was spoken in the hearts of those who sought beauty, tranquility and joy. Perchance Sawuura cometh from the ancient language of the Anasasi and Mogollons, even as from the Medes and the Persians. For is not Sawuura but a name for a quest, a journey, a dream – yea, even a life?

"And thus it is said by some, 'Sawuura does not exist, 'tis only a name.' And others say, 'If it hath a name there must be that for which it speaks!'

"Verily I say unto you, whether Sawuura be spoken by the ancient Habiru of the East or the Anasasi of the West, it's meaning doth speak in their hearts the same."

Thus having spake the truth of legends, he who seeketh the source of legends saith:

"I now speak for those who comprehendeth not the wisdom of legend but would be the solver of riddles.

To the solver of riddles, I say Sawuura can be seen as simply an acronym for Sierra Ancha Wilderness Unitarian Universalist Religious Association.

"Even so, beware that thou dost not deceive thyself in the solving of riddles, for there is much more to a name than its sounding in the air or its printing on a scroll."

Now you know how SAWUURA got its name. I hope it is still a haven in these mountains for you and others.

As we drove up the dirt road out of the canyon, we stopped for a half dozen wild turkeys to cross in front of us. Dick took pictures of them before they wandered into the underbrush.

When we returned, I checked our satellite dish for the news after supper. It was dominated by the presidential election that is still in question between Al Gore and George W. Bush. A recount of votes in parts of Florida is being requested and the Florida State Supreme Court has agreed to hear the case.

A comic relief in the news was another story, which was presented as a serious precedent setting matter. A three hundred pound pot bellied pig with a pink bow in her tail was flown first class from Philadelphia to Seattle. As the Boeing 757 landed with two hundred passengers, the pig, called Charlotte, tried to barge into the cockpit and stormed into the galley, according to the airline report. The pig was accepted on the U.S.Airways flight in a request "to transport a qualified individual with a disability and her service animal." Service animals are usually Seeing Eye dogs.

The pig owner, Maria Turotta Andrews, said she has a heart condition so severe that she needs the companionship of her pig to relieve stress. I wonder what other animals might be first class flying stress relievers in your time? If this is a serious precedence, I sure wish I could hear from you.

More from me later.

Your Great-Great-Granddad, Sam

FORTY-SEVENTH

Dear Great-Great-Granddaughters and Sons,

When you read this I know it will be ancient history to you, but on this ninth of December the Presidential Election dominates the world news. It is still not settled after more than a month since we cast our ballots.

The Florida Supreme Court has ruled for a recount. As reported this morning, Governor Bush leads Vice President Gore by only one hundred and forty-seven votes. There is speculation that Congress may ultimately decide this election. Of course you will know all about what happened. But as I write to you this morning, all is unknown speculation.

I remember how much speculation there was when I was attending Mount Hermon Prep School in New England as a fourteen-year-old freshman. That was in nineteen thirty-three, the year the Reichstag in Berlin burned down. At that time no one could have predicted the consequences of the Third Reich and World War II.

The present speculation points to nothing as dramatic, but the news media tries to portray it as such. Donna and I find it interesting to speculate on how a tie vote might ultimately be resolved. This morning it was reported that in one of the State's small community elections, which ended in a tie vote, they tossed a coin.

Since I mentioned being in New England in 1933, it was December the fifth of that year which made a dramatic impression on me. It was on December the fifth that fourteen years of prohibition came to an end. I was visiting New York as a winter holiday guest of a classmate's family.

That evening, with my older classmate, I accompanied him with a member of his family to a Forty Fifth Street Cabaret. There we attended a show in a "Speak-easy." That night it was opened to the public for the first time in over a decade. It was being celebrated as an historic occasion. I sipped my first legal beer and felt more adult and mature than I have ever felt since. I guess it was because I was accepted as a person and not just a kid.

As I am writing you, I wonder where that term, "Speak-easy," comes from?

I just looked it up in the dictionary which gave me no source, only "A place for the illegal sale of alcoholic drinks, as during U.S. Prohibition."

While taking this break in my writing to you, there was a news flash that the United States Supreme Court has halted the ballot recount in Florida. This countermands the Florida Supreme Court. Now we await the U.S. Supreme Court session on Monday. Isn't it interesting that when you read this you will know all about what happened? But now, while I am writing you, all I can do is speculate.

Since I mentioned New England, I don't think I wrote you that several years after my Prep School experience, I drove back there with my parents from Arizona. They attended a summer conference in Northfield, Massachusetts, where they had first met as conference employees and fell in love.

As a seventeen-year-old "man of the world," I was employed that summer in the dishwashing crew for the eight hundred attendees at the conference. In Northfield, my parents had traded in our old nineteen thirty-three Chevrolet sedan for a new Ford V8. As the family chauffeur behind the wheel of a new car, I took liberties to visit school friends of the past on my days off. Some of them lived as far away as Springfield, Massachusetts. One weekend I drove to New York City and spent an afternoon with friends at Coney Island. The beer I drank that weekend in New York was not sipped!

Driving back across the country to Arizona in nineteen thirty-seven, most of the major highways were paved. This was not so in nineteen twenty-eight, when I first crossed the United States with my parents over much of the same route. Today, we have friends who are amazed that our community here in Pleasant Valley is at the end of a thirty-mile dirt road. They consider it primitive. I wonder what the highway systems are like in your time? Maybe you have a different kind of transportation that I cannot imagine.

While driving my parents back to Phoenix in their new Ford that autumn, I could not imagine that I would be married and the father of a child within the next five years, and hold a degree in biology, be on the teaching staff of a University and a participant in a world war in secret weapons creation with the U.S. Office of Scientific Research and Development. Today, as I look back, it is hard to believe that was the way it was. But it was.

I once read of an ancient Chinese Curse, "May you live in historic times." I am not sure that I accept this as a curse. It could also be a blessing. I guess it depends upon a person's temperament or sense of adventure. As I look back at the way it was, I feel fortunate to be living in "historic times." I wish I could live into your historic times, but since I can't, I've tried to share with you a bit of the way it was for me in my time.

I'll write again later. But I have other tasks to do and it is late. So my warmest best to you.

Your Great-Great-Granddad, Sam

FORTY-EIGHTH

Dear Great-Great-Grandsons and Daughters,

The world news is dominated on this thirteenth of December by the acceptance of defeat for the Presidency by Vice President Al Gore thirty-six days after this very close election. Because it is history to you, you know that Al Gore won the popular vote but lost the Electoral College vote to Governor George Bush of Texas.

I wonder if the outdated Electoral College has been eliminated when you read this? I hope so. Ever since I learned about the Electoral College as a kid in an American History class, I questioned it. I was not very interested in history as it was taught in school. It seemed to be mostly dull, dead stuff of the past concerning who was President during wars and dates when things happened. Since I have been writing to you, history seems more interesting.

During World War II, when I was living in Albuquerque, a couple of friends and I would go down to Joe's Bar in "Old Town" for enchiladas and beer. There, we would meet with others to talk, laugh with Joe, and dance to the Mexican tunes played on a marimba.

One evening, a friend invited an Albuquerque reporter to share our table with us. He was an older guy and had been reporting on the war from Europe. He was home for a break before being assigned to the South Seas Area of Operations. Ernie had a great sense of humor. As the cheap bottles of "Rosebud" beer accumulated on the table following our plates of enchiladas, he kept us laughing with incidents where he had been reporting on guys in the infantry.

That evening in 1944, Ernie Pyle was just another guy sharing enchiladas, beer and good talk. The next year he was killed on the Island of Iwo Jima and became famous. There he became a piece of history. By 1945 Ernie Pyle was widely known throughout the United States as he reported from the South Sea area of combat. As I said, he was to us an older guy. He was forty-five.

At Joe's Bar in Old Town, we missed him and drank an extra Rosebud to him. He became a part of the history he reported. I remember that we toasted others who had gathered with us at Joe's Bar. They had less notoriety. Today I can't remember their names, but then they were just as "historic" to us who had known them.

It was with Ernie Pyle's death that I became aware that history (which is always in the past) is what is remembered. This is why I write you these letters about where I am and was, and what I remember.

Today I am again writing you from our hogan in Pleasant Valley. Donna and I will be packing our warm clothing, boots and skis, to take with us this week to Purgatory, a ski resort about thirty miles north of Durango, Colorado.

I am a downhill ski addict. I had never been on skis when I was a kid. Even in the northern Alaska wilderness as a trapper, I made my trails with snowshoes. At age sixty-eight, when I married Donna, she introduced me to downhill skiing at Squaw Valley in the high Sierra near Lake Tahoe, CA. Since then we have skied many slopes in California, Colorado, Utah and Arizona. We have been hoping for a decent snow base at Sunrise, a ski resort in the White Mountains of Arizona. It is only a three-hour drive from here. However, the pre-Christmas storms have dumped their snow further east in the Rocky Mountains of southern Colorado. I just checked the snow base and ski runs in the resorts in Colorado. I got this information on the World Wide Web.

I'm sure that for you the WWW is not as amazing as it is for me. This month, the World Wide Web celebrates its tenth birthday. Just a short time ago it was born as an unsanctioned project at a European physics lab in December of 1990. A young British computer scientist, Tim Berners-Lee, first proposed the web while developing ways to remotely control computers at the Geneva-based European Organization for Research, CERN. Six years ago, in 1994, he formed the World Wide Web Consortium to develop web standards.

Today I have access to web sites all around the world. I cannot conceive the interconnections that must be available to you, or what kind of global society it has created in your time.

I have to remind myself that globalization does not necessarily mean the golden age talked about in mythology. There were predictions of a golden age early in the nineteenth century. With its new technology and innovations, such as the automobile and airplane to telephone and moving pictures, many thought the golden age had dawned. But the so-called "civilized world" was soon in a war that lasted until shortly before I was born in 1919. Twenty years later, in World War II, that "civilized world" was again killing its members beyond anything history had ever recorded and I was a part of it. I, who intellectually called myself a pacifist, was an active part of it in weapons development under the U.S. Office of Scientific Research and Development.

Even so, I still have faith that we humans will ultimately care for our species if we have enough information and freedom to grow beyond the superstitions that once supported our tribal world of me against thee. Sorry. I didn't mean to start preaching. After fifty years in the profession it creeps in. I'm even preachy about skiing.

As I said, we are planning to leave tomorrow for our first ski trip this year. The last time we were on the slopes was over a year ago in the Sierra Nevada. I was serving as a minister in Reno where I wrote this piece about skiing as a religious experience; less than two hours from Reno you can see grandeur and beauty in mountains and forest and lakes at this ski time following the first deep snow. It is a religious experience to feel skis grip your leaning into fresh snow as you soar downhill in a world of beauty.

Skiing as Religious Experience

For thousands of years the purpose of religion has been to put human life in contact with all life: Cloud life, mountain life, sun life, human life, plant and animal life, rain and snow life.

Donna and I seldom use the word religious. But this was our experience on Monday as we slid off the ski lift near the top of Mount Rose and became one with snow, sky, trees, floating clouds and the mountain.

I find that we are not alone in calling this a religious experience. The brilliant philosopher Martin Heidegger, who was offered prestigious teaching positions all over the world, chose to stay in his little town at the small university of Freiburg because he cherished his skiing mountains in the Black Forest of Germany. The New York Times, in reporting his death, referred to him "as an expert skier well into his 80s, who liked to hold seminars with his students while skiing." Heidegger wrote of the"interrelationship of the fourfold earth, sky, gods and mortals. The skis bring together the united four, earth and sky, divinities and mortals."

Flowing with gravity and becoming one with the mountain, a skier glides, receiving the sky and hearing the crunch of snow beneath the skis in a divine world. There is freedom, grace and joy. Heidegger looked upon it as an ultimate spiritual experience and that we become authentic only as we live close to the earth and natural rhythms and stay in harmony with them. He found the finest expression of this in skiing.

It may be difficult for some to conceive of a "blue run" on a mountain slope at a ski resort as a spiritual path. But when the mountain, sky, trees, snow and wind in your ears become one, this swift white peace in life gives meaning to the daily round of clocks and chores and maintenance. This is the purpose of religion.

Enough said! Will write again after Christmas,

Your Great-Great-Granddad, Sam

FORTY-NINTH

Dear Great-Great-Granddaughters and Sons,

Merry Christmas!

We had a great ski trip driving to Colorado and spending three days on the slopes at Purgatory north of Durango. Donna's brother John and wife, Sandy, loaded their large suburban auto with our groceries, warm clothing, boots and other skiing equipment. We then strapped our skis and snowboard on top.

Last summer's newly weds, Sara and Jake Gold, along with Sara's brother, Mark, Donna and I filled John and Sandy's car to capacity. We stopped in Kayenta, on the Navajo Indian Reservation for fuel and snacks, both on the way and returning. In Durango we added to our groceries. The next day we were among the first on the lift to the top of the mountain. The days were bright with sunshine. It was a wonderful Christmas gift that we gave to ourselves.

Yesterday, the day before Christmas, Donna and I drove into the crowded parking lot of a huge shopping mall in Scottsdale. There she purchased last minute items for today's festivities. I wandered as an observer through the noisy crowd that streamed back and forth between the crowded shops. There, I became aware that people were careful not to make eye contact. As an experiment, I gazed directly at an approaching man in the mob and did not turn my gaze away when he did. He looked back again, then smiled and said apologetically, "Sorry, I thought you were someone I knew." I said, "Merry Christmas."

It is interesting to me how we protect our privacy and ourselves where people are crowded together in public. In our small community in Pleasant Valley we wave to each car we pass on the way to the Post Office. If someone fails to wave or acknowledge our wave, we assume the occupants are strangers from the city. At the Post Office we greet each other with a "hello," or a nod, even if we have never met and do not know each other. Not to make eye contact in our small community is a breach of friendliness.

More than that, it communicates a negative surliness, not a request for privacy.

When I was a "Native Counselor" on the Trans-Alaska-Pipeline Project, I found a striking contrast between Athabaskan (Indian) and Inuit (Eskimo) eye contact. The Athabaskan pattern was to avoid the straight gaze in contrast to the Inuit, who, in conversation made me wonder what he was trying to fathom behind what he saw in my eyes.

The pattern I grew up with among the ranchers and miners in the Southwest was a direct gaze. In the early black and white cowboy movies this separated the villain from the hero as much as the color of their hats. In that folklore, "If a man did not look you straight in the eye he was not to be trusted."

A Navajo friend of my youth once told me that to him a direct gaze was predatory, an attempt was being made to take something away. Even today, among the older generation, which is mine, Athabaskans innately avoid the direct gaze and react negatively to being photographed.

I've observed that wild animals react to a direct gaze as a threat unless it is fleeting. I learned that with wolves and grizzly bears, a directly held gaze triggers fight or flight; fortunately most often flight. Anyway, I found it interesting to observe these patterns while walking through the wilds of the Scottsdale mall.

I find the wilds of cultural differences fascinating. I wonder if you do? I imagine that the patterns in your time are not so different from those in mine. An example is the Christmas dinner we will have today.

We will gather as a family in John and Sandy's home to which their new son-in-law's parents, his brother Mike and family friend are invited. Jake and his family are active participants in The Church of Jesus Christ of Latter Day Saints (Mormons) in which they abstain from alcoholic beverages, tea or coffee. For Donna and me, as well as Brother John and Sandy, Christmas is celebrated with the cheer of a wassail bowl, wine and an after dinner coffee with brandy.

Do we curtail our traditional celebration, knowing others might feel it inappropriate? We also know it is their tradition that a prayer be a part of the Christmas meal. We concluded that the patterns should reflect the traditions of the host while recognizing a certain discomfort in the situation.

As a clergyman, I assumed the initiative in setting a theme as we sat down together before a table spread with all the traditional good things, including red and white wine. I spent several hours in considering what I would say to myself, and others, in the context in which we found ourselves. I finally wrote a prose poem, which I shared with them, and now with you, on this Christmas Day:

CHRISTMAS 2000
(A prose poem)

This Christmas morning I remembered some words from the famous Giovani Christmas Letter which begins, as I recall, like this:

"There is nothing I can give that you do not have. But there is much that you can take."

What can we take? Today I suggest seven things:

Beauty – Time – Silence – Joy – Existence – Love – Heaven.

TAKE BEAUTY: It is yours – wherever you see it, even in another's garden.

TAKE TIME: It's yours – to listen, to look, to feel, to smell, and to be.

TAKE SILENCE: Both inward and outward. In our day, outward silence is an endangered experience. Tranquility, inner silence, is still ours to take. It's a gift to treasure.

TAKE JOY: It is always there if we but look beneath the everyday, mundane acts of living.

TAKE EXISTENCE: Yes, take it for granted! For out of the millions of living things, your particular self is unique. There is nothing like you in this universe. So treat yourself kindly.

TAKE AFFECTION AND LOVE: Love and affection are easy to give, but not easy to take. Sentimental indulgence is easy to receive, even from strangers. Real love is synonymous with the awesomeness of life itself. Can you take it?

Back to Brother Giovani, who wrote:

"TAKE HEAVEN:" It is here in the midst of us if only we would look.

I invite you to look.

So at this ancient time of celebration,
when the earth turns back toward the sun,
we look both within and out
as we take these treasures we have received
but did not ourselves affect.
So be it. Amen.

Sam Wright
December 25, 2000

Until the New Year, when I'll write you again,

Your Great-Great-Granddad, Sam

FIFTIETH

Dear Great-Great-Granddaughters and Sons,

"Christmas passed" has always been a kind of let down for me. I don't think I am alone in this. For over a month one hears music of the season. Streets and stores are decorated in wreaths and red ribbons. Christmas cards and letters are written and received. Over-indulgence in cheer, food, drink and wrapping of gifts, along with their opening on Christmas morning. All of this ends abruptly.

There is still an attempt to have the Christmas momentum last until the New Year arrives. Christmas lights remain. Stores have after-Christmas sales, but it's over. I imagine it is much the same in your time.

I'm convinced that the Christmas season is for kids and their expectations. However, it does spill over among adults. I will never forget that Christmas morning, at age eight or nine, when a new red and chrome Hawthorne Deluxe bicycle was awaiting me beside the glittering Christmas tree. I recall peddling miles on that Christmas day. I went to bed with painfully aching legs. Later, I learned that my Dad had spent late hours on Christmas Eve assembling the bicycle. It had been shipped disassembled. The Sears and Roebuck Co. had shipped it by rail all the way across the country so this particular kid would have a Merry Christmas.

I too remember with pleasure the assembling and the making of Christmas gifts for our own kids. Today nearly everything is bought fully assembled and immediately functional, from electronic gadgets to bicycles and go-carts. However, some things seem never to change. I imagine, the expectations in your time will continue to be the latest style, whether in decoration, dress, household gadget or toy.

Anyway, Christmas 2000 is in the past. I write you today while sitting in front of a crackling fire in our stone fireplace. Here in Pleasant Valley, we still burn wood from the surrounding forest. Burning wood in fireplaces is restricted in the populated Phoenix area to avoid air pollution. When we were there, it was strange to sit with friends in front of their artificial logs and a gas flame in an electrically heated home. I learned of one family that had a television monitor in the opening of their fireplace. On the screen was a video of a crackling fire with accompanying music. This makes me wonder about open fires in your time? I wonder if they are possible?

Here, we have been watching The Antique Road Show, a Public Broadcasting presentation where appraisers evaluate the current worth of antique items. Someone was a collector of pie baking tins. Among them was a pie tin stamped with the name Frisbee Baking Co. of Bridgeport Connecticut.

As a kid, I remember my mother using Frisbee pie tins in her baking. Today teams of young people play games with plastic "Frisbees" about the size of the old pie tins. They are unaware that today's Frisbees originated in a dining hall at Yale University in 1925 when empty metal pie tins were sailed by students with a spinning backhand toss. I wonder if playing with Frisbees is still popular in your time?

As we watched the Antique Road Show, I felt a bit like an antique myself when someone spoke of the value of a baseball that Babe Ruth had hit for a record home run. It was the year the last model T Ford was replaced by the new model A. It was modern. It had shock absorbers and a speedometer. That was also the year Gene Tunney retained the world title as boxing champion over Jack Dempsey. These were important events in the world of us kids at the time.

At that time I was unaware that television had its first public demonstration, or that a spearhead had been found in a stone age bison's remains near Folsom, New Mexico. Both of these events dramatically changed the worldview in which I grew up. I wonder what events are changing the worldview in your time?

Today, globalization is a subject being widely discussed. Economic corporations now spread across borders around the globe. The World Wide Web and e-mail make it possible for everyone to connect. It is predicted that this new information age will transform us all for the better. I hope so.

In spite of the technological revolutions that today mend the human body and probe the universe, our adversarial tribalism seems slow to change. You can see why epistemology intrigues me. We know what we know because we have basic beliefs that are based upon how we know what we know. How we know what we know is our epistemology. For instance, the world as we once perceived it was flat. Now it is round because we changed our epistemological premises. It was round before we changed our epistemological premises, but we could not perceive it as round until we corrected our epistemology. Only when the world no longer makes sense, as we have perceived it, is it possible to consider different ideas and perceptions.

I wish I could look ahead into your time. But since I can't, I have to look for clues in the past.

Looking for clues in the past was one of the reasons I left my professorial role back in the nineteen sixties and moved into a subsistence life style on the shore of a lake in the wilderness of Alaska's Brooks Range. What I discovered there, I have tried to communicate in lectures and in my books. In summary, it was that we hold epistemological premises that we had better change or our survival as a species is uncertain. We have become accustomed to the support of outmoded social and corporate structures of the past while a new information age is coming into being all around the world.

Because I have such a curiosity about the outcome of this present day globalization, I'd give anything to be able to hear from you about what has taken place. But since I can't, I wish you a wonderful time and place in which to live, when and wherever you are.

My love to you. Your Great-Great-Granddad, Sam

FIFTY-FIRST

Dear Great-Great-Grandsons and Daughters,

I'm writing to you high above Canada's Channel Islands in British Columbia as Donna and I fly north to Anchorage on this January morning. We are on our way to greet the arrival of Donna's first grandchild, expected in the next few days.

Beneath us, an occasional white mark on the turquoise blue water points up the wake of a fishing boat. The snow-topped peaks of the islands are a dramatic contrast to the dark forests of spruce trees far below. Compared to my first trip to Alaska, these daily three-hour flights from Seattle still amaze me.

When the Alcan Highway was constructed, it took ten or more days driving over rugged sections of road to make the trip. Today it is still a seven or eight-day trip with its hard surface paving and rest and fuel stops. It was during the construction of the Trans-Alaska Oil Pipeline that the Alcan had its heaviest use. I made an overland trip then. There is still a lot of trucking. In the summer, tourists stream north in their motor homes and campers. I wonder if the Alcan Highway is a tourist attraction when you read this? I'll bet it is.

It was thirty-three years ago when Billie and I first drove those thousands of miles from the San Francisco Bay area to Fairbanks in our Volkswagon camper. It was a great adventure camping by pristine lakes and listening to the call of loons in the moonlight. At that time, I had no inkling that I would fail to return to the Bay Area at the end of the summer, or that Billie and I would move into a miner's isolated, twelve by twelve foot log cabin by a lake north of the Arctic Circle, and spend the winter there.

As you now know, it was during the following spring that we built our own log cabin on the shore and called it Koviashuvik. Since then we became the last of the Homesteaders under the old Homestead Act. I acquired our Home and Guiding Headquarter Sites from the Federal Government and built our winter cabin. Today I am again heading north with Donna to greet the arrival of our new grandchild who could be your grandparent or great-grandparent when you read this.

I wrote you in September about our daughter, Melea, and her partner, Thomas Roed, who are employed by the Girdwood ski resort facilities. We are expecting them to meet us at the Anchorage Airport and drive us the fifty miles along Turnagain Arm of the Cook Inlet to their small rented cabin beneath the Chugach Mountains in Girdwood.

Melea's due date is two or three days from now. Then she and Thomas will add another human life to the world's population. When I was a young professor, lecturing on eugenics at the University of Texas in El Paso, I recall that the world population was listed at two billion. Today it is six billion and the last billion was in just the last twelve years!

Much of this population explosion is due to antibiotics and medical knowledge during my lifetime. Before the twentieth century one-half of all children died before age five. When I was a kid I was vaccinated for smallpox. I remember people with faces bearing smallpox scars were common then. Today, smallpox has been virtually eliminated throughout the world. I remember a poliomyelitis and diphtheria epidemic that produced terror in our community, leaving several of my classmates in the grammar school I attended in Phoenix, Arizona either dead or crippled. If I rule out warfare, our new grandchild's odds for survival are enormous compared to my generation. I wonder what the survival threats are in yours?

With this expected birth of a new grandchild, I am reminded that today's world population explosion is itself a future survival threat. Optimists say that technological innovation will always keep food supply a step ahead of population. Pessimists warn that agricultural technology itself contributes to such problems as decreasing biodiversity, and the loss of arable land is expected to worsen as our numbers increase.

As I now look down on the emptiness of Prince William Sound, before our plane starts its descent to Anchorage, I have to remind myself that Alaska has been one of the least populated areas of the earth. However, in the short thirty-five years since I first visited here, the population has more than doubled. Most of the increase has been in and around the cities of Anchorage and Fairbanks.

I wish I could return here in your time to see what has happened to this pristine land, as I have known it. From what I hear and read of today's development mentality, I am not hopeful that it will be treated with care.

We have just been asked to check our seat belts and handbags in preparation for landing, so I'll close this letter and write you later from Girdwood.

With my affection,

Your Great-Great-Granddad, Sam

FIFTY-SECOND

Dear Great-Great-Granddaughters and Sons,

Last night we all gathered at Britany and Gary's digs for a potluck gathering. It was planned for the arrival of Thomas and Melea's baby. When I say "we all," I counted twenty of us, and two dogs.

What a feed it was, sitting on mats on the floor. Melea with her large, round pregnant belly was the focus of all this attention of well-wishers. The room was full of young adults. Except for Donna and me, the age range was about twenty to thirty.

One of the young people, driving in the snowstorm from Anchorage, pulled his car too far into a hidden roadside snow bank in the dark and slid into a deep run-off ditch. That shifted our focus of attention from the warmth of partying to the outside cold and dark until the car was pulled out.

Donna and I then sang a parody on last month's Presidential Election, called The Kennebunkport Hillbilly, to a tune of an old TV show called The Beverly Hillbillies. I'll enclose it.

This brought up a discussion of concern for Alaska's National Wildlife Range (ANWAR) that President George W. Bush had pledged to make available for petroleum exploitation. Afterward, we crawled into our sleeping bag on the floor of Melea and Thomas' cabin for the night.

The due date for the baby was today. We drove the fifty miles into Anchorage to the Birthing Center where Melea was examined. We listened to the amplified clapping of the baby's heart valves and the midwife reported that Melea's condition was not "ripe" enough for labor to begin. So we spent the day walking through parking lot slush into various markets to shop for our coming week's meals.

Anchorage has expanded a lot since I was here as the first full time minister of the Unitarian Universalist Fellowship some thirty years ago. At that time, the Fellowship met in their log cabin church in what is now downtown Anchorage. Today this historic building is a bed and breakfast place for tourists. The Fellowship now meets in its new quarters at 3201 Turnagain Street.

When I was minister in Anchorage, an exploratory oil well was drilled on the North Slope of the Brooks Range near Prudhoe Bay on the Arctic Ocean. It became headline news. This was the beginning of the Trans-Alaska Pipeline Project and construction of a haul road from Prudhoe Bay south across Alaska. As I have written to you, it is now hard surfaced and called The Dalton Highway.

The construction of the Trans-Alaska Pipeline made frenetic boom-towns of both Fairbanks and Anchorage that still continues. Traffic in Anchorage is as bumper-to-bumper before and after work hours as it is in cities in the lower forty-eight. The laidback, easy frontier quality I felt in the late nineteen-sixties disappeared with the North Slope Oil Strike and has since been replaced by a driving sense of need to succeed and Texas accents.

I recall listening to our little radio in the Brooks Range back in 1969 when Armstrong and Aldrich were reporting their walk on the moon. I stepped outside our small log cabin and looked up at its round, yellow surface where "One small step for man" had been taken. I wondered how long it would be before many others would be making that trip across space and beyond. Today I wonder if you will have the opportunity to look back at this earth as it was then seen for the first time?

Seeing for the first time, and knowing it is for the first time, has been for me the gift of adventure, as well as its definition. My first time recognition of words that I could read, the first time I fell in love at age seven, my first flight in an airplane, the first caribou I took and prepared for winter meat; even my first understanding that life itself is a gift that ends as surely as it arrives. All these are adventures that have led to others I cherish. I wonder if this is your experience? I hope you find wonderful adventures in your time as I have in mine.

And now, a first time adventure will soon begin for the child that Melea has carried the past nine months. I can no more predict the kind of world in which she or he will grow up than the one in which you now live. As I look back at my arrival time in 1919, it seems unbelievable that the astronomer, Harlow Shapely, had just presented our sun as a minor star in the vast galaxy of the Milky Way. And just ten years later, in 1929, Edwin Hubble would make us aware of those galaxies receding from each other in an expanding universe.

One of my adventures, back in the nineteen-fifties, was being on a panel with Harlow Shapely, discussing the philosophical and theological implications of science. He was then a famous elderly authority. I felt intimidated taking issue against some didactic statement he had made outside his field of expertise. It produced for me an insight that creative brilliance and knowledge in one area does not necessarily cross over into another. Since then, that venture still reminds me not to be down on what I am not up on. I'll bet it is even good advice in your time.

It is now time for Thomas to return from his late night clean-up job at the ski resort, so I'll end this note and write again later after the baby arrives.

P.S. Here is THE KENNEBUNKPORT HILLBILLY SONG.

THE KENNEBUNKPORT HILLBILLY SONG

"Come and listen to my story 'bout a boy named Bush.
His IQ was zero and his head was up his tush.
He drank like a fish while he drove all about.
But that didn't matter 'cuz his daddy bailed him out.
DUI, that is. Criminal record. Cover-up.
Well, the first thing you know little Georgie goes to Yale.
He can't spell his name but they never let him fail.
He spends all his time hangin' out with student folk.
And that's when he learns how to snort a line of coke.
Blow, that is. White gold. Nose candy.
The next thing you know there's a war in Vietnam.
Kin folks say, "George, stay at home with Mom."
Let the common people get maimed and scarred.
We'll buy you a spot in the Texas Air Guard.
Cushy, that is. Country clubs. Nose candy.
Twenty years later George gets a little bored. He
trades in the booze, says that Jesus is his lord. He said,
"Now the White House is the place I wanna be."
So he called his daddy's friends and they called the GOP.
Gun owners, that is. Falwell. Jesse Helms.
Come November 7, the election ran late.
Kin folks said "Jeb, give the boy your state!"
"Don't let those colored folks get into the polls."
So they put up barricades so they couldn't punch their holes.
Chads, that is. Duval County. Miami-Dade.
Before the votes were counted five supremes stepped in.
Told all the voters "Hey, we want George to win."
"Stop counting votes!" was their solemn invocation.
And that's how George finally got his coronation.
Rigged, that is. Illegitimate. No moral authority.
Y'all come vote now. Ya hear?"

Your Great-Great-Granddad, Sam

FIFTY-THIRD

Dear Great-Great-Grandsons and Daughters,

At one thirty in the morning on February eleventh, Granddaughter Acacia finally arrived. This was eighteen days later than she was expected.

She slid into this great, wonderful world still attached to mother Melea by her umbilical cord. After she took her first breath on this strange, new planet, she shouted the announcement of her arrival to all of us.

Thomas then cut the umbilical cord, relieving her of her connection to the past. When she was placed in her mother's arms, I called: "Welcome to our world, Acacia!"

This was so she and others might hear the name her parents had chosen for her. The acacia tree will be a symbol of her identity from now on. I try to consider the possibility of her being your grandmother, or even your great-grandmother, but it overstretches my imagination.

With Acacia now nursing and gaining weight, Donna and I left Alaska to fly back to Arizona, from where I am now writing to you on this snowy day in the Sierra Ancha mountains in late February.

The news of today from our satellite dish comes from Cape Canaveral, Florida, where, for the second day in a row, gusts of nearly twenty-five MPH forced the space shuttle Atlantis and its astronauts to keep circling the Earth instead of coming home. The weather at the back-up landing site in California was no better, so Mission Control ordered the crew to spend a thirteenth day in orbit and aim for a Tuesday afternoon touch down. Mission Control told Commander Kenneth Cockrell, "We do have three sites for tomorrow all of them have a 'go' forecast at this time."

The international project to construct a space station has now progressed to these shuttle trips in order to assemble this station in space. It appears that one of today's concerns is the weather here on Earth. I wonder if this is also a concern in your time as it is now?

Another concern at this time is bringing down the Russian space station MIR. It was designed to stay in orbit for three to five years but has just celebrated its fifteenth birthday. During this time, more than 100 astronauts from twelve countries have conducted thousands of scientific experiments on board, and Valeri Polyakov set a world record in 1996 for living 438 days in space.

MIR's 135-ton assortment of bolts and screws is planned to push out of orbit into the atmosphere and turn into a fireball on Friday. Fragments of the station should plunge into the Pacific, midway between South America and Australia. Fearing a deadly rain of space junk, Japanese authorities have ordered residents of southern Japan to stay indoors on the day of MIR's final descent and Australia has developed a national emergency plan.

As an advertising gimmick, the Taco Bell fast food chain has placed a 40-by-40 foot vinyl target in the area of the Pacific where debris is expected to fall. If the target is hit by a piece of the core of MIR, then everyone in the United States can receive a coupon for a free taco! The odds are far out, but this makes me wonder about the kinds of gimmicks that might be in use in your time to sell products to the public.

Anyway, as I said, it is snowing here in northern Arizona so Donna and I are looking forward to fresh powder on the ski slopes at Sunrise Resort on the Apache Indian Reservation. It may be our last chance for downhill skiing this winter. Will write more later.

My warmest,

Your Great-Great-Granddad, Sam

FIFTY-FOURTH

Dear Great-Great-Granddaughters and Sons,

This is another time that I find myself writing to you while sitting in a giant shopping mall north of Phoenix.

Day before yesterday Donna and I were skiing down the slope of 11,300-foot Apache Peak on the White River Apache Indian Reservation.

It was a glorious, clear, spring day on the mountain following a week of gray skies and snow squalls. Yesterday we drove down to the Valley of the Sun among the palms and green golf courses to shop for summer clothes before we leave for a tribal gathering on the big Island of Hawaii.

We already have our airline tickets to Honolulu, where I will be speaking about our life in Alaska at the Unitarian Universalist Church before we fly on to Kona on the big island.

On Hawaii, Donna and I will officiate and share in two weddings, as well as a naming ceremony for our granddaughter, Acacia. She will be two months old on April 11th, on her day of "Christening." At that time we will also be celebrating her parents' wedding.

The following day, at The Place of Refuge State Park, our tribe of Alaskans and relatives will gather again when Bianca Flores and Jeffrey Whaley share their wedding vows with us on this romantic mid-pacific island. Plans are underway for a grand party and reception as a climax to these Easter week events.

From where I am sitting at present it does not seem possible that I will soon be in Hawaii. I am writing to you at a small table in the mall to which food can be taken from the fast food booths. Here, the mob of shoppers, their echoing sounds of voices and background music, fill this vaulted space of Paradise Valley Mall like a crowded gymnasium.

Since I was last here, a dozen PC computers are now available for public use in the center of the mall. I took advantage of this free service to check my incoming e-mail and replied to friends, Betty and Bob Poynter, who are on an international aid project in Zagreb, Croatia. I still find it astonishing to communicate so easily to anyplace in the world. However, for you, this must seem like "old hat."

Isn't it interesting that I can communicate to you in this old-fashioned way by writing you a letter even though I will not be able to receive a response from you when you receive it?

Anyway, this noisy shopping center mall reminds me of how huge the Population of this Phoenix area has become since I was a kid and rode into town with my parents on Saturdays. They drove into downtown Phoenix to do their week's grocery shopping. The metropolitan area population was then estimated at about 50 to 75 thousand. Even back then it was considered enormous.

Today this same metropolitan area has a population approaching three million. And with these millions have come our crowded freeways and all the congestion that comes with it.

Back in the nineteen thirties, it was a pleasure to drive into Phoenix, eat a sandwich on the grass in a downtown park, and listen to the soapbox harangs where, on weekends, evangelists usually held forth.

One Saturday stands out in my memory when my dad and I were having lunch on the grass. An evangelist, standing on his soapbox (actually it was an orange crate), tried to convince the small crowd that the Bible prophesied all that has happened and will happen. He continually challenged the listeners with his literalisms.

My dad winked at me, then stood up and asked, "Would you be kind enough to point out where the safety razor is mentioned in the Bible?"

There was dead silence. There were then a few chuckles in the crowd. I don't remember what the evangelist said, but since then I have been acutely aware of dogmatic literalists, whether in science or religion.

Today, dogmatic literalists seem more numerous than ever. This may be a phenomenon of today's expansion of the soapbox to television and the Internet.

Anyway, this came to mind when I saw this news item: "ATHEISTS BATTLE FOR O'HAIR'S REMAINS." The story was in this morning's news, stating that the remains of Madalyn Murray O'Hair had been identified.

She was a strident evangelical voice for Atheism. At age 76 she disappeared in late September of 1995 along with her son, Jon Garth Murray, and granddaughter, Robin Murray O'Hair. Her headless and handless remains were found by an old man scrounging for aluminum cans on the bank of Trinity River Channel in East Dallas County near Seagoville, Texas. The remains were identified by a serial number on an artificial hip joint implanted in Madalyn.

Years before, she was carrying the cause against prayer in public schools to the Supreme Court. Our trails crossed when we shared the podium in a public meeting. Although we shared views, I was not impressed by her self-righteous dogmatism. Others obviously felt the same.

Her surviving son, William J. Murray, had become a born again Christian. When his mother, Madalyn, disappeared with son Jon and granddaughter Robin, he was quoted as saying: "You have these obese people. Robin requires two airline seats wherever she goes. My mother uses the F-word in virtually every sentence that comes out of her mouth... just singularly, they would be remembered. Together it's like waving a red flag in front of a bull. How could Madalyn, Jon and Robin hide anywhere?"

I am glad to know that Madalyn's disappearance is solved. She made headlines from coast to coast and put atheism in the news. I wonder if you have ever heard of her? I doubt it.

I see Donna coming toward me through the crowd so will sign off now. My best across our time belt,

Your Great-Great-Granddad , Sam

FIFTY-FIFTH

Dear Great-Great-Grandsons and Daughters,

Today, I am again writing to you from our lakeshore cabin at Koviashuvik, north of the Arctic Circle in Alaska.

It has been a long time since I last wrote you. Since then Donna and I have been to the Hawaiian Islands to officiate at the weddings of her nephew, Jeff Whaley and bride, Bianca Flores and also, for daughter, Melea, and groom, Thomas Roed. There, on the shore of the Big Island, we also shared in the naming and dedication of granddaughter, Acacia.

It is Independence Day, The Fourth of July, in this year two thousand and one, as we listen to National Public Radio's world news from Fort Yukon. The Palestinians and Israelis are still at each other's throats while talking conciliation, and the Stock Market is in its summer slump.

This summer we drove from Pleasant Valley in Arizona all the way north to Fairbanks, Alaska. In Fairbanks we parked our seventeen–year-old Volkswagen Camper next to long-time friend Syd Stealey's aircraft hangar near privately owned Metro Field. We then flew north of the Yukon, across the Arctic Circle to our home here on the shore of our lake.

It is a drizzly, wet morning and our little battery radio reports that it is snowing in the village of Anaktuvuk Pass at the top of the Brooks Range.

I remember writing to you from here last summer when my son Chip and his spouse, Lisa, were with us. They had retrieved a human skullcap and lower mandible in the shallows of the lake near our cabin.

On our way here in June, Donna and I stopped at the University of Alaska in Fairbanks to visit Professor Joel D. Irish, Curator of Biological Anthropology, and share with him our artifacts.

From the bone structure of the eye openings, and growth patterns inside the skull cavity, he said the person was probably an adult female. He said that Beta Analitical of Coral Gate, Florida could carbon date our material. He concurred that the remains could be as old as ten or eleven thousand years if they had been frozen in the glacial material that formed our lake. He said that legally, any human remains should be reported to the local coroner and would probably be confiscated. For this reason, he said his studies are now focused outside Alaska and the United States. Otherwise, human remains, no matter how ancient, might be claimed by an indigenous tribe and taken for reburial. In light of his comments, we have decided to proceed cautiously in determining the age of our human artifacts.

While we were in Fairbanks, Donna did her yearly shopping for groceries and supplies. With us, they were flown to our lake in a small bush plane on floats. The foodstuff has to last us through the next two months, before we are to be picked up in September to fly out. The heaviest items are flour, sugar, coffee and condiments. We try, as always, to avoid the weight of canned goods. Even so, we had six cardboard boxes packed in the small plane, plus the two of us, the pilot and our two full backpacks.

Last week, while shopping in the huge Fred Meyers and Safeway stores, I recalled that thirty years ago, when I was first in Fairbanks, there were no large grocery stores. Only small, so-called mom and pop grocers supplied the bush dwellers. When I was living here year-round as a trapper, I would send a grocery order by way of my monthly contact, whose plane was on skis. With him, I sent a signed blank check. Business and commercial relationships were very personal back then. The grocer would often include some oranges or bacon that I had not ordered. It was a community of mutual trust.

However, following the oil boom, this northern world has joined the distrustful legalisms of today's urban societies. I am glad I was here when our community had a personal context of mutual trust. I wonder about the time in which you live?

While we were driving north through Canada's Yukon Territory, I recalled my first trip up the Alcan Highway thirty-four years ago when large stretches were poorly maintained. On the trip we just completed, only a broken headlight and chipped windshield from flying gravel was our highway damage.

On our more than four thousand mile trip we camped in our yellow "Westfalia" Volkswagen by pristine streams and lakes, usually in public campgrounds. We saw four black bear, bald eagles, and other wild life, including gray-haired couples in huge motor homes towing automobiles behind them.

Anyway, here we are back at Koviashuvik, with fresh-caught char in our stomachs and a Great Northern pike is swimming in the small lakeshore holding pond I constructed last summer. The lake is about eight inches higher than when we were here last year. I hope our thirty-six inch pike doesn't leap and flop itself out as one did last summer.

This morning, when I took a sniff of our sourdough pot, it smelled ripe for the pinch of soda that makes the batter foam for our mouth-watering pancakes. Actually, they are "stove cakes" here since I cook them on the cast iron top of our wood burning Yukon Stove. Along with a strip of fried bacon and a cup of coffee, they are delicious!

As we finished breakfast, I glanced out the cabin window and exclaimed, "An eagle!" Donna and I rushed out on the porch overlooking our lake to watch the huge bird fly from a small island where a nesting gull swooped at it again and again until it retreated across the lake. We debated as to whether it was a golden or a bald eagle. Both are often here in summer.

I remember one year, climbing to the top of Aklak (the mountain 3000 feet above our lake) to look down from a cliff edge to a nest in a golden eagle's aerie. Two young birds were about ready to take their first flight. With a screech, the returning parent swooped down at me. I shall never forget the feeling of that rush of air from its wings where I teetered and retreated from the cliff edge. Like the eagle, which we watched flying away from the island this morning, I too scrambled away from the nesting area. A protective parent, even a seagull, can be fearless.

I have had Arctic terns swoop and strike my head while filming their nests on our lakeshore, and I've had to protect my face from a male ptarmigan, which flew at me while I attempted to catch a young chick from a brood that was following their mother over the tundra.

This is why it is dangerous to cross trails with a grizzly bear with her cub. Nothing is more fearless than a concerned parent. I find it strange that I, as your great-great-grandparent, have a concern about you, who have not yet been born. I wonder if this biological sense of responsibility for the future is latent in our species?

Enough for now. Will write more later.

Your Great-Great-Granddad, Sam

FIFTY-SIXTH

Dear Great-Great-Granddaughters and Sons,

This past week has been pretty much a gray one with snow whitening the surrounding mountains.

However, this morning is warm. The sun is brilliantly reflecting itself from the mirror of the lake surface, so much so, that I have to protect my eyes from the glare as I now step out on the porch with my cup of hot coffee to continue this letter to you.

Backlighting picks up the fine gossamer strands of cobwebs that cover the spruce trees like Christmas decorations. Except for this kind of light, the works of small busy spiders are unseen and would not be noticed.

"What is it about sunlight and sparkling water," I ask myself, "that speaks of life and joy, while the dark and colorless times infer the opposite?"

As I casually crushed a mosquito that settled on the rim of my cup, I became aware that it too carries that spark of life we all share, and wondered if it responded this sunny morning as I do? I notice that I used the past tense as I flicked its dark, lifeless spot from my cup's edge. Does a mosquito fear death?

Life is present and death is past, I thought to myself. And to paraphrase Socrates: "The fear of death is the pretense of wisdom. A pretense of knowing the unknown. No one knows whether death, which men in their fear apprehend to be the greatest evil, may not be the greatest good..."

As a biologist, knowing how important mosquitoes and their larvae are in the food chain that produces fat grayling for our evening meal, I wondered about the one I had just euthanized. This then recalled Albert Schweitzer's reverence for life ethic, and I was aware of a guilty tweak in myself as I so casually sent Ms. Mosquito into the unknown.

But then there is that delicious grayling that excitedly grabbed the luring fly I presented at the end of my line. His high dorsal fin flashed rainbow as it broke the surface and I swooped it into my net. At supper, its savoryness repeated in taste those images of its brilliant colors that were fed by relatives of the mosquito that I had so nonchalantly crushed on the rim of my cup.

Life is the miracle which death makes possible. On a glorious morning like this, I could make a good case for death. This does not mean that I would welcome it. I doubt that the mosquito did. But I wonder about that flashing-finned grayling, unaware that the artificial fly I dropped on the surface of its world would mean its demise?

The problem for us self-conscious humans is our awareness that as soon as we are born death is inevitable. Again, as Plato has Socrates say, "The fear of death is the pretense of wisdom. A pretense of knowing the unknown." This morning I ask myself, "What did I know in those centuries before I was born"?

It is curious that we have no fear of the unknown that preceded our birth. Why is it that we react to the unknown with manufactured images of Rebirth, Heavens, Hells and other fancies after our demise and few before?

Speaking of "before," I wonder if curiosity about the past in biological and human history is a response to the miracle of our being?

Somehow, we seem to recognize that life is a miracle as the dictionary calls the term, miracle: "An effect in the physical world which surpasses all know human or natural powers." To be aware that one might lose the experience of the miracle of life makes our speculation about death inevitable.

Since I only know what I think when I write or talk, you are the receiver of what goes on the head of this eighty-two-year-old epistemologist this morning. And what does eighty-two years have to do with it? Very little. Such questions have intrigued me since my early teens and are no less intriguing now. I'm just more comfortable with them today and make no apology that you, who are in the "unknown" as I attempt to communicate with you across the gap of time, existing only in the projection of my imagination. And when you read this letter, I will have joined the "once was" of the mosquito and grayling.

As I write you in the glorious sunshine of this July morning, I recall how many neighbors in the vastness of this sparsely inhabited area have ended their lives during my residency here at Koviashuvik.

The four old prospectors who were the only permanent residents in Wiseman when I arrived are all gone. The last to die was Harry Leonard, who had practically owned the old mining town. Victor Knor died in the Pioneer Home in Fairbanks where I visited him the week before. Oliver Chappell, who remembered Robert Marshall's winter in Wiseman back in the nineteen thirties, was flown out to die outside Alaska. And Ross Brockman, who was the only vegetarian resident I have known in the Brooks Range, literally starved to death one winter refusing caribou and moose that his neighbors tried to offer him.

And others I've mentioned before: Meador, my neighbor who lived at Wild Lake and inadvertently stepped into the whirling propeller of a float plane on the Koyukuk River at Bettles. And friend, Ackerman, who lived at Chandalar Lake, who was lost when his plane in a storm crashed in the lake. I can count ten others who died in aircraft, including the Bettles Airfield Manager, who disappeared one winter in a snowstorm and his plane not found until breakup. All of these, and more, whom I knew, and who are now in the unknown, came to mind because of that one mosquito this morning.

And here you are now reading about a time and place that you can imagine and know about because I am writing to you. It is your time that is unreal for me. To conceive of what will be in your time and life is beyond my imagination no matter how hard I try. I'd like to hear from you, but know I can't. In the meantime, I'll keep writing to let you know how the miracle of life appears from here.

Because that mosquito also reminded me of Jim Pitts, I'm enclosing a copy of a letter I wrote to his mother, in whose cabin I spent my first winter here.

My love to you,

Your Great-Great-Granddad, Sam

Dear Joanne,

I just learned that Jim lost his battle with cancer and my heart reaches out to you from here at the lake where Jim spent so many happy days.

Scott, husband of Heidi Rekoff, in Wiseman, brought our groceries from Coldfoot when he came on his ATV to fish and to tell us that Jim had died.

When I talked with you on the phone in April, before we were flown in on skis, you said Jim was taking a new treatment outside Alaska and sounded optimistic. So the news startled us both. I'm so glad that Donna had a chance to meet Jim at his optimistic best. Is it possible that it was only eight years ago?

We were hoping for the possibility of his coming in to visit this summer, so the news of his death was a real shocker.

Many memories flooded back over the 28 years since Billie and I spent our first winter here. How generous you were in making your cabin available and sharing your family in Fairbanks!

I remember the long hike to your cabin following a wet night at Eight Mile. Upon my arrival, I said to your two startled kids and Wes Redhead, "I brought your hats. Your mother said you'd forgot them."

As I recall, Jim was twelve and his brother ten years old then. There were a lot of memories I'd forgotten, such as the year of the bear's damage after you and Wes separated, and when you were last here with your long time friend and new husband, Ernie Wolff.

Anyway, I'm sure you have many past memories to treasure of Jim. He was special as your first-born, conceived in your small cabin.

After Billie's death, I carved a stone with her name and date as a marker, and Donna and I scattered her cremated remains at Rooney's plot and Nakutchluk's gravesite.

I am now making a marker for Jim with a stone from Lake Creek. I remember joking with him once that I, or my ashes, would someday be there. Now there will be a marker for him.

Donna and I are not sure when we will head outside. Maybe next month. We always touch base with home in Pleasant Valley, Arizona to pick up mail and catch up on maintenance. Will try to give you a call on the way out.

Again, our touch across the years and miles.

Our love to you, Donna and Sam
June 29, 1996, Brooks Range, Alaska

⟵ FIFTY-SEVENTH

Dear Great-Great-Grandsons and Daughters,

Today, I am again writing to you from Koviashuvik. When I return here to our wilderness home, I'm reminded of how little change appears to take place in our surroundings.

In these mountains, north of the Arctic Circle, the white spruce trees grow so slowly that those larger ones beside our cabins are as familiar thirty years later, seemingly to have changed little in three decades.

When I flew out of Phoenix on our way to Anchorage in January this year, I looked down on the urban sprawl of Phoenix and the Salt River Valley trying to remember it as I knew them three decades ago. However, my memory goes back six decades. It was when I was taking flying lessons from a dirt airstrip near the Salt River and Sixteenth Street before World War Two. Camelback Mountain, Squaw Peak, Tempe Butte, and a few other landmarks still give familiarity to the area, but little is as it was sixty years ago, or even thirty, or ten. From the air, crowded freeways with their heavy trucking are what every large American city has become as old buildings are destroyed and new high rises replace them.

What a contrast in being here at Koviashuvik! We are still the only two people in miles, and our life in a log cabin on our lakeshore seems much as it was over thirty years ago.

Our little battery radio brings us today's news of the world as it did then. However, our reception is better today because National Public Radio now broadcasts from both Point Barrow on the Arctic Coast and from Fort Yukon, southeast of us. Ten years ago, the nearest broadcasts were far to the south in Fairbanks.

We consider ourselves fortunate that change here has a different sense of time. Here, the years speak to the hours instead of the other way around. I remember counting the annual rings of a large white spruce log that runs lengthwise, supporting the rafter poles and tundra on our cabin roof. For over five hundred years it spent long dormant winter nights before its summer spurt of growth to produce a new ring. A prospector for his cabin early in the Alaskan gold rush cut the tree down at least a hundred years ago. He abandoned the cabin after panning for gold among the sands and gravel of King Creek without success.

As I counted the growth rings, after I reused this old patriarch for our shore cabin, I noted how tiny the young tree must have been in the year 1500. I recalled that it had to grow another hundred and twenty years of rings before the Pilgrims landed at Plymouth in 1620. It was over two hundred and seventy-six years old when the Declaration of Independence created the beginning of our nation.

And here it is now, in the year 2001, with light shimmering along the ancient adze-marked surface from the morning sun as reflected from the rippling edge of the lake.

When I placed the log in our shore cabin, I inscribed on it, "SEEM WHAT YOU ARE." At that time, it was not addressed to the log, but as I read it today it seems appropriate. Another purlin in our cabin has a quote from Plato: "BE WHAT YOU SEEM." Neither of these aphorisms are any more duplicates than the spruce logs on which they are printed. Another aphorism I have in our cabin, as well as elsewhere, is in the form of a prayer: "SECURE ME FROM SECURITY NOW AND FOREVER. AMEN."

This reminds me of a long discussion I had with Alan Watts when I was living in the San Francisco Bay area. Alan had written a small book of essays, published under the title: "THE WISDOM OF INSECURITY – A Message For An Age Of Anxiety." As an interpreter of Zen Buddhism, Alan was invited for an evening of discussion with several of us whose fields of interest were either science or religion. Mine were both.

What I remember is that the perspective Alan and I shared was incomprehensible to the other participants. What we shared was that religion wants to assure the future beyond death, and science wanted to assure it until death and to postpone death. Our shared dogma at the time was that there is no other reality than the present reality.

Here, this morning, a vital sense of NOW is the real world, which words and ideas can never pin down. We cannot define the ultimate, and this insecurity is paradoxically our security.

Shortly before Alan died in 1973, I had written a piece for a winter issue of VIEW FROM THE TOP OF THE WORLD, a small publication I produced here, in our isolated cabin. I had sent Alan a copy of the short essay, but never heard from him. I'll enclose a copy of it for you. I wonder if it makes sense in the context of your time?

Anyway, you can see I'm always the epistemologist! If these letters bore you, you can always use them to start a fire in the Yukon Stove. Sorry! I forgot that you may not know what a Yukon Stove is or have much contact with starting a fire. I was made aware of this when we were trying to find

"Strike Anywhere Matches" when gathering supplies to bring north. Apparently there is little market for "the old fashioned" wooden kitchen matches today.

One of the delights of being here at Koviashuvik is this recapturing of a sense of time. I guess that in a way this is what I'm doing in writing to you across these years. As I said, I'm enclosing the piece from VIEW FROM THE TOP OF THE WORLD, written during my first winter here at Koviashuvik. That was more that thirty years ago but it seems like yesterday as I write you across the years this morning.

More at another time.

Your Great-Great-Granddad, Sam

BEYOND THERAPY – KOVIASHUKTOK – 1968/1969

The Inuit Eskimo calls it being koviashuktok. One translation of the concept is general happiness. Another is self-respect. It is so subtle a value that it translates as commonplace. But like many concepts that are simple to state, its practice is another matter. So when I say I am learning koviashuktok – selfhood – from the Eskimo, the statement can be put aside as old hat. Doesn't everyone have a sense of self?

Of course, but there is a subtlety here we miss at our peril, particularly as the bulldozer of western culture rolls over the values of the Eskimo as it has others. It may be that the Eskimo has succeeded in preserving something, which we need now more than any other thing.

The snow, ice and darkness here, north of the Arctic Circle, help the Eskimo teach me what he has learned in this environment which puts a premium on life. Whatever exists, the Eskimo himself shares in bringing it into being. With each act and statement his world is created, brought into existence, and each act accomplished is as quickly lost. His ecological relationship to the world is not passive. Man is the force that reveals form. With the human, creation becomes.

For example, the Eskimo language is not one that simply names things that already exist, but brings things and actions into being as spoken. There seems to be unlimited words for snow because snow never exists in itself but takes its form from the actions in which it participates –blowing, sledding, falling – distinctions possible only when experienced in a meaningful context. I recently mentioned to an Eskimo friend how difficult it was to see white ptarmigan in the snow. The response was, "Oh, it is not hard when you know the color of snow. Ptarmigans are different...Pink, I think. The snow is different too. You just have to learn."

The point is, that different kinds of snow are brought into existence by the Eskimo as they experience their environment and speak. All Eskimo words are in effect, forms of the verb "to be" but which itself is lacking in Eskimo.

Today's psychological, scientific and sociological thought, which gives a measure of therapeutic comfort, convenience, power and prosperity, tends to deprive a person of respect for his own nature and his own powers.

Only by recovering his selfhood, becoming koviashuktok, can he move beyond therapy to a natural practice that honors life and growth in the individual above all "practical" considerations. Somehow our concept of the good life must be more than comfort, convenience, power and prosperity.

What I am learning from the Eskimo is not how to live in Utopia, when and if we achieve it, or even how to promote possible Utopia. It is how to live before that glorious day which may or may not come, and live like the Eskimo in taking satisfaction in the world in which we are compelled to live, no matter how bad or good it may be.

We cannot be indifferent to the suffering of others or the fate of humanity, but refusal to accept what IS becomes what theology calls the sin of melancholy. This seems to be one of the sins into which contemporary man easily falls, but is not in the Eskimo frame of reference. As Samuel Johnson put it, "He who sees before him to his third dinner, has a long prospect."

From our point of reference, it is easy to criticize the immediacy of the Eskimo, but he lives beyond therapy. Those who find life a trial because it is not perfect in their eyes are not likely to find it much improved in the foreseeable future, and those who have transformed life into existence by living continuously second-hand can only survive in a therapeutic environment.

They might do better to realize as Thoreau did – that the first business was to live in this world – be it good or bad. The Eskimo did not resolve this. It is where he is.

Sam Wright

FIFTY-EIGHTH

Dear Great-Great-Granddaughters and Sons,

It's the first day of August, and when I went out to the cache to bring in bacon and an egg to make our sourdough blueberry pancakes this morning, I thought I heard music in the distance coming from someone's portable radio.

My first thought was that fishermen had come in to our lake in last night's summer light. We would have heard a floatplane, so they must have driven in from the pipeline haul road on all-terrain-vehicles. Then I recognized what I was hearing was a chorus of wolves! Not strangers.

Donna met me as I came in the cabin door, saying, "Did you hear that choir of elation? I thought at first I heard someone's boom-box."

I said that I'd had a similar response. And then I howled back, hoping for an answering chorus, only silence followed. We thought the wolves might have taken a moose calf as we have seen its tracks on the lakeshore.

Having been informed by our small battery radio that weather was moving into Alaska from the northwest, we left after breakfast to fish for our supper before the clouds thickened with the threat of rain.

After casting for great northern pike, without success, we decided to troll for a Char and Donna hooked a beautiful eight pound male lake trout which will grace our table this evening.

Yesterday evening at supper we were also graced by a huge colorful arch in the sky. It was a brilliant rainbow that reached from shore to shore across our lake. With the sun just above the mountain behind us, we were aware that such a rainbow could only exist as a relationship between water particles, sunlight and our eyes, while looking out from the shore at that moment in time. Without any of these four, in this relationship, that rainbow would not have been. I know this could be the same experience for you, but not the same rainbow.

It is curious that we can share the experience called rainbow across this gap of time when neither of us exist, and in this sharing have communication. It is much the same as these funny shaped black marks I am making on paper this morning in this letter I'm writing to you. When you read this, yesterday's rainbow is again present for both of us in these marks on paper.

I will close this off for the present as we hear the engine of an airplane in the distance. With field glasses, Donna noted it has floats and is landing on our lake.

LATER

It was the arrival of son, Chip, and Lisa, in the small bush plane that flies from the float pond at Bettles Field. As you recall, they were here with us in August last summer when they found the human skullcap, mandible and other bones in the shallows near our shore cabin. They too have been exploring sources for radio carbon dating of the artifacts and have brought with them tools to aid in further exploration of the area where the remains were recovered. They also brought in with them fresh fruit and other perishables such as bacon and eggs to add to our larder.

As this bush plane was the first contact we've had since we arrived in June, Donna had a dozen letters ready to go out and we passed on word to the pilot to change our day of departure, as we plan a to fly out later this month with Chip and Lisa when they leave to return to Yakima, Washington.

I think I once wrote you that my son and namesake, Chip, is minister of the Unitarian Universalist Church in Yakima. Lisa is also UU clergy and will be serving a small group in Coeur d'Alene, Idaho this winter. I may have told you they have a small house and apple orchard in the community of Tieton near Yakima. I wonder if the Yakima area is still one of the great fruit producers in the Northwest when you read this?

When I was a youngster, living in the Salt River Valley in Arizona, the Phoenix area was known as one of the great citrus fruit producers, rivaling southern California. Today, the orchards have been replaced by subdivisions and golf courses where winter visitors swell the population as the snows arrive in the Northeast and Midwest. This is why I wonder about Yakima, and for that matter about our isolated home here on the south slope of the Brooks Range. By sheer luck we have been fortunate during the past decades, to have escaped what I call the bulldozer of the population and subdivision tidal wave that today, like an avalanche, is engulfing all in its path.

I apologize for having stated this to you over and over again. As I look back at what I have experienced in what to me is a short lifetime, I find my imagination unable to project the context in which you are now living. Of course, in your time, I assume there still are those concepts which the ancient Greek philosophers called verities, such as beauty, truth and goodness. However, they always occur in a context that defines them. It is your context that I am unable to imagine. I'm sure that in many ways you cannot imagine mine, no matter how much of it is presented to you by sound or visual reproduction. In the same way, I cannot translate the reality of the time before my birth from its black and white photographs, phonograph recordings and history books.

When you get this letter I will only exist in your world of the "once was." While for me, you are presently in the "not yet." And so I try to put myself in your place and wonder what I would like to hear from my great-great-granddad. Wish you could let me know? Since you can't, I will continue to keep in touch and tell you how it is for me from time to time.

Again, my love to you,

Your Great-Great-Granddad, Sam

FIFTY-NINTH

Dear Great-Great-Grandsons and Daughters,

It is September here in Pleasant Valley.

After flying out of Koviashuvik, we picked up our Volkswagen Camper, which had been parked in Fairbanks, and drove the four thousand six hundred miles home to Arizona.

Early in the morning of the eleventh of September, we were in southern Idaho and drove into a Burger King fast food restaurant for breakfast. It had just opened and we were the first customers. The woman at the cash register said, "Did you see the news?"

She pointed to a television screen on the pick-up counter, and with a sense of unreality we saw an aircraft disappear behind a smoking New York Trade Tower, and then the flaming explosion from its crash into the other one. It was that morning's national news broadcast shortly after the event. As we drove south through Salt Lake City, we followed the national commentary on our radio.

When you read this letter, September Eleventh will mark a long past event to you, much like the bombing of Pearl Harbor. President George W. Bush has addressed the world at a special joint meeting of Congress, stating that it was an act of war and the enemies labeled "Terrorists".

At present, this nebulous enemy is personified in an Islamic leader, Osama Bin Laden in Afghanistan. The terrorist movement, which is currently focused on the United States, appears to have no geographic or centralized leadership other than an Islamic fundamentalism not supported by so-called Islamic countries, but apparently nourished within their borders.

Anyway, this is the way it looks from here, and as extremists in the Mid-East call for a holy war, I hope the extremists in the Western World do not respond in kind.

You (fortunately I hope) can look back upon this time and event as it has worked itself out in history. I find it exciting and heartwarming to see and hear the leadership of the world's major nations supporting this "War on Terrorism," but I am apprehensive by what is meant by "War," knowing how easy it is to use the tactics of the so-called enemy for so-called noble ends.

As you know from my letters, I was deeply involved in World War II, which produced the technology to wipe us all out as human beings. I'm sure that technology has improved. Today I am wondering about our improvement as human beings, as we attempt to deal with ourselves in a world where a very few can dramatically affect the lives of all.

I wish I could be looking back, as you can, but today's world is in the present where we must function with what we know as best we know how.

At the end of this week we are driving to the foothills of the Sierra Nevada Mountains in Auburn, California to participate in the dedication of the new Church Meetinghouse of the Sierra Foothills Unitarian Universalists. Five years ago I served as their first minister while they were meeting in the gymnasium of a school. Donna and I made many warm friends and we have been invited to share the congregation's joy in having a home of its own.

Acquiring a home of one's own, whether for a congregation or a family, is not easy today. When I say "home," I do not mean a rental, such as a flat or apartment, or even a condominium or house. I mean a structure in which one lives with the intimacy of a sense of possession and permanency.

I've found great pleasure in literally constructing the homes in which I have lived for the past thirty years. Donna and I are now looking forward to again building a home on the acreage we share with our family tribe near Chickaloon, Alaska.

When we visited the land this summer, Bianca and Jeff had already begun cutting trees and preparing their site for a future home. And we just learned this past week that the proposed well on the property has now been drilled. This means we will no longer have to haul our water.

Anyway, having the opportunity, and being able to construct one's home has become rare in my lifetime. I wonder how possible it is for you?

For the past two weeks, flags have been flying at half-mast throughout the country. This was following the attack on the Trade Tower buildings in New York City with the loss of more than five thousand lives. Today, after two weeks, they have been returned to full staff on all government buildings. However the television, radio and internet, have been full of commentary as have all other means of communication.

Suggestions have been made to bomb the Taliban Headquarters in Afghanistan, believed to be harboring the terrorist, Osama Bin Laden.

On the internet appeared the first suggestion of a bombing with which I could agree:

Here it is, attributed to a Dr. Joshua David Stone:

A military response, particularly an attack on Afghanistan, is exactly what the terrorists want. It will strengthen and swell the small but fanatical ranks.

Instead, bomb Afghanistan with rice, bread, butter, clothing and medicine. It will cost less than conventional arms, posses no threat of US casualties and just might get the populace thinking that maybe the Taliban don't have the answers. After three years of drought and with starvation looming, let's offer the Afghan people the vision of a new future, one that includes full stomachs.

Bomb them with information – video players and cassettes of world leaders, particularly Islamic leaders, condemning terrorism. Carpet the country with magazines and newspapers showing the horror of terrorism committed by their 'guest.' Blitz them with laptop computers and DVD players filled with a perspective that is denied them by their government. Saturation bombing with hope will mean that some of it gets through. Send so much that the Taliban can't collect and hide it all.

The Taliban are telling their people to prepare for Jihad. Instead, let's give the Afghani people their first good meal in years. Seeing your family fully fed and the prospect of stability in terms of food and a future is a powerful deterrent to martyrdom.

All we ask in return is that they, as a people, agree to enter the civilized world. That includes handing over terrorists in their midst. In responding to terrorism we need to do something different. Something unexpected... something that addresses the root of the problem.

We need to take away the well of despair, ignorance and brutality from which the Osama bin Ladens of the world water their gardens of terror.

Of course, today, in my time, such a "bombing" would never be considered possible or practical. But we do "need to do something different, something unexpected, something that addresses the root of the problem."

Symbolically, people have identified New York and the Trade Towers with their sense of home. Deep in our psyche, I think that not only Americans, but those we call the civilized world, have seen this tragic event as an attack, not only on innocent individuals, but on what I called, a sense of permanency, of ownership and that intimacy symbolized in a home of one's own. As I said, I wish I could look back with you. I would like to see if we acted with that unexpected something that addresses the root of the problem.

Until you again hear from me, I send my love to you across time.

Your Great-Great-Granddad, Sam

SIXTIETH

Dear Great-Great-Granddaughters and Sons,

I'm writing you this morning as I wait in line to have the oil in our car changed in Flagstaff, Arizona. We are on our way home from a meeting-house dedication in the Sierra Nevada foothills in California.

Donna and I spent the night in a motel in Kingman, Arizona, where large numbers of truck drivers and tourists gather for fuel, food and a break from their miles of driving on Interstate Highway #40.

Today Highway 40 has replaced what is now known as "Historic Route 66." I find it strange that old highway 66 is now called "historic."

As we drove east this morning, I recalled my many adventures here in Northern Arizona when I was a teenager living near Phoenix. When we passed the Ashfork, AZ turn-off, I told Donna about my seventeen-mile hike one night from there.

It was a hike along old Highway 66 up into the pines toward the town of Williams. I was hitchhiking from the Salt River Valley to Mormon Lake, south of Flagstaff, where my family was spending the summer. I remember that it was June and I had just passed my seventeenth birthday. However, I do not recall any of the rides I caught before being dropped off at the Ash-fork, AZ turn into Highway 66 at dusk.

Back in 1936, hitchhiking included hiking as well as hitches. A pick up was less frequent then. I started hiking up the hill along 66 in the twilight. Several cars passed me, ignoring my outstretched hand and thumb. Then darkness fell and I knew there was little chance of a car stopping to pick me up.

After a five or six hour climb along the highway, I was up a thousand feet in the ponderosa pines, tired, and feeling the mountain's chill. So I stopped and built a fire away from the road. There I curled up in my bedroll for the night. I still vividly remember those brilliant stars that night, and the yapping howl of a coyote before I drifted off to sleep.

Since then the old Highway 66 has been replaced by heavily used Interstate #40 on which huge trucks and traffic roar by. If there are any hitchhikers on Highway #40 today, we saw none. There are few places where one could safely hold out a thumb and try for a ride.

Anyway, here in Flagstaff, the railroad still parallels old Highway 66 through the city but heavy trucking and east/west traffic on the interstate bypasses the town. I wonder what kind of highway system and railroad exist in your time?

Today, long-range passenger railroad travel is nearly non-existent. Except for commuter traffic near east and west coast cities, railroads today are primarily haulers of freight. The last time I rode a passenger train, and had a meal in a dining car, was nearly forty years ago on a trip between the west coast and Chicago. I wonder if there are any cross-country passenger trains when you read this?

At present, air travel has become minimal, following the September eleventh hijack airplane crashes into the New York Twin Towers. Many people are afraid to fly and several airlines are facing bankruptcy. All U.S. planes were grounded following the attack on the towers, and though the ban has been lifted, air travel has not picked up.

I've just been asked to start the engine to see that the oil pressure is OK. I'll put away this pad for now and finish writing to you later.

LATER

I had hoped to finish this letter to you soon after our return to Pleasant Valley. However, we only had one day at home before leaving to drive to Puerto Penasco, south of the Mexican border on the east coast of the Sea of Cortez. I remember writing to you from there last autumn.

Here we are again at the annual gathering of church families during the first full moon of autumn. This is a special blue moon month with two full moons. Donna and I were married over thirteen years ago under a full blue moon. Here we sun on the beach, eat fresh shrimp, guacamole and papaya. In the evening we sip our tequila beneath a palm frond palapa and watch the pelicans soar above the waves along the shore.

Much of our conversation is about the "War on Terrorism" in which we and other countries of the world are now engaged. Most of us share a concern that the military action which may result, could precipitate an escalation of violent acts involving biological and other weapons of mass destruction. I find it interesting that the families gathered here this weekend share a common perspective of caution about how our country proceeds in this so-called war on terrorism.

However, as I am sitting here writing you this Sunday morning, someone came down to the beach and reported that the United States and Britain have attacked Afghanistan. He reported that there was little other information. Since it is night in Afghanistan, we assumed that there would be no new information until more time has passed. However, several people left the beach to watch television in their motor homes.

Since Donna and I are camping here in our "pop top" Volkswagen, we will later join with a neighbor to get the news in their fully equipped house on wheels. Many of the motor homes parked here along the shore have every conceivable convenience, from satellite television and air conditioning to hot and cold running water. I wonder what motor homes are like in your time or if they even exist?

Since we leave in the morning to drive back to our home in Pleasant Valley, I'll close this note and write you from there.

My love to you 'til then.

Your Great-Great-Granddad, Sam

SIXTY-FIRST

Dear Great-Great-Grandsons and Daughters,

It has been over a month since passenger airplanes, with suicide hijackers, crashed into the trade towers in New York City and the Pentagon in Washington D.C. The number of people missing at the World Trade Center stands at 4,688, with 450 people confirmed dead and 375 of those identified. death toll at the Pentagon is 189 and 44 at the Pennsylvania hijacked plane crash site.

Since then the United States has retaliated in its war against terrorism by heavily bombing targets in Afghanistan where terrorists are believed to be. Scenes on television this morning show the rubble of crumbled structures reported to be centers of terrorists' informational activity.

I know that this will be ancient history to you when you read this, but I want you to know the context in which I'm living while writing to you.

Last week I wrote you from the beach at Puerto Penasco in Mexico. After a leisurely breakfast, sitting in the shade with friends, we packed our camper and drove north to the border. There we found cars and motor homes backed up nearly a mile while each was being searched for possible bombs and other illegal contraband. Slowly we crept forward, as two cars at a time were searched. Engine hoods and trunks were opened and cupboards, closets and ovens in motor homes were explored. It was interesting to me that no one seemed irritated by this invasion of privacy caused by last month's attack.

At lunchtime we stopped at a Dairy Queen fast food outside the former mining town of Ajo. As we sat out of the sun under its tin roof shelter eating a banana split, I commented to Donna how safe we felt here in the desert southwest compared to those in other parts of the world.

Just then a violent tornado-like whirlwind swept through the area nearly taking off the metal roof and filling our banana splits with dirt and sand. As the dust devil spun weeds, sand and debris across the highway, I said aloud: "I got your message!"

Donna asked, "What do you mean?"

I reminded her of the prayer we have carved on rafters in both our homes in the mountains of Arizona and Alaska: "Secure us from security now and forever. Amen."

Anyway, as we drove home to Pleasant Valley, we talked about the contrasts between different parts of the world at this time. We noted how many Afghans are living a medieval world of the past while western technology has projected us unto a place in history that has no precedence.

I recalled a discussion I had with Clyde Tombough, when he was teaching geography at New Mexico State College in Las Cruces back in the nineteen fifties. Tombough had become a name in science because, as a graduate student, he was credited for the discovery of the Planet Pluto at the Lick Observatory in Flagstaff, Arizona in February of 1930.

Since that conversation in Las Cruces, men have not only walked on the moon and sent probes into space, but are awaiting the return of a NASA Spacecraft from Mars with rocks and soil samples to answer questions about life there. Although we talked until late in the night about what the future might bring, neither Clyde nor I could have imagined what has happened during the past fifty years.

It never occurred to me that the shift from ignorance to enlightenment might not occur as rapidly as implied in this space and information age. Somehow, ignorance has kept pace with knowledge in my time. I trust that it is not the same in yours.

As I pointed out to Donna on our drive home, one area of ignorance is the one we call religious faith. Few people know anything about faiths outside the one with which they have a connection.

The faith of Islam has been given an evil connection by association. Since Islamic fundamentalists were those whose suicide missions destroyed the Twin Towers in New York, I've become aware that most Christians actually know very little about the history and tenets of their own faith and less about Islam. Their ignorance and misconceptions are amazing to me. This is why my subject as guest speaker at the Prescott Unitarian Universalist Fellowship next Sunday is "Islam, the Religion of Mohammed." I may enclose it for you.

Since Islam is presently the second largest and fastest growing religious faith in the world, I wonder if it has become the dominant faith in your time?

Until you hear from me again, my affection,

Your Great-Great-Granddad, Sam

SIXTY-SECOND

Dear Great-Great-Granddaughters and Sons,

Tonight is Halloween and the moon is full.

This October is a blue moon month because it has two full moons. As I have mentioned before, Donna and I married on April Fools Day in a month of the blue moon, so to us blue moons are special. I wonder why it is called "blue?" Tonight it is in its traditional golden yellow.

Although it is Halloween, when kids go from house to house for "trick or treat," few are expected to do so tonight. With the news of several anthrax bacteria deaths believed to have been introduced into mail by terrorists, people are apprehensive. Even our small, isolated post office has been affected.

Our local Postmaster said he couldn't sell pre-stamped envelopes, which would normally be licked to seal them. He is required to use a wet-mop on the Post Office floor instead of the usual vacuum cleaner, and the public is requested to wash their hands after handling mail. No wonder there is a sense of tension and stress everywhere.

On the bright side tonight, baseball fans were ecstatic. Tonight's World Series game, between the Arizona Diamond Backs and the New York Yankees, was tied. The Yankee batter, Derek Jeters, hit a home run in the tenth inning after midnight in New York. The game was played there. Here, in Arizona, with Mountain Standard Time, it is still Halloween.

I wonder if the World Series is still being played in your time? Does it include the "World" and not just the United States?

Tomorrow is the "Day of the Dead" in Mexico and the Spanish speaking communities here in the southwest. Tonight it reminds me of my first letter to you when I commented that you were dead (at least not born), and I would be dead when you read my letter. I think I once wrote you that I called this a time binding of our lives.

We cannot know in advance how long we shall live. I've been lucky. When I look back at close calls of which I was aware, and the many friends I've lost whose life-calls were too close, I'm especially aware tonight that life is a gift so precious that we would accept it on any terms rather than never to have had it.

I can only speak for myself, but once we accept the fact that we shall disappear, we also discover the larger self that relates us to our family and friends, and to our neighborhood and community. And beyond that we relate to nation and humanity, and to the whole creation out of which we have sprung. Both of us are a part of this in all these related groups and persons. We live on in them, dead and unborn.

As an epistemologist, I used to wonder why the Hindus included Shiva, the destroyer, in their trinity. I could understand Brahma, the creator, and Vishnu, the preserver. But why the destroyer? After visiting care centers where human beings live on after reason, locomotion and pleasure have left them, I understand. We are not imprisoned by death but freed.

As a naturalist in its broadest sense, I see everything in a very essential way alive and moving and related – not just through material qualities but through belonging within a unified design of such magnitude and beauty that we can hardly grasp its meaning.

Because it is late at night, and because it is Halloween, and tomorrow is the Day of the Dead -- and because my brothers (our soldiers) are dropping bombs on others in Afghanistan, I am acutely aware that the connection between life and death is, in the end, a mystery, but real.

Out of the great wheel of the seasons new life comes, yet always dependent on the old. The dead plant transmits its seed to the future. Last year's leaves make compost for this year's garden. The mystery of the living seed is a tie that binds us both to the past and to the future.

Enough of this stuff! For me life is mostly fun. I hope it is the same for you. It's fun to think, to read, to walk and hike when the smell of rain on dry grass and creosote bushes drifts across the desert. Its fun to eat a meal, drive a car, mow the weeds, take a shower, open a letter or write one, and to hit the sack after a hard day's work. What is not fun? You can answer that for yourself, and so can I. But most of the things I do are fun. I hope it is the same for you.

Donna and I expect to be traveling soon to Thailand. It was called Siam when I was young. I assume the musical, "Anna and the King of Siam," may be still around in your time.

Anyway, it may be some time before you hear from me again. In the meantime, remember that this relatedness, as it binds us to all that has passed, surely binds us to the future as well. Whatever is kindled in us can never really be extinguished. So live life to the hilt. Whether long or short, it will have been a full one.

As ever, my love to you,

Your Great-Great-Granddad, Sam

SIXTY-THIRD

Dear Great-Great-Grandsons and Daughters,

When I turned on our satellite dish for news from Berlin, Germany this morning, I learned that my friend Ken Kesey died yesterday of complications from liver cancer.

This astonished me because I had been told that Ken was to speak at the Throop Memorial Unitarian Universalist church in Pasadena where my colleague, the Rev. Paul Sawyer, is minister. Paul had called me last week to invite me for a reunion of several of us, with Ken, to recall a conference week at Asilomar in Monterey, California.

It was thirty-five years ago that Kesey and his Merry Pranksters were invited there to participate. They arrived in their gaudily painted school bus, with a large American flag draped from the top and two blaring loud speakers on either side. It was during that bizarre week that Ken and I became friends.

I remember writing you about my wild ride on the back of a motorcycle in South San Francisco one Halloween night. It was the night of the so-called "Graduation Ceremony" that was underwritten by Kesey to persuade people to go beyond drugs and achieve a mind-altered state without LSD.

He had brought a rock band, called "The Grateful Dead," for the gathering. His wife, Faye, and their small children were there in Halloween costumes as were the rest of us. As I wrote you before, I was in a priestly clerical collar and dark suit.

During a break in the raucous music, Ken spoke of this "graduation." He then looked at me, offering me the floor. I guess I let him down. I did not respond.

Because I was dressed as a Christian priest, and because I had been mistaken for a Roman Catholic cleric by the Hell's Angels motorcyclists on arrival and because the context had become jovial with the odor of pot, I realized that my anonymity would be gone when the San Francisco Chronicle appeared next morning. Publicity would certainly not be helpful for the new Graduate Theological Seminary, or Starr King School for the Ministry where I was professor.

Ken, in his red, white and blue Mr. America costume, tried to say something about this being a graduation, but the evening had taken on a mood of its own. The drummer started a beat, the dance went on, and I was relieved to be able to slip away after midnight.

I shall miss Ken. I wonder if his books and the film, "One Flew Over The Cuckoo's Nest," are still around in your time?

Another news commentary from Europe this morning dealt with the terrorists who committed suicide by crashing hijacked planes into the New York Trade Towers.

I can understand suicide where life is seen as totally negative. When there seems to be no out, or where physical suffering is intolerable with no end in sight. However, a deliberate suicide for a so-called cause is hard for me to comprehend.

The phrase, "He gave his life for his country," in my experience does not ring true to fact. The truth is that "His life was lost in defense of his country."

Following the eleventh of September and its suicides, I remembered the Japanese Kamikaze pilots in World War II. They, and the nineteen "terrorists" who flew into the New York World Trade Towers, are a psychological puzzle for me.

However, in seeking for insight into such motivation, I ended up with a moth. Yes, a moth!

Remember the cockroach, Archie, of New York newspaper columnist Don Marquis', *Archie and Mehitabel*, who learned to write to Don by jumping from the top of the typewriter down upon one key at a time and thus unable to print capitals?

I never expected to learn from a cockroach, much less from a moth. But, through Archy's conversation with a moth, I now have some insight into a martyr's mind.

Here is the conversation as Don Marquis published it.

What do you think?

The Lesson of the Moth – Don Marquis
(Written by Archy the cockroach on Don Marquis' typewriter)

i was talking to a moth the other evening
he was trying to break into an electric light and fry himself on the
wires
why do you fellows pull this stunt i asked him
because it is the conventional thing for moths or why
if that had been an uncovered candle instead of an electric light bulb
you would now be a small unsightly cinder
have you no sense
plenty of it he answered but at times we get tired of using it
we get bored with the routine and crave excitement
fire is beautiful and we know that if we get to close it will kill us
but what does that matter
it is better to be happy for a moment
and be burned up with beauty than to live a long time
and be bored all the while
so we wad all our life up into one little roll and then we shoot the roll
that is what life is for
it is better to be a part of beauty for one instant and then cease to exist
than to exist forever and never be a part of beauty
our attitude toward life
is come easy go easy
we are like human beings used to be
before they became too civilized to enjoy themselves
and before i could argue him out of his philosophy
he went and immolated himself on a patent cigar lighter
i do not agree with him myself i would rather have
half the happiness and twice
the longevity

but at the same time i wish
there was something i wanted
as badly as he wanted to fry himself
                        archy

My coffee has become cold while writing to you this frosty November morning, here in the Sierra Ancha Mountains, so I'll say adios, until you hear from me again.

In the meantime, I'm still

your Great-Great-Granddad, Sam

SIXTY-FOURTH

Dear Great-Great-Granddaughters and Sons,

It has been three and a half months since suicidal hijackers flew passenger planes into the World Trade Towers. Their collapse has changed the familiar New York skyline.

When I first saw the city's skyline as a teenager, I was attending prep school in New England. The new Empire State Building, as the "tallest in the world", entranced me. It had been dedicated the same year as the George Washington Suspension Bridge, which was "the longest suspension bridge in the world." Then, a few years later in 1937, the Golden Gate Bridge became "the longest in the world," with 80,000 miles of wire cable. That year the Hoover Dam created Lake Mead in Arizona as "the largest man-made lake in the United States." Everything seemed to be the biggest, tallest or newest at that time.

As a kid from Arizona, where a twelve-story building in Phoenix was a marvel, the Empire State Building was literally a "sky scraper." In the nineteen thirties, the World Trade Towers would have been to me, inconceivable. Today, rubble from the September 11, 2001 attack is still smoking as huge portable cranes load trucks with the towers' debris.

It was in the nineteen thirties that the dirigible Hindenburg exploded at Lakehurst, New Jersey. I remember watching those first newsreels of the tragedy. It never occurred to me that this was the end of our dream of huge dirigibles replacing cruise ships and ocean liners.

It was also in the thirties that I got my first official job in a drugstore in downtown Phoenix. I say "official" because the Social Security Act had recently been passed and I had to acquire, what to me, was a long social security number of nine digits to make me a legitimate employee. Since 1935 that number 526-20-#### has identified me on driver's licenses and in many other ways far more than my actual presence. I wonder if it is the same for you? Anyway, I find it interesting the way numbers have taken over since I was a kid. Our first telephone number I remember was simply number 312.

Today our tickets arrived for our flight to Thailand. The invoice number was 0000208683, and account number 9284623255. I then recognized that this last number is our current telephone number!

Anyway, it is December 1, 2001 and we are leaving tomorrow for two months in Thailand. We are flying there by way of Phoenix, Los Angeles, Taipei and Bangkok with our ten-month-old grandchild, Acacia, and her parents. We have found that at present the cost of living along the Andaman Sea in southern Thailand (including transportation) equals the expense of being at home in Arizona and Alaska during these winter months.

Having never been in southern Asia, I'm looking forward to this adventure in a strange land with travelers who know how to live there simply. Thomas and Melea spent many months in India and Northern Thailand a couple of years ago, and it was their experience that has encouraged us to join them this winter. When they asked if we would like to accompany them we responded enthusiastically with "You bet!"

So yesterday Donna and I drove to Payson where she had a dental check up. And there we had extra passport pictures made for visas that we might need.

Since the attack on the New York Trade Towers, fewer people are traveling by air. Our tickets on China Air are more reasonable than we expected. The current War on Terrorism has had some positive effects for us.

I am not promising to write you while we are gone, but I'll tell you all about it when we return in February.

In the meantime my love to you.

Your Great-Great-Granddad, Sam

SIXTY-FIFTH

Dear Great-Great-Grandsons and Daughters,

I'm writing to you from where I sit under a coconut palm tree. The sound of the surf on the beach of this island cove in the Andaman Sea makes me sleepy. Or perhaps it is the light breeze in this humid heat after long hours of travel on a bus from Bangkok.

Since I last wrote you, the five of us (ten-month-old granddaughter Acacia, her parents, Donna and me) flew across the Pacific Ocean to Bangkok,

Thailand. There we spent a couple of days among mobs of tourists before taking an all-night bus down the Malay Peninsula to Rangon.

It was there we crowded on to an open boat with a dozen others. After a two-hour trip on a blue-green sea among other islands, we landed on Ko Phayam, a small tropical island where we expect to stay through Christmas.

As this is my first time in what is called "The Far East" (although we traveled west to get here), I carried images from books and stories I've read by travelers in the past, from Rudyard Kipling and Somerset Maugham to Mitchner's Tales of the South Pacific. My bare and sandaled feet, along with exotic foods and unfamiliar language intonation, still carry a certain romantic image in spite of mobs of tourists, Internet access and air-conditioning. I wonder what you will find in your time? Today's western culture appears to dominate everywhere.

When Donna and I were on an island in Lake Titicaca, high in the Andes of Peru a few years ago, we were paying guests of an indigenous Indian family. There was no electricity or so-called modern conveniences. We slept in their courtyard in an adjoining hut on a straw mattress and ate meals of their homegrown potatoes with them. Their protein was cooy (guinea pig). These free running rodents occupied a corner of the kitchen next to the cooking fire. Outside income came to the family through tourists like us, who were willing to adapt to their life style. Our Peruvian hosts continued their basic way of life, sharing it with us for the income we provided.

I wondered (and still do) if the next generation of islanders would be able to resist the pressure of modern technology and its so-called affluence? However, this will be something you can know. Not me.

Anyway, we expect to be here on this small tropical island in the Andaman Sea for the next several weeks through Christmas. By then, we should know more of other places we want to visit and that we can afford here in South East Asia.

One of the reasons we are here is that the monetary exchange rate makes it so reasonable. It would have cost us more to remain home in Arizona. Currently we get 43 Thailand bhats for a U.S. dollar; also, food and lodging are more reasonable here than there. While we were in Bangkok we sampled many Thailand dishes and found them savory to our taste. A few were a bit painful with hot spice, which I will avoid.

Flies, mangy dogs and traffic in the sweltering, humid heat were a contrast to the modern tile and glass of the air-conditioned International Airport where we were held for several hours and searched due to an anonymous bomb threat. With the U.S. war on terrorism, security measures in air travel have meant several searches on our way here.

Now that we are here, I'm going to join Donna, who is wading out in the surf, with Acacia. This is Acacia's first dip in the Andaman sea. The western horizon is broken with silhouettes of fishing boats, back-lit by a golden sun. I think we are going to like it here in our bamboo huts on the beach of Aow Yai.

I hope there are still a few un-crowded tropical beaches in your time. Thinking of you on this unusual December day for me,

Your Great-Great Granddad, Sam

SIXTY-SIXTH

Dear Great-Great-Granddaughters and Sons,

We have now been seven days here on Aow Yai (Aow is Thai for beach and Yai is big).

When the boat pulled up next to the pier on the other side of the Island, we were met by several small motorbikes whose drivers had us climb behind with our backpacks to be carted across the island through the jungle of cocoanut palms, bamboo, and groves of cashew and latex trees. It was an exciting ride for all of us as we each clung to our driver's waist and bounced through the steamy undergrowth.

That evening, Donna and I shared a large bottle of beer and we watched brilliant horizontal sunset ribbons of surf give way to blinking fishing boat lights on the horizon.

We recalled that it was Pearl Harbor Day, and that was sixty years ago! I was twenty-two years old and could never have imagined what has taken place in my life and times since that day any more than I can imagine your world and the time in which you will be reading this. I hope it is as interesting for you as mine has been for me.

Anyway, having been on this tropical island for a week, it has become familiar – from the sound of waves breaking on the beach to the spicy taste of Thai cuisine. This morning I took granddaughter Acacia on my shoulders while we walked a quarter of a mile along the beach to another small resort of bamboo huts. There, we could get fresh ground coffee with our breakfast of fruit and eggs while sitting under an overhead fan to discourage the flies. The proprietor had a basket of children's toys with which Acacia played on the floor of the cabana. But most significant to me was finding yesterday's English language newspaper: *The Bangkok Post*, that someone had brought from Ranong on the mainland.

Like a thunderclap, the news of the world outside caught my attention as if I'd never been away from the media that so dominates our lives. The headline was about a suicide bombing of the Indian Parliament, followed by more clashes between Palestinians and Israelis. And of course there was an update on U.S. troops searching for Osama bin Laden in Afghanistan.

As I sipped my coffee, looking out across the island dotted sea, broken by sweeping prowed fishing boats, the turmoil of our times seemed distant. Now the angry, black headlines shouted for recognition. And as a dutiful reader, I read on and on about the world's problems and concerns. I became aware of how few of our joys and achievements are considered newsworthy. I suppose it still the same in your time.

When we arrived in Thailand on December fifth, and ordered a meal after our long flight, I asked for a glass of beer and was told that it was not available. Nor was liquor or coffee, as it was the king's birthday. The deference paid to his majesty, King Bhumibol Adulyadej and his family is evident in the large colored photo posters of his majesty surrounded by gold frames in shops. He also appears larger than life along the central boulevard in Bangkok.

It is much the same here on the small island of Ko Phayam. Every Thai hut has pictures of the king (often with the queen) attached prominently on a visible wall. There is also a separate shrine in prominence, usually with several gifts presented before a statue of the Buddha. I wonder which takes precedence? Both idols seem venerated about the same. This veneration is strange to my experience. I wonder if kings and queens still exist in your time? I feel sure the image of Buddha is still around.

Here, the cashew trees are in bloom with tiny pink blossoms on the ends of drooping branches. I found one tree, along a jungle trail I was exploring, that had already developed green fruit (cashews). I was intrigued that the green nuts hung in clusters like grapes. I cut open and tasted an unripe kernel. It had a cashew flavor with which I am familiar, but left a stinging sensation in my mouth and around my lips. I was told later that Burmese harvesters wore rubber gloves because the sap of the fruit is so caustic.

I find it interesting to listen to conversations among the travelers at the dining table. Most are northern Europeans. A New Zealander came in yesterday. And Yuli, the owner of this 'Bamboo Bungalow" retreat, is an Israeli by way of Los Angeles. He is married to a Thai woman whose family lives here on the island. Most who are here have traveled widely and are still on the go. One couple, from the Netherlands, said they had left never to return. They were ultimately seeking a place to settle.

I am by far the senior traveler on this island. Most here are of the twenty-five to thirty-five generation. As a biologist, I sense that those who are single are traveling unconsciously seeking their "perfect mate."

What am I seeking? Not my mate, which I have. But I ask myself, what is this curiosity that has brought me to where I have never before been? What do I expect to discover? Is it T.S. Eliot's journey, ending in what he discovers to be the beginning? A "for the first time?"

This appears to motivate my curiosity that never seems to be satisfied. Each discovery, whether inner or outer, piques my curiosity for further discovery. It is as if one could somehow, in time, know what is ultimate. But time is endless and the term "ultimate" infers a stopping place. I find no beginning or end in discovery. It is always new.

As I write, I am aware that what I communicate across the years is always in the context of where I am and what I am seeing, hearing and sensing at the time. I am also aware that this must be the same experience for you in your time.

Again, I send you my affection across the years that try to divide us.

Your Great-Great-Granddad, Sam

SIXTY-SEVEN

Dear Great-Great-Grandsons and Daughters,

My calendar today marks the Winter Solstice. However, on this lush, tropical island I have no sense that it is the shortest day of the year.

Early this morning we hiked the seven kilometers through humid vegetation, across the island, to where a resident has an e-mail connection with the mainland.

After cranking up the generator to power his computer, for three bhats a minute (less than ten cents), we could receive and send messages to friends and family elsewhere in the world. I am sure that for you, such communication may seem crude, but for us to instantaneously send and receive messages halfway around the earth from this small island still seems a bit miraculous.

I remember on my birthday, when I was eight years old, going with my dad to the railroad station in the mining town where we lived in New Mexico to send a message to my favorite uncle in Denver, Colorado. It was to thank him for my birthday gift of a bone-handled pocketknife.

It was also a birthday gift from my parents that I could send a telegram to him, a message that would reach Uncle Ed in Denver the same day! I remember Mr. Tolsen clicking the telegraph key, using the magic of the Morse code to send my "Thank You" to Uncle Ed. On that warm June afternoon, Mr. Tolsen sat under his green eye-shade with sleeves pulled up near his elbows by black, elastic bands and explained to me how every click that he made went along the telegraph wire and was repeated at the same time in Denver, many miles away. He showed me how he could spell out my name in clicks of the telegraph key.

I was so intrigued at that time I thought of some day becoming a telegraph operator. I wonder if my lifetime interest in communication in its many forms began in that small telegraph office along the railroad tracks in New Mexico?

Anyway, here I am on an island in the Andaman Sea trying to communicate with you across time from a once familiar world that has changed dramatically since that eighth birthday. I cannot imagine the changes in your time.

This makes me wonder about what appears not to change, such as the sound of the surf on this beach and the smell of salt in the humid air. I hope the coral reefs, with their exotic fish, are still around for your enjoyment and wonder.

As I look out at the many fishing boats between the shore and the distant horizon, I see no gulls flying. I'm also aware that I've seen no shore birds on this beach with its plentiful small crabs and sand dollars. As an ecologist, I am curious about this lack that I've never observed in fishing areas elsewhere in North or South America. It makes me wonder about ecosystems in the future, specifically in your time.

Since this is the time of the winter solstice, I try to imagine what it is like today at our home at Koviashuvik in arctic Alaska. There it is locked in winter cold and snow. The only sound in miles would be the song of wolves, and overhead the aurora would be dancing in bright, gaudy curtains of light across the heavens among glittering stars.

We do have glittering stars here, and the constellation of Orion is as familiar as it is in northern Alaska. It just appears in a different place in the sky. What I find curious is no sign of aircraft are overhead either day or night. Flight patterns apparently by-pass southern Thailand.

Today we celebrated the solstice with a toast of rum and Coca Cola, which intrigues our hosts. They asked about winter solstice, and with drawings on the sandy beach, I indicated why it was the shortest day and its significance to us northerners. Although they had seen movies with snow and cold, it was difficult for them to grasp the shifts between summer and winter in a place that only recognizes wet and dry seasons.

Also today, an unusual event brought us all to the beach where four large fishing boats towed a fifth into our cove. It had been sunk on its side. The crews of the fishing boats spent hours attempting to pull the sunken boat close to the beach. Finally they hauled it partially upright between the four ships. I suppose it was to await the incoming tide in order to beach it tonight. We shall see.

The sound of the diesel engines of the fishing boats, in contrast to the single cycle motor bikes that are used by the islanders on their trails, recalls to me my first motorcycle, whose large four cylinders sounded more like the boat diesels that the poppity-pop of the single cylinder motorbikes that seem to be everywhere in Thailand.

My first motorcycle was an Indian, and had what we called a "suicide clutch." If your foot slipped off the spring-loaded clutch pedal, the powerful engine could throw you from the heavy bike. I still carry scars from it and other motorbikes I once owned.

Isn't it interesting that the sound of a fishing boat engine on a south sea island can bring back the recall of a motorcycle I had not thought about for more than sixty years? Back in 1940 I was a newly married twenty-two-year-old, employed in Phoenix by Standard Stations Inc., a subsidiary of the Standard Oil Co. With my big Indian motorcycle between my legs, I felt I could lick the world.

At that time I could never have predicted the events that followed and changed not only my life but also the whole world, following the Japanese bombing of Pearl Harbor.

So here I sit, sixty years later, watching a fishing boat being repaired off this tropical beach and wonder about you and the world in which you live. I hope it is as interesting as mine has been so far. I'll try to keep you informed.

My love to you.

Your Great-Great-Granddad, Sam

SIXTY-EIGHTH

Dear Great-Great-Granddaughters and Sons,

On Christmas Eve Donna and I walked under bright stars along the edge of the sea. Phosphorescence sparkled at our bare feet in the warm edge of the ebbing tide.

How strange it seems without the commercial Christmas of "Jingle Bells," "Santa Claus Is Coming To Town," and "Away In A Manger." Just a lulling of surf and the lights of fishing boats on the horizon accompanied our hand in hand stroll along Aoi Yai (broad beach).

The day after Christmas we were up early in the morning with our backpacks on and astraddle motorbikes. We gripped the waists of our drivers as we tore across the island to catch the boat to the mainland.

As the open boat banged against the pier, we were delayed, awaiting a cart of life vests for us to wear before departing on a rough sea. Wet with spray, we arrived in Ranong. There we boarded another open boat for Myanmar (Burma) in order to leave and return to Thailand for another thirty-day visitor permit.

Crossing the bay to Myanmar, with its many boats and coastal shipping, recalled a harrowing experience that I'd forgotten when I crossed the San Francisco Bay from Sausalito to Alameda in a small pontoon houseboat in which I had planned to live following my sabbatical year leave from the seminary where I was teaching in Berkeley.

The two-room houseboat was powered by an outboard motor and steered by cables from a wheel inside the front windows. There was no way to avoid the main shipping lanes beneath the Oakland-San Francisco Bay Bridge. The wakes of steamers, tugboats and barges threatened to swamp my small, clumsy craft. When I pulled up at the mooring site at Alameda Island in the East Bay, I was asked where I'd come from in my clumsy craft? When I told him, he said, " I don't believe it. You are lucky to be here!" I agreed with him.

Actually the houseboat was not in a "lucky" place because several months later, when I was away, someone opened the outside pontoon valve and my houseboat disappeared beneath its mooring place in the Bay.

Crossing to Burma, it must have been the sea traffic, waves, and sound of the motors that transported me back thirty-four years from the Thailand-Myanmar border to San Francisco Bay. Isn't it interesting how sounds and scenery can recall forgotten experiences? I'm sure it must be the same for you.

Anyway, we had our passports stamped in Myanmar and then returned to Thailand to board a bus for an all night trip to Bangkok.

There we boarded a train north to Phitsanulok where we spent the night in a youth hostel before catching our early morning bus to Sukhothai. In Sukhothai we visited ancient temple grounds in the Historical National Park.

Sukhothai was Thailand's first capital in the thirteenth century. There we rented bicycles to visit its forty-five square kilometers of temple ruins. I wonder if you will have visited these ruins or others in Southeast Asia when you read this? As I stood before a huge, white, restored statue of the Buddha gazing down at me, I imagined you in this same spot years from now.

Today I am writing to you from the village of Pai (pronounced "Bye" in English). It is one of the few Thailand cities, besides Bangkok and Chang Mai, that I can recognize when I hear it spoken. We are here among the mountain people to greet the New Year 2002.

This heavily forested mountain area has been a crossroads for ethnic minorities, and today it is undergoing a tourist boom. At this time the "farang" (non-Thais) appear to be primarily European back-packers who help fill the crowded streets.

Main streets are jammed with food stalls, native cloth products and vehicles. The one-cylinder motorbikes, made in Japan, dominate in both sound and mobility in every thoroughfare. I was told that motorbikes outnumber cars and buses in Thailand ten to one.

The many dogs everywhere also intrigue me. In particular, bitches with pups. They are in nearly every entryway to a dwelling and in eating places on the streets. Wherever we go, I usually have to step over a dog. They appear lethargic and remind me of the mangy dogs in rural Mexico.

Outnumbering dogs are chickens. Gamecocks and their round, bamboo cages have been everywhere we've traveled in Thailand. Sitting in a street café, sipping a cold drink, I watched a street-wary black hen with half a dozen lemon size chicks, keeping her brood from wandering out into the motorbike traffic as she led them under our tables for crumbs.

About three kilometers from Pai we rented a couple of bamboo bungalows beside a gurgling stream lined with banana trees. It is called Muang Kon Garden. (Muang is the name of the stream.) For us it is luxurious as the resort's toilet and shower room has an electric water heater so we can bathe with hot water. What a treat!

At dusk, Ting (our Thai host and owner) kindled an open fire around which logs were placed for sitting. There, guests from Japan, Europe, Canada, Thailand and elsewhere joined us with beer, smokes and conversation. From them we learned of travel routes and places to stay. Of interest to me were their perspectives on world politics, in particular how they viewed the current United States war on terrorism. Their perspectives were affirmative if not enthusiastic, which seemed to match those of travelers we met from the United States.

However, I reminded myself that these were generally adventurous young people, well educated, between the ages of twenty-five to forty. In our travels, gray haired people like Donna and me, have been so scarce as to be non-existent. Believe it or not, so far in our travels here, I've found no one my senior. When told my age (over 80), the questioner usually expresses disbelief and often questions me, or others, about my being here in this context as if it were unique. A forty-nine-year-old Thai asked me, "What is your secret? Food? Exercise? Religion?"

I said, "Religion."

He then asked, "Buddhist, Christian, Muslim?"

"No," I said. "My religion is to keep my feet warm, my head cool, my bowels open. But most importantly to keep a sense of humor because ultimately life is a conundrum."

He smiled as if I were joking. I wonder how you would answer such a question? Anyway, this is the last day of the year 2001. And tonight we plan to eat Indian curry and share tequila imported from Mexico that Thomas found in the market.

I wonder what this northern area of Thailand will be like in your time? It is obviously being discovered by Europeans and Americans as a unique winter vacation place.

I'll write you more about it next year in 2002. Until then, my love.

Your Great-Great-Granddad, Sam

SIXTY-NINTH

Dear Great, Great Grandsons and Daughters,

Here it is the year 2002 in Thailand as it is in the rest of the world. Our awareness of "the rest of the world" comes to us today on the Internet from friends vacationing in Italy and families in Alaska and "the lower forty-eight."

New Year's Eve we sat on the floor around an eight-inch high table drinking East Indian chai while awaiting the special curry we'd been promised. The context was certainly unique. A dog was tied to a support of the room. At the end of its leash, it could just about reach where we sat. There it endeavored to defecate. The dog was curtailed by the proprietor. Background music was an old Bob Dylan song, "Blowin' in the Wind" in English, and followed by his repertoire of thirty years ago.

As for the Indian chai and curry, they were delicious. When we walked out under the stars, a flaming, orange New Year Thailand balloon, called a "Klom Loy," rose above us and dropped explosive sparklers as it slowly disappeared next to a nearly full moon directly overhead.

By midnight we had walked back the mile or so to our bungalows. There we sat around a campfire sharing tales and toasts with other travelers. We watched the glowing sky balloons rise above the village of Pai and drop their trails of sparkling fire to welcome the New Year.

At breakfast in Pai on January first, Donna and I watched an international television review of the year 2001 as we sat in a street-side café. The smells of hot fat, tobacco and motorbike exhaust accompanied the repeated reviews of the year in French, Serbian, Arabic, Russian and German. We left before a repetition of the attack on the New York Trade Towers, and the repeated comments by world leaders were finally presented in English. Even so, we had not missed the communication about conflicts in Malaysia, Israel and Afghanistan, or the initiation of the "Euro" as Europe's new monetary symbol of exchange.

However, here among the rice fields, in a village beside a sluggish river in the mountains of Thailand, the world's concerns seemed more like a redone video presentation than reality.

For me there is a needful reality in "getting away." However, as I look back, the most interesting and meaningful times in my life were initiated as much by "seeking for" as "getting away." I suppose in reality they are the same thing. I find it curious that venturing is usually considered in physical terms. But as an epistemologist, the ventures of the mind are just as exciting as a strange land or new planet.

Although I am writing to you today from the mountains of northern Thailand, I carry with me other mountains, from the Brooks Range of northern Alaska to the Torres del Paine in the Andes of southern Chile. Although strangely different, I always seem to find a familiarity in the context I bring to their drama.

As I observe the "farang" (foreigners) here in this unfamiliar land, I'm curious about the contexts they bring from their homeland, their culture and experiences.

I find squat toilets, and sitting cross-legged on a grass mat on the floor to eat a meal, a bit uncomfortable. But this may just be a symptom of my more than eight decades.

Anyway, so-called western culture patterns are now dominating indigenous ones wherever tourists gather. It is another form of the globalization that is taking place in this so-called instant information age.

I wish I could project myself into your time. I wonder if I could find in it a context of familiarity as I do here. I hope your world is not as uniform as I tend to project it.

At this beginning of a new year in the twenty-first century, in an unfamiliar land, I am sitting in the morning sun watching our granddaughter, Acacia, learn to balance as she takes first steps into an unfamiliar waiting world. It is hard for me to project her as possibly your great-grandmother when she grips my finger and leads me with her wavering steps into her world-to-be. Her curiosity is a continual reminder that the world is ever new and interesting to those who continue to see, hear, taste, smell and observe, "as if it is for the first time." I find this particularly true when traveling in new and strange contexts, both physically and mentally.

Here in the village of Pai I became aware of the many water tanks above roofs at the back of buildings. I learned they were for water pressure from gravity. In our Arizona hogan, the electric power pump in our well continually replenishes water to our pressure tank at the expense of our electric bill. What I have repeatedly learned is how many trade-offs that define our lives we make without being aware of them. I notice that even ten-month-old Acacia, who is attempting to walk, has to make a trade-off between watching her balance and taking a step.

One of the major trade-offs, of which most people I know seem unaware, is time. Nearly every technological gadget, from a dishwasher and microwave oven to a personal computer, are considered time savers. The question I raise is time for what?

Sitting here, writing to you, I am aware that I have taken this time for us. I am aware that it is yours and mine although we are years apart. I wonder if I were elsewhere, say at a job or profession and had a cell phone to answer, if I would take time to write? I wonder about your time. Does it define you in the way it does so many of us today?

My writing has been interrupted by the "Call to Prayer" from electronic speakers in a minaret at the village mosque. Although this population is primarily Buddhist, with its many wats, temples and gilded Buddha images, there are also the veiled Islamic women and bearded men in their distinct costumes who maintain street stalls for food and goods.

As I observed an entranced audience watching the same news shows we see on our television by satellite on the other side of the world in Arizona, I wondered about time and trade-offs for them. I wondered about you?

Time has caught up with me so I will have to make a trade-off with time and close this letter with my love to you.

Your Great-Great-Granddad, Sam

SEVENTIETH

Dear Great, Great Granddaughters and Sons,

This morning I am sitting on a bank of the river Nam Lang, which flows south through the jungle into the famous Tham Lod Cavern. We will explore the cavern later today.

Four fat water buffalo are grazing across the river bend. One lies in the shade chewing its cud. Except for the gurgle of water over gravel and rocks, it is quiet in this sultry air.

I'm happy to sit awhile this morning after our seventeen-kilometer backpack yesterday. We hiked from Mae La-Na up into the dramatic mountain ridges along a dirt track. It gave us grand views of jungle covered limestone peaks high above deep valleys.

In the mountain village of Mae La-Na, we spent a night on the sleeping pad of a resident. Hers was a simple room, rented to us while she was away. A pet monkey with a gray ruff around its face, looking like the winter hood of an Inuit Eskimo, was on a leash at the front of the open café where we ate. The usual chickens and dogs were underfoot. After dark we followed the sound of unfamiliar musical instruments and were lucky to discover a presentation of dance and drama by these mountain people for a tour group of Thais from the city of Chiang Mai. We joined the locals, squatting on the sidelines as the costumed dancers imitated wild animals to the beat of gongs, followed by stylized hand dances and patterned feet.

To the local mountain people there, we were as much a center of interest as the staged activity. Acacia's red hair and Donna and my gray were obviously unfamiliar. The children in particular were intrigued with us, and wanted to touch and play with Acacia.

However, what intrigued me, in this village of Mae Hong Son, were two dominating presences: The huge Buddhist temple with its saffron robed monks, and the Thailand military presence with its camouflaged uniforms and vehicles. I suppose this is because we are close to the border of Burma (Myanmar). As I was sitting here writing you, a military helicopter flew overhead reminding me that this "Golden Triangle" of Laos, Burma and Thailand in south East Asia still carries many tensions.

To us, however, it is an exotic and strange land, one familiar to us only in pictures, stories and film. Although coconut palms, papayas and bamboo were not strange to Donna and me when we were back-packing in Central and South America, here the terraced rice paddies and the open, woven bamboo family dwellings on steep hillsides let us know how heavily populated the world has become outside its dominating cities.

In contrast, when I first visited Alaska to search for Robert Marshall's tree plantings, the total population of that new state, which is larger than the country of Thailand, was less than three hundred thousand people. Since then it has doubled its population. But here, the population of the city of Bangkok alone numbers over six million. I wonder what the population ratio of Alaska and Thailand will be when you read this?

When people here ask us where we are from, and we say "Alaska," they often cross their arms in front of their chest and give a shudder, saying "Cold!" Somehow only winter cold and snow are among the images they carry. In much the same way, I brought my images here of illiterate people working in their rice paddies, and others parading with elephants in front of gilded temples. It is strange how we carry such stereotypes.

Beyond the stereotypes, what I have found here are good paved highways that are well marked with yellow passing stripes, and electric power even in remote areas, carried by square, reinforced concrete poles! Television is everywhere, and the Internet is available in any village large enough to be labeled a town. Even with television in hillside thatched bamboo houses on the terraced slopes, rice is still sown by hand and transplanted in paddies by people working ankle deep in mud.

Speaking of "ankle deep in mud," I wonder if this is why nearly every one wears strap-on sandals under bare feet. Here it is the custom to remove them and proceed barefoot in restaurants, stores and dwellings even in towns and cities with paved streets and sidewalks. Wet feet cannot be avoided in bathrooms where the squat toilet is flushed by dipping water from a container, and the shower uses a general bathroom floor drain, even when a western "sitting" toilet has replaced a "squatter."

So far, in our weeks of travel, I have not seen a bathtub. This does not surprise me, as we have no tub in our hogan in Arizona. I wonder if bathtubs are no longer in use in your time? Anyway, here on a misty morning, bare feet in sandals contrast with a wool cap pulled down over ears, and a heavy scarf around the neck above a warm jacket, roaring down a paved boulevard on a motorbike.

I find writing to you this morning helpful in recalling yesterday's long hike. A dozen people intrigued with Acacia stopped us in a mountain village. An eleven-month-old with red hair and with pale skin, attracts attention everywhere. In this mountain village she made it impossible to simply hike through by becoming a center of attraction.

My interest was an old man with gray hair chewing betel nut, and with few teeth in his red gums. I would have judged him to be far older than me. And because Acacia's age was of interest, and I could ask ages by signs about their children and others, I was informed that he was VERY OLD, nearly sixty. When I signaled my age over eighty, there was no doubt that I was not believed and caused much amusement, as if I had made a joke.

In this mountain village of Red Lahu there seemed to be as many dogs as people, and a few small, beautifully marked cats reminded me of miniature ocelots. I presumed they had been domesticated from current wild ancestors.

I was also interested, to note while hiking the high ridges of these mountains, pine trees were growing along with bamboo and banana trees. Down here in the Nam Lang river valley, there are no pines. As a biologist I am always interested in the effects of altitude on vegetation. Here at this tropic latitude, colorful red poinsettias, bougainvillea, and calla lilies give their burst of color high in the mountains as well as in the jungle below.

This evening we are all going underground into Tham Lod Cavern. The river by which I am sitting disappears into a large limestone cave. We are told that it is one of the longest known caves in mainland Southeast Asia and it takes two to three hours to see the whole thing. I'm curious to compare it with caverns I've visited in past years in the United States.

I see it is lunch time, so will close and send you my love from Northern Thailand.

Your Great-Great-Granddad, Sam

SEVENTY-FIRST

Dear Great, Great Grandsons and Daughters,

I am writing to you today from Chiang Mai, the old caravan crossroads from China at the north of Thailand, while sitting at a street-side table watching traffic and pedestrians pass by.

Since I last wrote you, we explored a limestone cavern that compares in size, and in the drama of its huge stalagmites, and stalactites with other caverns I have visited in the past. This one in northern Thailand had ancient wooden coffins left in their present placement nearly two thousand years ago.

At dusk, we sat for an hour watching millions of swallow-tailed swifts fly into the cavern where they roost for the night. Clouds of bats flying out under the stars soon replaced them. I was reminded of Carlsbad Caverns in New Mexico that I first visited as a kid and about which, I think, I once wrote to you. Like the Carlsbad Cavern in 1928, a guide, carrying a gasoline lantern, led us through this one in 2002 in Thailand.

On our way here to Chiang Mai, where we came to get a visa to enter Laos, we caught a ride in the back of an open pick-up truck. It took us over the mountains and beneath limestone crags with great trees, bamboos and vines. We passed terraced rice fields in the foothills and valleys before being let off in the tourist town of Mae Hong Son with its dominating Buddhist temple high on a hill overlooking the city.

While there, we hiked to the temple where vendors were selling curios in front of golden Buddhas. However, for me, it was the western tourists that were the curiosities, with their toe rings on sandaled feet, exposed tattoos, weird hairdos and (nearly without exception) some kind of fabric anklet, along with bracelets, rings on many fingers and smoking cigarettes.

The Thailand people, including shopkeepers and those on the streets, in comparison, present a modesty of appearance and dress. Yet the tour advertisements and pictures encourage visiting the few mountain villages where people still dress in colorful, traditions and costumes. One area in particular is stressed, where women wear brass rings extending their necks.

I remember first seeing pictures of what are here now advertised as "Neckies" in a National Geographic Magazine over sixty years ago (before photography in color) as a weird custom in the mountains of a far away, isolated, unexplored land.

Today, the "Neckies" observe us weird "farangs" who come to see them as curios. We bring income to their villages. I wonder if the communities we are visiting in this mountainous area of northern Thailand are still seen as curios in your time?

Here in the city of Chiang Mai, with its swarms of tourists, anything marketable throughout the world can be found. In the major market area, an artificial, "sheer-rock climbing wall" is lit up at night. There you can test your skills with purchasable climbing equipment.

Thirty-six years ago, when I first visited northern Alaska, the city of Fairbanks had only a few small grocery stores. At that time I could not envision the huge shopping malls and chain drug and grocery stores, along with fast-food outlets that are now there. I imagine much the same has happened here in this ancient city of Chiang Mai, which still has a wall and moat around its early original settlement.

As I sit beside this ancient wall and water-filled moat, trying to imagine the way it was when first built as a protection from invasion, I find it hard to close out the roar of traffic and babble of sounds from radios and street vendors. I'm sure the street vendors have changed little in the past hundred years, but loud speakers, automobiles, trucks and motorbikes have changed the language of sounds as much as our means of transportation.

I grew up with the radio and automobile, which were very primitive when I was young. At that time they were unknown in this part of the world. Now they are everywhere on earth and define our lives.

I find that writing to you from an unfamiliar location gives me a different perspective on my own life and times that might not otherwise surface. An unfamiliar location is not just a physical place or a cultural one. Where people are psychologically located, in relation to meaning and values, defines them as much as the physical landscape.

A case in point is the difficulty I find in understanding the action of so-called terrorists who commit suicide in their act of righteousness. If I could put myself in their context (location, landscape, history, belief system), my perspective might be quite different. This is what makes me curious about you and your "landscape." Today we are in many ways creating it for you when you may not need walls and a moat, or superhighways and global corporations.

As I have often written to you, I wish I could look back from your (unfamiliar to me) location in time in order to get a perspective on my own time and life. However, in a small way, perhaps I am doing so by trying to correspond with someone who can only respond in my imagination.

Anyway, in my imagination you are as real as tomorrow's sunrise. So you will keep hearing from me, whether in Alaska, Arizona or Chiang Mai.

My love to you.

Your Great-Great-Granddad, Sam

SEVENTY-SECOND

Dear Great, Great Granddaughters and Sons,

Today I am writing to you from the city of Siem Reap in northwestern Cambodia. Donna and I are here to visit the famous ruins of Angkor Wat and the many others discovered in its vicinity.

When you read this, these world-renowned ruins may be well known to you. I learned of them when I was called as the first minister of the Unitarian congregation, north of the Golden Gate in Marin County, California in 1953.

Donald Greame Kelley, a member of this new congregation, was then editor of the California Academy of Sciences publication, Pacific Discovery, and had received a Fulbright Scholarship award to visit Angkor to photograph and report his observations.

Upon his return, his descriptions and photographs captivated me. I hoped to some day visit these ancient temple ruins in Cambodia.

Since then, Cambodia has gone through civil wars, revolutions and saturation bombing by the United States. During the Vietnam War, and in the 1970s and 80s during the Pol Pot regime, millions were starved and executed.

Today, in front of the sidewalk restaurant where Donna and I sat, several beggars, each with one leg, held out a hat. They were victims of the leftover land mines from that time.

We learned from the driver of our tuk-tuk (a two seated cart behind a motorbike) who took us to the ruins that his parents had died of starvation during that period. He said he acquired enough rice, as an eight-year-old, to stay alive by gathering water buffalo excrement as fertilizer. I asked him how old he was. He said, "Thirty."

We learned that there were very few Cambodians over forty-five years of age. This was evident to us as every gray head we've seen is a tourist from elsewhere.

I remember reading, during that period of civil strife under the Khmer Rouge, that many who maintained the temples were executed. And, during the Vietnamese army's occupation of Cambodia, an enormous number of artifacts disappeared, robbing the temples of irreplaceable statues and lintels. Also, that indelible scars were left where pieces were hacked off from the temples structures.

Knowing this, and with the images and photos my friend Don Kelley had shared with me before these terrible times, I was curious about what my impression would be of what is now included on the World Heritage list of endangered natural sites.

Well, I have been overwhelmed by the experience of being here among these stone temples in the jungle the past few days. They are unique and unequaled as human artifacts, in their acres of carved stone and in both their proportion and form after a thousand years of history. The camera can in no way catch the drama and proportional relationships of the parts to the whole of these human structures surrounded by their moats. I hope they can be preserved so that both you and I share the unique experience they bring to those fortunate enough to visit them in person.

There are few places and sights I have visited in the past eighty years that measure up or exceed my expectations. One, in my home state of Arizona, is the Grand Canyon. From the first time I viewed it at age nine, and during the summer I worked there as a teenage wrangler, and later spent vacation breaks at Toroweep on the north rim, its grandeur always impressed me. And, among human creations, in a terrifying way, was the atom bomb, set off near Alamogordo, New Mexico in 1946. It still fills me with awe as I recall that early July morning.

And now, among human creations, in a very different way, as a work of art, perspectives and architectures, I must admit the Angkor Temples in their dramatic settings, were beyond my conception and expectations.

I assume that by the time you read this, your context will be so different from mine it will be hard to imagine us backpackers walking the dirt streets of Siem Reap; sitting on their edge in restaurants where mangy dogs, chickens and small children are at play around us as we sip a cold drink. Of course there are several large, "walled-in" hotels for well-heeled tourists, but they are not in our travel budget.

One airline flies in here from Bangkok in Thailand, and we plan to fly there to make contact for our return home. Getting here, after many hours on a poorly maintained dirt road from Thailand, where we were crowded in an over-packed vehicle with no legroom was a physical chore we do not want to repeat.

Anyway, I mention our stay here in Siem Reap because it recalls so vividly the dirt, animals and lifestyle in villages of southern Mexico and among the hill people of Guatemala where we visited a few years ago.

I also recall, as a kid, the mining camp town of Hurley, New Mexico where there was no pavement. On my bicycle I had to dodge chickens and dogs that strayed there from Mexican town.

Here in Cambodia, I am again reliving what was once the rural life style of much of the south and western United States of eighty years ago.

If I try to picture Angkor and villages of Cambodia eighty years from now, I expect the temples and their environs will be much the same but with better restoration.

As for the villages, I would not try to guess. In those that now have electric power, satellite dishes feed television screens in nearly every thatched bamboo dwelling. And beneath them is a motorbike or two that vie for space with pigs and chickens. I just wish I could return in your time for a comparative visit. But since I can't, I'll pass on to you a bit of the way it was while I was here this week.

Since today is Chinese New Year, barrages of fire crackers exploding in front of our guesthouse and down the tree-lined, rutted street awakened us. Shortly after, when we went out for breakfast, we followed a loud drumming, shouting and oriental music to its source of exploding firecrackers.

There, a lion headed dragon was accompanied by red and white pantaloon dressed figures. They were bobbing it up and down from underneath to the beat of the drum. Other musicians accompanied the celebration in their red and white costumes along the dirt track. As firecrackers exploded, children ran out to retrieve those unexploded with a burning fuse, so as to throw them at others to explode with a loud crack.

Since this community, along the Siem Reap River, has been on the ancient Khmer Highway from China to the Mekong River Delta for centuries, this New Year celebration has probably changed little in the past thousand years. If you happen to be here on a Chinese New Year, I'll wager that the ritual we share will be much the same.

As for dirt, pregnant mangy dogs, and chickens under foot; along with two cycle motorbikes and one-legged beggars, I expect you will find an environment that I can only imagine. In some ways I am sorry you will have missed the way it is now. But then, I too missed the way it was when the stone artists of a thousand years ago created Angkor. This we share.

More later, Your Great-Great-Granddad, Sam

SEVENTY-THIRD

Dear Great-Great-Grandsons and Daughters,

This morning we sat for breakfast on the edge of our guesthouse's dirt street with the traffic of motorbikes and cars streaming by. A dog miscalculated the traffic and was run over twenty feet from us. Its shrill cries of agony as it tried to gain its feet drowned out all else as vehicles moved around the desperate animal.

To our relief, its cries soon ceased and I said to Donna, "It's gone," as it appeared to have taken a last breath. A group of seven or eight curious Cambodians stood about commenting. While we wondered about the dog's disposal, our attention was distracted as someone pulled the animal from the street out of our sight.

Then the stricken animal again began to howl in mournful agony. It was not dead but terribly injured. No one made a move to put it out of its misery. A tourist asked for the dog's owner, who only shrugged his shoulders in non-comprehension and left.

As we listened to the unavoidable, desperate cries, I looked about for a stout stick or club to put it out of its agony. It was then I recalled many paradoxical problems that such an action could create in an unfamiliar cultural context. Even in my own cultural climate in the United States, the action of putting an animal out of its misery would be criticized by many. Here in Cambodia, where we observed the slaughter and preparation of animals for food, and their treatment as commodities, my ending a dog's suffering by taking its life would (believe it or not) be incomprehensible. It could seem evidence that white westerners are arrogant killers, not respecting the natural process of death by the means, destiny or fate or one's karma has decreed.

So I controlled my urge to relieve this terrible suffering and we walked away down the dusty street to where we could no longer hear the painful cries.

I mention this to you because Donna and I talked about the event as we walked away, aware that mercy killing, or euthanasia, as it is currently called, holds a similar psychological set in the United States today. This makes me wonder about questions like this in your time?

When Billie (my former late spouse) was ill with what was diagnosed as terminal cancer, we acquired lethal drugs to put her "out of her misery" if and when she did not feel life was worth the effort. Since this was an illegal act she contemplated, we had to be secretive. Although it was her choice, we had to be careful that I not be seen in any way as a supporter of such a decision. By law, I could be guilty of manslaughter, or would it be called "woman slaughter" in your time?

So, after we shared our last nightly "mogollon cocktail" together, we said our goodbyes and she left us.

Later that evening I called the mortician. And since Billie was ill with what had been diagnosed as a terminal disease, no questions were asked and no autopsy required.

However, if we had been living in a different place at that time, or if she had been confined in a hospital, such choices could not have been ours.

I wonder how much freedom of choice exists in your time? During mine, it has become illegal to ride a motorbike without a helmet, or drive a car without a seat belt. I could make a long list of other public controls curtailing my freedom "for my own good."

I remember that phrase from my parents, "It's for your own good that we want you home before midnight." "It is for your own good that... etc." What they meant was, "Until you become an adult, we are in control for your own good."

More and more in my lifetime, social legal control has replaced parental admonition far beyond the age of adulthood. This is why I wonder about how much freedom of choice there is in your day?

I'm writing to you while Donna and I are sitting in the Siem Reap Airport awaiting our plane to Bangkok, in Thailand. We hired a tuk-tuk to the airport at about 5 p.m. to give us time to check in our backpacks, and to share a drink and perspectives together before leaving Cambodia.

After our episode with the dog this morning, we met a young man from Poland who was studying in Vietnam, living in Hanoi and doing research here in Cambodia. He shared with us the digital photos on his notebook computer of land mines and other weapons in the War Museum outside

Siem Reap. For me it was a re-living of the tragic recent past that left this country one of the poorest in Southeast Asia.

Our short flight to Bangkok tonight, in contrast to our long, grueling, dusty trip over miles of rutted road, reminds us of how privileged we are because of our wealth. Our plane ticket cost us $300.00 in comparison to $5.00 for the same trip we took coming here overland. This $300.00 was not in our travel budget but we decided to join our kind as we headed home. None of the passengers waiting to board the plane with us appear to be Cambodians. With one or two exceptions, they are older tourists from afar who have come for a sightseeing visit to Angkor.

I expect that in your time the temples of Angkor will be high on the list of special places to visit in the world and that there will be roads throughout Southeast Asia leading here. I hope so.

We have been called to board our flight, so I'll sign off for now and get in line to climb the ramp with the other passengers.

My love to you,

Your Great-Great-Granddad, Sam

SEVENTY-FOURTH

Dear Great-Great-Granddaughters and Sons,

By nine-thirty last night Donna and I had passed through Bangkok Immigration in Thailand.

Waiting in the airport for our hotel transportation, we talked about the contrasts of the past two months traveling in Thailand, Laos and Cambodia, compared to this air conditioned glass and tile terminal with its soft background music playing "Amazing Grace."

We grinned at each other, then hoisted our backpacks and were soon in a small hotel with air conditioning, a television, shower and a comfortable bed.

At six-thirty this morning, our driver was calling us through a balcony window because he had misplaced the lock-card to the entrance of our small hotel. However, by the time we had flown to Chiang Kai Check Airport here in Taipei on the island of Taiwan, we enjoyed a full breakfast with orange juice and two cups of coffee. We are now ready for the long wait before our plane takes off across the Pacific for its eleven-hour flight to Los Angeles.

Before we can board our China Air flight, all passengers were searched for possible weapons (items) that could be used in hijacking the flight. We even had to remove our shoes and pass them through an x-ray machine. Since the declaration of war on terrorism by the United States, flights such as ours from Asia are given particular scrutiny.

LATER

We are now in the crowded Los Angeles Airport. It was a long uncomfortable night with hundreds of other passengers (mostly Asians) traveling in family groups. We exchanged seats with a young Asian woman, traveling to the United States with her eleven-month-old child on her lap, so she could be on an aisle with more room. Sitting eleven hours in a crowded flying auditorium, with poor acoustics for its third rate movie that was dubbed in another language, was no treat after our months of Southeast Asian travel. But now, Donna and I are sitting at a fast-food counter awaiting our flight to Phoenix.

I started this note to you while waiting to board our flight in Taiwan. Since then we left the Far East, crossed the Pacific Ocean, gained a day, and (flying east) arrived in the Far West at dawn.

For you, I imagine this is nothing unique. But for me, (who took his first flight in a two seated wood and canvas bi-plane from a dirt landing strip less than a lifetime ago) it's a bit unbelievable. In trying to imagine your time, I cannot conceive of what would be unique or unbelievable for you.

When flying into this Los Angeles Airport over fifty years ago, I then wondered how it might handle the air traffic that was already being shifted to other outlying terminals, like the one in Ontario. As we flew in this morning, I had the same question as we taxied for many blocks past acres of huge aircraft pulled up to hundreds of loading gates.

In this context, it is hard to conceive that two days ago in Cambodia, Donna and I watched women with woven bamboo rice-winnowing baskets, loaded with rocks, carry and place the stones individually.

In that tropical sun, they worked paving a street. And in the countryside outside Siem Reap, rice was being sown and transplanted by hand as it was when the temples of Angkor echoed to the gongs and drums of their saffron robed monks many centuries ago.

Here in this crowded airport, the psychological shift from the medieval world of Southeast Asia to the ordered, technology of our disinfected western society is somewhat unsettling with its escalator stairways and faucets that flow only when hands are placed beneath them. In some ways I felt more at home in that other environment, including its discomforts. However, I remind myself that this often seems to be the case when in transition.

Right now, Donna and I are looking forward to being greeted by our long time friends, the Mankers, at the Phoenix airport. From there we will be driven to their home in Paradise Valley where our car has been awaiting our return.

As we wait for our boarding call, it doesn't seem possible that tomorrow we will be driving through the mountains on our familiar unpaved road to our rock home in Pleasant Valley, or that we have been traveling nearly two and a half months in environments unfamiliar to us where we met many people who had never been farther than a hundred miles from where they were born.

Of course, in your time, this kind of localization will be past history to you. In some ways I feel sorry that your world may not have those un-climbed mountains and unknown regions that were mine to explore. As my great-great-granddad could have written the same to me.

Somehow, I feel that my time in history has been particularly unique. And I feel fortunate that I am, and have been, here. Even so, I'd sure give a lot to look over the horizon into your time, as I try to envision it as an im-provement over mine.

However, the time has come to board our plane to Phoenix. So I'll sign off and write to you next from home in Pleasant Valley.

My love to you.

Your Great-Great-Granddad, Sam

SEVENTY-FIFTH

Dear Great-Great-Granddaughters and Sons,

So much has happened since our return from Cambodia it does not seem that a year has passed since I wrote my last letter to you.

Since then we moved from the hogan I built in Pleasant Valley to a many-windowed home among Emory Oaks in an arroyo south of Tucson. It is about thirty miles north of the border of Mexico.

After our moving here, the United States and a small coalition of coun-tries, including Great Britain, invaded Iraq with thousands of troops and are currently attempting to set up a new democratic government.

I know that for you this is ancient history, but the unrest in the world that it has caused makes many of us nervous about the future. Anything can happen. And it nearly did for Donna and me when we were moving here to Sonoita.

We had our big Dodge Ram pick-up truck loaded with stuff and were halfway between Globe and Tucson, on our way here, when another pick-up pulled onto the highway without stopping. There was no way to avoid crashing into it. If we had not had seatbelts and an effective airbag that exploded between me and the steering wheel, my last letter to you would have been just that. My last!

Anyway, it was the last of our big white truck that had carried us and provided our sleeping quarters all the way to Fairbanks, Alaska and back last summer.

That close to death experience recalled many others. And how lucky I am to be alive and able to write you and remind myself again that you are yet to be born.

This accident also reminded me that many other "close calls" that I recognized as such, were in northern Alaska. Several were when I was employed as the Native Counselor on the Trans-Alaska Pipeline Project.

One of them was a slide off the icy haul road that winter. The vehicle rolled over several times. Luckily I was only bruised.

There was also an attack that winter by a psychotic native with a hunting knife, who missed my throat by half an inch.

Another "close call" was a break through winter ice with my snow machine on the Dietrich River. I was rescued by an errant helicopter pilot who " just happened" to have taken a shortcut up the river at that time. Several other "close calls" in Alaska were in aircraft, which reminds me of other times when "luck" saved my life.

One was when I was flying in gliders for sport in the eastern hills above San Francisco Bay. I think I once wrote you about that incident. Anyway, I've learned that being alive for more than eighty years on this planet is really a matter of luck. For me, "good luck." I hope it is the same for you.

Today is Earth Day, April twenty-second. Because of the war in Iraq I've seen no mention of Earth Day in the news. I remember the original first Earth Day celebration.

It was when I was called as the first minister of the Unitarian congregation in Anchorage, Alaska. Services were held in our little log cabin church building that is now a tourist bed and breakfast. Today, it is designated as an Historical Site: "Anchorage's Oldest Church Building In Continuous Use." Therefore, it may still be there for you to visit some day.

Here in sunny Sonoita, as I sit on our patio writing to you in the shade of a large oak, I am caught with the contrast of our home at Koviashuvik in Alaska's Brooks Range with its trillions of sparkling reflections glittering from the frozen lake this April morning. I try to imagine your world, whenever and wherever you are reading this letter. I hope it appears as wonderful to you!

With my affection,

Your Great-Great-Granddad, Sam

SEVENTY-SIXTH

Dear Great-Great-Granddaughters and Sons,

It is the longest day of the year north of the Arctic Circle at this mid-summer Solstice at Koviashuvik.

I find it hard to believe that it was thirty-five years ago when I first flew into this isolated wilderness and constructed a cabin of spruce tree logs that has become home.

Since I wrote you last, after our return from South East Asia, much has happened internationally. The Bush administration declared war on terrorism and invaded Iraq to seek reported weapons of mass destruction that have still not been found months later. Before that, our troops, with the British and others, invaded Afghanistan seeking Osama bin Laden, believed to be the leader of the terrorist movement responsible for the September 11 attack on the Trade Center Towers in New York City. I wrote you about this attack nearly two years ago.

Last year Donna and I moved to the cross roads community of Sonoita in southern Arizona where we share 125 acres of scattered oaks with other home owners in a cattle grazing area thirty miles north of the Mexican border.

Our home is a beautifully designed Santa Fe style, built into the hillside with full facing windows and doors opening onto separate, connecting patios. The kitchen patio encloses a large Emory Oak under which we often lunch in the shade.

On the twelfth of May, we loaded our car with backpacks on top and headed north for Alaska. After a stop in Yakima, Washington with Lisa and Chip, we drove the Cassiar Highway through British Columbia to Chickaloon, Alaska where we spent three weeks enjoying our two-year-old granddaughter, Acacia, her parents and other members of the Chickaloon-landowners tribe.

There we celebrated my eighty-fourth birthday before we drove on to Fairbanks, where we left our car with friends Syd Stealey and Beverley Prince. After two days with them, we flew north, arriving here at Kovashuvik yesterday.

Whoops! I'll have to pause.

A cow moose wading in front of the cabin on our lakeshore needed to have her picture taken. The moose stood curiously watching Donna with the camera. It then sauntered along in the shallows, nipping at the reeds poking up above the mirrored surface.

Soon after we put our cabin in order following the year's absence, we boated to the bay south of us and caught a Great Northern Pike. I filleted it. And after a late supper we pulled curtains over the windows to keep out the midnight sun and crawled into our familiar bed.

I apologize for this long gap in my letters to you. But with our move to Southern Arizona and all it entailed, my writing to you has taken a long pause. Now that we are back in our isolated cabin in the Brooks Range I will try to fill you in on our busy lives.

As I mentioned above, we were busy moving to Sonoita, Arizona where friends, Judith and Howard, who had left to live on the Bay of Fundy in the state of Maine, sold us their house. We had previously seen it, enjoying their hospitality, and thought it an ideal place for us during the winters we are not in Alaska. As the saying goes, "We were delighted to take it off their hands!"

We began our moving last November, so we have not yet had a summer experience there. However, the elevation is about a mile high, as was our six-sided hogan under the Mogollon Rim. We expect temperatures to be about the same, but near the Mexican border, there is more sunshine in the winter. Anyway, we are pleased with our beautiful winter home and looking forward to returning at the end of this summer.

Here at Koviashuvik we've found our upper cabin ankle deep in spruce cone litter from red squirrels that made nests on tabletops, chairs and high overhead on stored snowshoes. As in times past, they denuded shelves of books, chewing pages for nesting material and chewed holes through the inner wall cardboard linings. They are geniuses at pulling hair from moose hide rugs. I just eliminated two with the .22-rifle.

After a preliminary sweep-out, we decided to take our time during the next week in repairing and putting things back in order.

Apparently arriving with us on this summer solstice are arctic terns returning from their winter in Tierra del Fuego, South America. A flock of eight or ten flew excitedly along the eastern shore by the island where some had originally hatched. They will pair off in the next few days to lay their eggs. Like us, they are delighted to be home and express it in their familiar cries that sound like: "We're here! We're here! We're here!"

It is good to be home. In this sub-arctic world where little appears changed since I first moved in here back in 1968, spruce trees that were waist high near the cabin are now at my shoulder.

However, large spruce seem much the same, and the lake shore appears the same even though great ice chunks are pushed up at break-up, clearing the beaches year after year. The yellow-legs, jays, ravens, loons and shore birds greet us the same as in the past but are of another generation, as are the ermine, grizzly bear, moose and occasional caribou.

This contrast between the frenetic life and activity of civilization's freeways, commitments, and cell phones, and our time here at Koviashuvik, I find astounding. I do not find it a retreat, though some would call it that. I call it a return to sanity.

The American College Dictionary here in the cabin defines "sane" as: "Free from mental derangement; having or showing reason, sound judgment or good sense [from the Latin sanus: sound; healthy]."

I will write more later once we've settled like the terns, here in our nesting spot.

As ever,

Your Great-Great-Granddad, Sam

SEVENTY-SEVENTH

Dear Great-Great-Grandsons and Daughters.

Yesterday Donna and I took the flat-bottom aluminum boat to the southeast end of our lake to climb "Gun-sight mountain." We called it Gunsight because the swale on top imitated the groove on the back site of a rifle. In the center of the groove could be seen from our shore cabin porch, a dark object like the front-sight on a rifle. We were curious as to what the vertical dark object might be. Even through the binoculars it stood stark and dark well below timberline, obviously behind the mountaintop groove.

It was a three-hour climb from the lakeshore through alders, willows and spruce trees to the steep upper, open mountainside above timberline. What we discovered was a rare, unique copse of a dozen isolated spruce trees about twenty feet tall just behind the swale of the mountain's top. This was the vertical "front-sight" we could see through field glasses but not identify.

However, the real reward of our mountain climb was the view of snow-capped mountains in the range far beyond the lake below us. But best was the myriad of alpine flowers that covered the tundra on the open, steep mountainside. The tallest were bright yellow Alaskan poppies only ankle high. These were in contrast to the pink and blue campion blossoms in their mossy beds. Our feet sank in the mattress-like cinnamon, white green and yellow lichen on the steep sloping tundra.

The wind that swept beneath scattered cumulus clouds was exhilarating and kept mosquitoes away as we sat on our mountain top paradise munching granola bars, mixed nuts and raisins.

Trolling for fish on our way back to the cabin in mid-afternoon, a six-pound lake trout (char) took my red and white spoon bait.

Donna cooked fresh fish for our supper as the gathering clouds gave us a welcome shower before crawling into bed. It was a great Sunday in June. We wondered how stiff we would be in the morning.

I guess we are physically in good shape with no aches or pains after yesterday's five-hour up and down climb. I am amazed that at age eighty-four I still feel more like half that age. Mentally I see myself like others of my generation in finding it difficult and slow to come up with words and names that were once on the tip of my tongue. It is not the person, object or concept. They are as clear as ever. It is their symbol – a name, a specific word that seems hidden in the brain's synapses until it floats up in its own time. What a nuisance!

I need to split some wood for the Yukon Stove so will close this note with my affection.

Your Great Great Granddad, Sam

P.S. Donna just finished an eight-page letter to our in-laws (Acacia's other grandparents) and read me her view of yesterday's hike. She described it so well I'm enclosing her description in this postscript of the first two pages of her letter:

Dear Pauline and Bill:

We've just returned from a mountain top above our lake. Yesterday the weather was perfect and we had seen through our binoculars an outcropping on a mountaintop at the other end of the lake. We couldn't believe it was a tree it looked so large. Anyway, it was our excuse to go see. We left in the morning. It's about an hour by boat to the other end. We're always curious to look along the shoreline for tracks. We did see tracks of a bear and her cub, and moose and wolf tracks. We haven't heard wolves yet this year and nothing has taken our fish scraps from our feeding station about 100 yards from our cabin and in our sight through the cabin window. So we know no bear or wolverine has been near.

We hiked about 2 hours up. Walking where there's no trail and on tundra that's like walking on mattress is slow going (at least for us seniors). In about two hours we hit timberline and we hiked about another hour in what I call "Heidi Country", alpine tundra above timberline where everything is dwarfed. We walked in an array of small arctic, early summer flowers. We did find our outcropping. It was a copse of trees, about a dozen, all within a 12 ft. diameter area well above tree line but in a semi-protected area. It looked like one giant tree from afar.

We really enjoyed our lunch of granola bars, raisins, nuts, yogurt pretzels in a strong wind on the high top. It was just warm enough to dry our sweat and keep the mosquitoes and other insects away.

We really enjoy, as well, coming in by bush plane over the lake be-

cause we are high enough as we descend to see moose, caribou, tundra swans and the shape of the whole lake. But mountaintop sitting has that beaten by far. No obstructions to seeing and all the time in the world. You don't even have to worry about getting down the mountain before dark. There isn't any dark. We could see the whole lake and up the Bettles River drainage. It was glorious!

Donna.

Enough for now.

Your Great-Great-Granddad, Sam

SEVENTY-EIGHTH

Dear Great-Great-Granddaughters and Sons,

It is the first of July here at Koviashuvik, north of the Arctic Circle, and the Public Radio news from Fort Yukon mentioned a fire near Tombstone, Arizona.

It caught my attention for two reasons: Tombstone is the area of Southern Arizona where we recently moved. And Tombstone is where I gave my first sermon in its Congregational Church in the fall of 1941. That was sixty-two years ago!

I still remember its title: "The Field Is The World." There were only about a dozen people in the congregation and the town itself was then a small, deserted mining camp on the road to Bisbee. I was newly married with a seven-month pregnant wife, Jean, who played the treadle organ for the anthem and hymn singing.

The young President of the Church Board was the owner and publisher of "The Tombstone Epitaph," the newspaper that dated back to the days of Wyatt Earp and the shoot-out at the OK Corral. The owner-editor had just received a contract to publish the Arizona Highways photo magazine the coming year and was delighted to be able to give the town some publicity. He had a key to the old Bird Cage Theater Opera House and took us there after showing us archives of old billings and news clippings of past performances.

The building was then decrepit, with peeling wallpaper and a water stained ceiling from the leaky roof. In 1941, Tombstone was just a road stop for gasoline on the road from Tucson to El Paso Texas.

On a Saturday last May, Donna and I drove from our new home in Sonoita to visit Tombstone, AZ, now a tourist center with shops and old style redesigned buildings. The crowded town had people in nineteenth century costume wearing pistols, moustaches and black sombreros, also with tight waist, full skirted dames, inviting tourists into the hundred or so shops lining the streets.

The Tombstone Epitaph had a display of its old printing presses and a presentation of tombstone's famous past Sheriff and other personalities were enlarged for public viewing. Some difference from the quiet little town of sixty-two years ago!

This morning the direct international news on our radio is primarily from Baghdad in Iraq, where a reporter commented on the difficult time invading United States forces are having keeping order. A couple of soldiers were killed when a grenade was thrown into a vehicle. No change in the news from Israel where Palestinians and Israelis continue to kill one another. I wonder if there is peace in the Middle East in your time? It is hard for me to imagine it.

Here at Koviashuvik I spent most of the day repairing squirrel damage in the upper cabin. The little red devils chewed holes through the cardboard wallboard in a dozen places, using the litter for their nests.

From a squirrel's perspective, they are not malicious. That is our perspective. They have to gnaw and chew to keep their biting teeth of workable size. Their front incisors never stop growing. It is the same with beavers that are committed by nature to chomp down trees whether they build a lodge or dam with them or not.

One year a pair of beaver came north to our lake and destroyed all but one clump of the few poplars here. Fortunately, they then returned south. So far this has been our good luck with human invaders who came in on all-terrain vehicles and carried out their compelling need to shoot animals, cut down trees, pack out our fish and leave garbage. They too returned south.

However, I am aware that our luck cannot continue indefinitely, so I am grateful for the thirty-four years of relative privacy we've had on this lake's shore. I wonder about the concept of privacy in its many forms where you are in your time? I cannot even guess.

Last weekend, a little after eleven p.m., we were startled by voices that awakened us. And as I stood undressed, with my head poked out the door, three young men with large back-packs, who had obviously been hiking in the range, asked if they might take pictures of the cabin.

By their broken English and strong German accents, I surmised they were tourists visiting the wilds on foot. My first inclination was to ask them to wait while I got dressed and then invite them in. Instead, I said, "You are welcome to take pictures, but we have just gone to bed."

They asked about a mine of which they had heard, and I directed them up the hillside to the Lake Creek mining site and we went back to bed.

I felt uncomfortable, not inviting them in. In the past, when we were much more isolated, there would have been no other response than an invitation.

Times seem to have somehow changed. I felt our privacy was being invaded. I cannot blame the young hikers. It is still daylight after eleven p.m. this far north. They may not even have been aware of our isolated dwelling until arriving here. I was aware that the privacy problem was mine, also the changing contexts in which most of us now live.

In the city of Anchorage, or any other, being awakened at eleven o'clock at night by strangers coming in would seem offensive. Here, it is different, a different context. It was I who changed our context in my attitude. It makes me uncomfortable acting like a city dweller in the isolation of the Brooks Range. This is why I wonder about the concept of privacy in your time. I feel it is changing in mine and I don't like it.

What is privacy? I remember spending a night with an Inuit family when weathered in at Anaktuvuk Pass in nineteen sixty-six. There were nine of us altogether: four children, their parents and another non-Eskimo beside myself in a small sod hut, about twelve by twelve feet square. The pee-pot was curtained off in a corner and a caribou skin hung from the willow pole ceiling separating sleeping quarters of the family from where we were invited to bed down on skins placed on the willow bows covering the floor.

Everyone, including the children, gave others a sense of privacy. Nothing was said about it. It was just physically done. Psychological privacy was the same, although I knew the children were as curious about us as we about them. Like their parents, they did not pry beyond asking our names and where we came from. Of course we volunteered much more, and conversation was lively. I felt at home. Never did I feel a sense of invasion of my privacy. Ever since that night at the top of the range I've been aware that privacy is something that can be given if not easy to take.

I wonder what your experience is in your time? I'll have to use my imagination.

As ever, Your Great-Great-Granddad, Sam

SEVENTY-NINETH

Dear Great-Great-Grandsons and Daughters,

On this Fourth of July morning at six a.m. a pair of mew gulls nesting on the small island called to us and one landed on the cabin roof. They are aware that we are the source of fish entrails placed at a feed station a couple of hundred yards away for scavengers to clean up. So far this summer, only these gulls have fed where wolves, ravens and grizzlies visited us last year.

As I stirred the batter for our sourdough pancakes, I recalled Fourth of July mornings when I was a youngster. I was up at sunrise to set off firecrackers with older boys next door. Firecrackers could be heard all over town, along with an occasional blast of a shotgun.

On Independence Day flags were flown in front of houses throughout the mining town and at night roman candles and sky-rockets filled the sky. Children lit sparklers from each other's and waved them in the smoky din. Anyway, that is the way I remember it.

Except for a gull's mewing call and crackle of our Yukon Stove, this Fourth of July is quiet. Here, there will be no fireworks tonight, primarily because there is no night north of the Arctic Circle at this time of year.

From Fort Yukon, southeast of us, the National Public Radio (NPR) news mentioned a delay in launching the rocket destined to carry a "lander" to the planet Mars. If the delay (due to mechanical problems) is too long, the launch may have to be canceled. It seems the trip has to take into account the Earth and Mars orbits around the sun. If it is not launched before July fifteenth it will be another two years before the orbits are such that the launch can be repeated.

Twenty-seven years ago, at this time of year in nineteen seventy-six, Viking One landed on Mars and sent back first pictures and data from the planet's surface. Just to get a radio's signal through space from Mars took twenty minutes, and the trip from Earth's launch pad, over two hundred and thirty five million miles to Mars, took nearly a year.

I am intrigued that the question of whether life exists on Mars is given such support and attention. I'm sure that it is based on the question: "Are we alone in the universe?"

If life emerged or persisted on such a hostile spot, it would mean it must abound on other planets in other galaxies. If life is found on Mars it will be the most important philosophical discovery in my lifetime.

So far, only in stories and science fiction do we populate the universe with life and consciousness. I wish I could hear from you in your time. By then you will probably know if Mars had life. Since I cannot hear from you I shall await the success of this expedition to the red planet.

Here at Koviashuvik we never feel alone as we share with each other the life that surrounds us, from fish in the lake to the many birds that nest around the lake. When we hike up to the winter cabin, a pair of shore birds, yellow legs, call excitedly from the tops of spruce trees that they have a nest nearby on the tundra and try to lead us away. The arctic terns pause in front of our cabin on the shore and call to us before swooping on. Of course the mosquitoes are particularly friendly if we fail to use repellant. Their hum along with other insects reminds us that they make up the food chain from which we get our trout, pike and grayling. So, are we comforted by the hum?

Even the crackle of wood in the Yukon Stove is a shared delight before the sound of percolating coffee drifts its aroma throughout the cabin.

We are fortunate to be sharing partners in this life together. Our conversation may pause, but never ends. For those who do not have this good fortune, I feel for their loneliness. And so I ask myself, "Are we alone in the universe?"

I say, "No way!"

If there is no life on other planets, so what? Here is where life is abundant. I think it is exciting to explore the unknown, but to worry about being alone on this planet in the universe seems pretty dumb to me.

If ours is the only planet with life in the universe, how privileged we are to be here. We are not alone. Not only do we have each other but are connected to life in infinite ways. In my writing this letter for you to read after I am gone, I am with you. You are not alone, nor am I, as I write to you before you have been born.

Whoops! My apologies for getting philosophical. But as you are aware, it is who I am. And since you cannot tell me what you want to hear from me you will have to take what you get. Just know that it is with affection.

From your Great-Great-Granddad, Sam

EIGHTIETH

Dear Great-Great-Granddaughters and Sons,

This morning we were awakened by a soft, hushed rustle outside the cabin.

I was immediately up to discover it was the sound of a brief sprinkle of rain. Two hours later the sun had broken through misty clouds reflecting itself from the mirror of a ripple-less lake surface. Not a breath of air this humid morning. It made my sourdough pancake preparation on the Yukon Stove a sweltering task although the outside thermometer was only 70 degrees F. This rare, still, humidity was gone by mid-morning.

According to the National Public Radio from Fort Yukon, scattered thunder-showers are predicted today in the Brooks Range. We need the moisture to keep the tundra alive on the roofs of our cabins.

News of the outside world reported President George W. Bush visiting countries in Africa and the usual economic concerns of international trade and the stock market fluctuations. And there was a report of a summer youth camp that had banned the use of electronic devices such as cell phones and internet games connections so the youth could have a better natural-world experience. The major problem was the parents. It was reported that they objected to not having cell phone connection with their kids. That same report talked about space-phones and their use by wilderness trekkers.

"Satellite phones" caught my attention because we have no way of calling out from our wilderness home here in northern Alaska. A satellite phone was suggested to us by a friend who was concerned by our inability to call-out in case of an emergency. I had not heard of a satellite phone and was told that it was connected to communication by satellite.

When I asked what "a case of emergency" might be, he said, "Being attacked by a bear, or being able to buy or sell if your stock portfolio is in trouble."

I said, "You must be kidding?"

He said, "No way! If I didn't have a phone connection in my plane I wouldn't fly."

We had an interesting conversation about the meaning of emergency, isolation and the value of privacy. When he told me the cost of a satellite phone, and I pointed out that we could not afford one, all he could say was, "I think it damn stupid to isolate yourself at Koviashuvik."

I had no answer that he could hear except the word "cost." The only way he could interpret that word was "money."

There is no way I can measure the value of the years here in our isolated home on the shore of this beautiful lake that has provided our fish, berries, caribou and moose. But more important it has provided the beauty, solitude and time for reflection, so rare in today's world. I wonder about your world?

This reminds me of another bit of today's news about a congressional bill to control telemarketing. Telemarketing is the unasked-for solicitation for goods and services. Some people I know, in urban areas, will not respond to their phone's ring after five p.m. They do let their friends, who might care, know this. Then that question again comes up. "What about a case of emergency?"

Here, by mid-morning the sky was blue with piles of cumulus clouds. So Donna and I took off in the boat to catch a great northern pike for supper. We lost three lures in the process but did return with a five-pound pike that I filleted for our evening meal.

When I took the leftovers to our animal feeding station, north of the cabin, no remains of the past were there. Bears (possibly a mother with a cub) had cleaned up all of last week's fish remains while we were away and left only their scat. There was no sign of animal bones in their droppings. They must have found those fish remains a treat.

Tonight we sat on our cabin porch watching arctic terns hover and dive into the shallows for small fresh water sculpin. When a pair of loons gave their evening call, we decided it was time to go to bed even though the sun will not drop behind craggy Mount Truth until after mid-night.

As usual, I will read aloud before we drop off to sleep tonight. We are starting Herman Melville's "Billy Budd." Some day, when you read it you might picture us sharing the same story in another time and place, another connection we will have across the years.

"Good night," from Koviashuvik.

Your Great-Great-Granddad, Sam

EIGHTY-FIRST

Dear Great-Great-Grandsons and Daughters,

The bear was back at the fish remains last night and carried its spoils about fifty yards up into the forest where she, or he, ate and defecated. In my mind's eye (actually my mind's ear) I could hear her belch, lick her chops, and then shit.

"Shit" is a word never used in polite society. But since I don't consider you or the bear "polite society," it seems O.K. in writing you today.

I know of no one unaware of this word, although it does not appear here in my American College Dictionary or in Roget's Pocket Thesaurus on our cabin bookshelf. I think the word "shit" was the first one I could recognize in print. It was scratched on the walls of public toilets and back alleys. Although I heard terms like "doodoo" and "poop," I never saw them in print. And "feces" was not a word I knew until I was in my teens. Anyway, I wonder if the word "shit" is still a no-no in your time? I'll bet it is.

Historically, I've heard that before today's commercial fertilizers were known, bundles of manure were transported by sailing ships in a dried out form (primarily because of weight). However, at sea, if water got into it, the process of fermentation began again with a by-product of methane gas.

If bundles of the manure were stored below decks, the first time someone went below at night with a lighted lantern, BAROOM! The ship was on fire.

So bundles of manure were stamped with "Ship High In Transit," which was usually abbreviated to S.H.I.T. and has come down through the centuries to today in such a phrase as, "I've heard enough; don't give me any more of that shit!"

At seven o'clock this morning the thermometer registered 37 F degrees and the wind chill factor would put it below freezing. The mountaintops to the north are white with snow and the contrast from last week's warm, sunny days is dramatic. We are delighted with this break in the weather that will put a huge dent in the mosquito population. Also, it is cozy reading in our warm cabin.

Here, reading is a pleasure, where we have a sense of time that is ours to use at our pace, in contrast to the time demanded by society in the outside urban world. Here, no telephone rings to be answered. There is no lawn to be mowed, or newspaper to be read before going to work. The collection of books that line our shelves is a bit much; from classics to current travel and fiction. When I look at the shelves in our winter cabin, I'm aware of what a neat library we've accumulated over the years, although as many volumes have been used as fire starters.

A recent survey that I read indicated that fewer people actually read the many books provided in today's media because their content is available in sound and films and on CDs. This makes me wonder about your time? When a book is passed along to someone, the question often heard is, "Are you a reader?"

Are you?

I guess I assume you are, as I write you these letters.

One interesting book Donna and I just shared, written by Bernd Heinrich, a biologist at the University of Vermont, is titled: Mind of the Raven.

With the unique experiences we have had with birds here at Koviashuvik, his research, observations and experiments, particularly with ravens, validated a raven experience I had a few years ago. It began when "Eap" attached himself to us by way of the fish remains he was given after we prepared fish for dinner.

The raven acquired the name, Eap, after the sound he made when I spoke to him, but mostly referring to Edgar Allen Poe and his classic poem "The Raven".

After Eap's arrival with several other ravens one August, he adopted us and remained after the others flew off. He seemed to see himself as human. He spent most of the time on the beach in front of the shore cabin and would waddle after me talking raven talk, then leap up on the waist-high sawhorse and watch while I split wood. He adopted the fourth rung on the ladder up to the door of the eight feet high log cache where we kept our supplies. There he would roost after we went to bed, and then call in the morning with pleasing bell-like notes. Because he never flew, I thought he might have an injured wing and discovered us as a food supplier while it healed. It was the only rationale I could come up with for his human-like behavior. I never fed him out of my hand or tried to touch him, nor him me. He would waddle up within three feet of me, look me in the eye and ruffle his feathers. I was careful never to spook him and he responded the same.

Eap became a pal who waited for us, jumping up into the air a couple of feet as we pulled our boat onto the shore after fishing. He stood on our outdoor table where I filleted and gutted the fish, and then carried the liver and other parts off under the willows and alders where he buried what he had not consumed. I thought of him as an intelligent pet. He appeared to feel the same about me.

Near the end of August, after the first heavy frost, we decided to move to our winter cabin, two miles along the shore of the lake and a mile up a trail, to our winter home. We wondered about Eap as we loaded the boat with supplies and took off.

I missed his call the next morning but we spent the day readying our winter home and retired soon after sunset. Shortly after bed, I heard a familiar, bell-like sound and stepped out to find Eap perched for the night on the log sawhorse beyond the cabin door. He had moved with us.

Then I heard a "cluck" from a tall spruce tree beyond. There was another raven perched on top, outlined against the evening sky. Eap had a friend. His mate? We wondered.

Next morning both birds were gone. And so far as I know, Eap has not been seen since. I'm always hopeful. Whenever a raven calls, I call back, "Are you Eap?"

This summer our bird friend is a mew gull we call "Lefty." He is identified by his left foot, where a piece of webbing between his toes is missing. Lefty keeps track of us night and day from where he parks atop a spruce on the shore in front of our cabin.

I'll try to remember to tell you about him at another time because the weather has just shifted with a relatively still lake and broken sunshine. We need a fish for supper, so off we go! I'll close with my love.

Your Great-Great-Granddad, Sam

EIGHTY-SECOND

Dear Great-Great-Granddaughters and Sons,

Believe it or not, it is snowing heavily at ten o'clock this morning as I write you following our usual bacon and sourdough pancake breakfast.

It is thirty-two degrees Fahrenheit and we seem to be under snow clouds that have cut off any visibility of mountains, while the huge flakes pile up on the fish-cleaning table outside our cabin window. The radio from Barrow, on the Arctic Ocean, reports a sunny thirty-four degrees. The Brooks Range has apparently caught the storm reported there yesterday and is now giving its white moisture to us. We need it because the tundra on the roofs of our cabins has been drying out and shriveling the mosses. Besides, it is beautiful, with trees decorated in white among the huge, falling snowflakes!

It looks like a socked in day for reading and sewing. Donna has been piecing a Grandmother's Flower Garden Quilt at spare times since we left southern Arizona in May. She now has most of the gay flowers created from her hand-sewn, one inch hexagonal pieces. She will soon be literally creating her garden, as it is to be an heirloom for granddaughter, Acacia. I wonder where the quilt will be when you read this? With you, I hope.

In yesterday's letter I mentioned "Lefty", the mew gull who has been with us since we flew in last month. We think this gull was here last summer when he and his mate had a nest on the island and produced two offspring. It would fly overhead as we headed home after fishing and await the results of my fish cleaning from a treetop by the shore cabin.

This summer we are not sure that Lefty has a mate although there are several other mew gulls now nesting on the island. Lefty seem to spend most of his time here with us, either on the cabin roof or on his favorite spruce tree perch. When I eviscerate a trout (char) or a great northern pike on the table beside the cabin, Lefty lands on the table and watches my progress until I hand him the liver and other fish entrails. He then chokes them down and flies on to the lake surface where he washes his head in the water before returning to his tree- top or cabin roof. There, he loudly exclaims his appreciation in mew gull meowings.

As I told you, we call him "Lefty," because part of the membrane between the toes of his left foot is missing. It could have been caused by a great northern pike that attempted to take him for a meal in the past. For us, it provides a name and a feature that distinguishes him from other mew gulls in the neighborhood. Also, Lefty's personality, and his obvious identifying with us, not only as his food supply, but as his personal property, makes him one of the family here at Koviashuvik.

One of the first sounds in the morning is his wake-up call from the top of his spruce tree perch on the shore. After I greet him and turn on our battery radio for the news from Fort Yukon or Barrow, he flies to the cabin roof and listens with us before returning to his perch in the sun. However, his world with us is not as simple and pleasant as it was.

A few days ago a large herring gull, with cold, yellow eyes and a blood-red spot on its lower bill, flew in while I was cleaning fish. Lefty, being only half his size, gave his spruce tree perch to the aggressive stranger, also the fish guts I left for him. The Herring Gull then flew on but returned a day later and again usurped Lefty's perch and grub. We shall see if the yellow-eyed stranger stays around. He certainly has changed Lefty's style. Our guide book, "The Birds of Alaska," lists the herring gull as "rare and uncommon" in our area. So, we shall see.

As I watch these falling snow flakes thicken on the spruce boughs outside the cabin window, I am reminded of the many winters spent here when the frozen lake was our landing field, and we listened each month for the sound of the two seated Piper Cub on skis bringing us our mail.

Not much has changed here since then. The winters are still eight months long and the lake ice doesn't break up until early June. Except for a song from wolves and an occasional call by a raven, it is quiet. I recall it so quiet that I became curious of the sound of my heart's beat and the internal gurgle of my digesting caribou and sourdough hotcakes. The first drips of melting icicles from the cabin roof at break-up were startling and loud.

Today, in this unexpected summer snowfall, it is the quiet flakes and the still air that makes us aware of the occasional crackle of wood in the Yukon stove. We are reminded that it is silence that makes sound meaningful.

The radio station in Barrow, on the Arctic Coast, reports that this storm has already passed to the south and tomorrow we can expect sunshine here on the south slope of the Brooks Range.

So I'll close this note to you, hoping that you too can find meaningful silence in your time as I in mine watching these huge, white flakes settle on the spruce boughs to the accompaniment of the occasional crackles of embers in the stove!

As ever, across the years and miles, my affection.

Great-Great-Granddad, Sam

EIGHTY-THIRD

Dear Great-Great-Grandsons and Daughters,

This coming weekend we are expecting Lisa and my son, Chip, to be flown in for a twelve-day visit. It means that we must get our mail ready for the bush pilot to take out when he brings them in. Donna has a stack of letters to go to friends and relatives, and I feel I should send my letters to you.

Since you have not yet been born, I have no address for you. Therefore, I will keep these letters in my three-ring notebook until they can someday get to you after you arrive on this planet.

As I write you today, I am aware that all of the experiences I've shared from our lakeside, here at Koviashuvik, speak the joy and wonder that is ours in this wilderness home. However, it has not always been that way.

One summer, about thirty years ago, I seriously considered setting the cabin on fire and leaving, never to return.

While we were outside one winter, a thief came in and took our small boat and sled, filled with our tools, traps and other supplies. Then, pulling them with our snow machine, he headed out by way of the Dietrich River where it meets the winter haul road that was then being constructed for the Trans-Alaska Pipeline Project.

If we had returned that winter, as we expected, the ski plane would have dropped us on the shore of the frozen lake, where we would have hiked to our decimated cabin and cache after the plane took off, leaving us without the tools and supplies necessary for survival.

It was a learning experience about myself. My anger was such that I spent the summer attempting to hunt down the culprit. I knew who he was, and would have shot him on sight if he had resisted my confrontation. He had put our lives in jeopardy. If we had returned in mid-winter as planned, I might not be here alive to write you this letter.

With my rifle, I hiked our area, checking with miners at Garnet Creek on the Dietrich River, who had also had equipment stolen. The single state trooper, whose area of hundreds of square miles included us, was stationed over two mountain-passes at the construction camp in Coldfoot. To contact him meant a two-day hike and he could do no more than I could, except provide a symbol of authority.

So, I posted signs like the following in large letter at every mining claim and vacant cabin and let our bush pilot pass the word throughout the north that the thief was a hunted man:

"RYAN CONNLEY – YOU ARE A DEAD MAN IF I AM EVER IN RIFLE RANGE OR IF THERE IS ANY OTHER MEANS OF GETTING RID OF YOU IT WILL BE DONE!
THE TROOPERS HAVE YOU ON THEIR WANTED LIST –BUT YOU ARE ON MY DEATH LIST.
BY YOUR LARCENY YOU HAVE PUT US IN LIFE AND DEATH JEOP-ARDY AS WELL AS OTHERS IN THE KOYOKUK.
IF I HEAR YOU ARE IN ALASKA AND STILL ALIVE I'LL HUNT YOU DOWN, SO HELP ME. S.W.

As I said, from this life and death experience I learned a lot about myself that was otherwise only speculation. I could never have seen myself on the hunt for another individual with the intent to kill. In fact, even now it is hard for me to believe how I felt and my intentions at the time. As I said, I seriously considered burning our cabin and leaving the state of Alaska forever.

What would be considered an act of vandalism to be brushed aside in many urban settings, was here, literally real. Vandal, as defined in my dictionary: one who willfully or ignorantly attacks or mars anything beautiful or valuable.

This was only part of the desecration I felt. Not only were our lives in jeopardy, but something sacred in the whole wilderness experience, so tenuous in our world today, seemed at stake.

Fortunately, the vandal left, or someone else carried out my intention. Neither the people who knew him nor the state troopers ever heard of him again. Anyway, you can read more about it in my book *Edge of Tomorrow*.

Obviously, I did not burn the cabin and leave. But what still bothers me, reminding me like a scar of an old wound, was that I was changed by the experience. And I am not sure I was for the better. I do not have the trust I once had that those who hike into this wilderness honor it as we do. Nor do I trust myself to honor others in the way I did before.

This time and place of joy in the present moment, called Koviashuvik, has a smeared blur that I cannot erase even though I know it is not out there, but in me. No other animal I know kills for revenge ("eye for an eye and tooth for a tooth"). Only humans. It was a real shock to discover how human I was – am. This is one of the reasons I would like to be able to talk with you about being human in your time.

As you can see, the question of what it means to be human has been with me all my life. As a professional biologist and epistemologist, I'm continually intrigued about how we know what we know but feel trapped by the past. This is perhaps one of the reasons I'm writing to you in the future. I guess I'm seeking for clues as I try to project myself into your time. But since time's arrow goes only one way, I can only report mine to you.

As I looked up from this writing, an Arctic tern hovered above the shallows before dropping into the still water to rise with a fresh-water sculpin dangling in its bill. It immediately swooped away across the lake to feed its young on the distant island. His concerns are obviously not mine. Nor were they in the past when I was debating a decision to walk away from the evil in which I felt caught.

By the middle of next month, this bird with its mate, young hatchlings and others, will be winging thousands of miles south to Tierra del Fuego at the other end of the earth for the winter. And then, next June, they hopefully will have returned to Kovashuvik, their home, as will we.

I find it strangely comforting that the terns and I share many things in common, as you and I do, although we are years apart in time. These terns remind me that I, too, have chores to perform today. So I will put down my pen and gather fishing gear to hook a pike or char for supper. Wish you could be here to join us.

Your Great-Great-Granddad, Sam

EIGHTY-FOURTH

Dear Great-Great-Granddaughters and Sons,

As I may have told you, the top of our cabin is roofed with tundra that acts as a sponge. When it is soaked with two days of rain, particularly after a dry spell, water finds its way through. Last night I hooked a plastic tarp over our bed and we went to sleep with the drip, drip, drip on it from the spruce pole raftered ceiling. At least, we were dry, warm and comfortable. I wonder if this is why beds in medieval times had canopies over them? I recalled wet nights in a tent at the other end of the earth in Tierra del Fuego, as well as here, north of the Arctic Circle.

Before falling asleep I thought of a particular fish breathing its last in the bottom of our boat two days ago. After its agony, we ate it for supper. When I eviscerated it, there was another small fish in its stomach. And in this smaller fish was a tiny fresh-water sculpin for which our Arctic terns dive to feed their young. I didn't explore the stomach of the sculpin but I'm sure the organisms it has consumed were not at the bottom of the food chain.

Anyway, with the drip, drip of the leaky roof and the recall of that food chain, in which I considered myself at the top, I fell asleep and dreamed that I had drowned and found myself (not at the top of the food chain but at the bottom) as a corpse washing up on the shore.

Well, that dream ticked off my reaction to those sentimentalists about "mother nature," who see, feel and sense her as kind and beneficent. They do not look into the depths of nature and see their own wars, pursuits, tribes, and in particular, their search for security.

As I write you today, I can glance up and read the prayer I had lettered years ago above our bed in the cabin: "SECURE ME FROM SECURITY, NOW AND FOREVER, AMEN."

One thing I have learned, at least for myself, is the wisdom of insecurity. That life is a verb, not a noun. One of the exasperating things about nature and the universe is that they will never stay put. To be passing is to live. Life, change, movement and insecurity are so many names for the same thing (which is not a "thing"). Life is a verb. Trying to cling to life is like holding you breath. If you persist you will kill yourself.

Life and death are not two apposing forces, but two ways of looking at the same force, CHANGE. I am aware that the dictionary itself is circular. It defines words in terms of other words. However, it does come closer to life, when alongside some word it gives a picture (like that of a sculpin in the New College Dictionary). But all dictionary pictures are attached to nouns.

We are bewitched by words. We confuse them with the real world when they are only symbols. I've become aware that we symbolize the universe this way, which loses much of the joy and meaning of life itself.

However, in these letters to you, the symbols I have to use are marks on paper. Hopefully they will share with you more than I expect. To use a phrase I have grown up with: "I hope you catch the drift."

Anyway, the storm has moved on so it will be possible for the floatplane to fly in with Chip and Lisa as expected. To get ready for them, I'll put this letter aside until later.

Here it is three days later.

While Chip and Lisa are out fishing for our supper, and Donna is picking blueberries, I'll finish this letter to you.

I believe I have mentioned that Lisa and Chip are both Unitarian Universalist clergy. Therefore much of our conversation was about our denomination because they had just attended the General Assembly of congregational representatives in Boston where they gathered for the annual conclave.

When I first attended an annual meeting, as a new minister fifty-five years ago, we all met in the Arlington Street Church in Boston, representing less than a hundred thousand Unitarians throughout the whole of the United States and Canada. I do not know how many were represented by those gathered in Boston last month, but Chip and Lisa mentioned that over eight thousand delegates and attendees were in the city's huge convention arena. It was the largest General Assembly gathering of liberal religionists of which I am aware.

I must admit that I am glad I was unable to be there. I would have enjoyed meeting colleagues and friends I've not seen in many years, but organized crowds are not my thing.

However, this has not always been the case. During the Vietnam War, when I was living in the San Francisco Bay area, I was an active organizer and participant in marches for peace that proved effective in helping bring about the war's end.

And as I once wrote you, I participated in the "March on Washington" during the Civil Rights Era. I know that these are bits of past history to you, but they did their part in producing changes that have followed since.

Even so, today I wonder about our country's role as the dominant force in the world militarily, economically and socially. Already Americans are being looked upon with fear, and even loathing in many parts of the world. So much so, that Donna and I have withdrawn plans to visit places that were once on our agenda in Asia, Africa and the Middle East.

As an American, looking back at history, world dominance by Asians, Romans, Europeans and the British Empire raise a question about us today. I wish I could hear from you and learn what has happened.

Here at Koviashuvik, the newly hatched gulls are begging their parents for food. The white-crowned sparrows flit from branch to branch in the spruce trees to feed their hatchlings, while Lisa and Chip troll for fish to feed us at supper tonight. These remind me of those circles of life that, like a spiral unbroken, appear to move beyond the now. For better or for worse, we judge their direction of spin.

Thank you for being. Even though at this time you are only in my imagination as one with whom I can share my world.

My warmest best to you.

Your Great-Great-Granddad, Sam

EIGHTY-FIFTH

Dear Great-Great-Grandsons and Daughters,

We have decided to fly out when the bush pilot comes in to pick up Chip and Lisa the day after tomorrow. This means tomorrow's chores will be the preparing of our cabins for the winter even though freeze-up is nearly six weeks away. Preparation means making them as bear-proof as possible by boarding up windows and doors, hanging up skin rugs and other nesting materials so they are out of reach from squirrels that may find their way inside. Also, putting away non-perishable foodstuff into the high cache.

Leaving Koviashuvik this early in August will give us more time with granddaughter Acacia and her family in southern Alaska before we drive the thousands of miles south to Sonoita, Arizona.

By the way, Lefty, the mew gull, brought his three new kids to join us on the lakeshore. Here, they peep and beg him for fish guts that he regurgitates for them. In their gray plumage they now appear larger than their white-feathered dad.

An Arctic tern's chicks are now swooping down to the surface of the lake with their parent in order to scoop up insects. This will be first summer that Donna and I will be heading south before the terns. Their exodus to the other end of the earth will be later this month.

Another pair of birds that have nested on the lakeshore is a pair of loons. Their plaintive call, after the sun disappears behind Mount Truth, can be mistaken for a wolf's mournful cry. Their newly hatched chicks ride on their parents backs when not learning how to dive for food below the surface. These two baby loons will also be flying south after we have gone but before the lake freezes.

Late September and October are freeze-up time here. By November only

Chickadees, Alaska jays and northern ravens will stay for the winter.

As we prepare to leave for the winter early, one of the many things we do is empty our sourdough crock-pot and dry the residue in it so it can be restarted next year when we return. The original yeasts in our starter were given to me my first year here by an Inuit Eskimo woman in whose family the yeast was passed on from whalers who were wintered on the Arctic coast over a hundred years ago. We have shared dried starter from our pot with others for the past thirty-four years, so these ancient yeasts continue to be re-grown throughout the U.S. today and are being passed on to others. I wonder if you will be enjoying this handed down sourdough, with its taste of the Arctic in your pancakes and waffles?

One of our concerns, as we now leave the cabins empty for a month before freeze-up, is the grizzly bear. In the past we have had one break-in. With his bulk and curiosity he destroyed not only stuff on our shelves, but he bit through every packaged item and metal container. He then tore apart the Yukon Stove to explore its insides. I may have written about it to you.

Today I have boards to bolt over windows and doors. We put all foods outside, up in the high cache. The bears will not hibernate until freeze-up. Until then they will have time to explore during our absence. However, blueberries are now ripe, so we hope they will feel well fed and avoid our cabins and the smell of humans.

Before I forget, I want to mention that one of the reasons I first came to Alaska was my interest in ancient living trees. I may have written you about my involvement with the world's oldest tree, known as "Mathusala." It is a Bristlecone Pine, four thousand seven hundred and sixty eight years old, growing in the White Mountains on the border of Nevada and southern California. I mention it because a news item on our radio spoke of cloning this particular tree that was a seedling at the time of the building of the great pyramids of Egypt. The tree is still alive. The reason given for cloning is that the decline and death of many species of trees has become a concern with weather changes and advancing environmental attacks of acid rain, ozone pollution and imported exotic diseases and insects.

Shortly after these Bristlecone Pines were discovered to be so ancient, I explored them in the Inyo Mountains and wrote a piece about them for the California Academy of Science's publication, "Pacific Discovery." It was through this that I learned about Robert Marshall's exploration and his interest in Alaska's northern timberline. I'm sure that I have written you that this is what first called me to Alaska. It was in that summer of nineteen sixty-six, on my hundred mile search across the Brooks Range for Bob Marshall's tree planting plots, that I fell in love with this wilderness and returned to make it my home.

I think I wrote you one Fourth of July that there had been a question of a rocket delay carrying a lander to the planet Mars. Apparently the problems were resolved with the new announcement that a robotic lander and two rovers, loaded with scientific equipment, are on their way to this unexplored world. Mars is as close as it has been in sixty thousand years.

The year before I left to explore for Robert Marshall's spruce seed plantings in the Brooks Range was the first time the surface of Mars was photographed from a spacecraft. In 1965, Mariner 4 photographed a Martian surface that looked more like the moon than the earth.

I just learned that in December and January three missions are expected to land on Mars and a lander from Great Britain, delivered by an orbiter from the European Space Agency, will search for chemical indications of past life. An orbiter from Japan was also announced on its way to Mars.

I find all this exciting, as there have been only three successful landings on Mars. In a few months these present missions will observe the red planet at close range and hopefully answer many unanswered questions.

Of course, you already know more answers to questions I have about life on Mars and elsewhere. I wonder what kind of questions you have, that are seeking answers to be found in your future? Somehow I feel you will have as many questions in your time as I have in mine, perhaps even more.

I wish I could be there with you. But more than that, I wish you could be here with me to tell me about what has happened that I will never know.

I must end this letter and begin getting ready to leave Koviashuvik. So I send my love to you.

Your Great-Great-Granddad, Sam

EIGHTY-SIXTH

Dear Great-Great-Grandsons and Daughters,

As I sit looking across the sparkling lake this afternoon I try to imagine your world years from now, and wonder if there will still be a place anywhere like this on our planet.

I know it will be ancient history to you, but our world has been uneasy since the United States invaded Afghanistan and Iraq, as part of its war on terrorism following the "September eleventh, two thousand and one," terrorist attack on the trade center buildings in New York City.

I wish I could step into the future where you are and see where this all plays out in the world. However, I'm not so sure I want to know. My optimism, after four score and five years, is again as tentative as it was following the atomic explosion at Alamogordo, New Mexico during World War II.

It has been a fun summer with Chip and Lisa, who flew in to our lake for a ten day visit to enjoy our being together, fishing and eating the catch of char, great northern pike and grayling – also, talking philosophy and singing folk ballads.

One of the ballads, "Lavender Cowboy," I had written when I was in prep school in New England at age fifteen in nineteen thirty-four. I sang it back then to my classmates. And then sent it to a pulp-paper magazine called Red Hot Pepper. I received something like five dollars for it. Recently I learned that it was now in a collection of ballads attributed to someone else. I learned from son, Chip, that he had sung it many times in the nineteen-sixties among music groups with whom he had contact such as "The Grateful Dead" and others. Strange, that after seventy years, it has returned to be sung on the shore of his Arctic lake. Here are the lyrics of LAVENDER COWBOY in case they get lost again:

LAVENDER COWBOY

He was only a lavender cowboy.
    The hairs on his chest were two.
    He wanted to follow the heroes
    And fight like the he-men do.

But he was in mortal trouble
    By a dream that gave him no rest.
    When he was a hero in action
    He wanted more hair on his chest.

    Bear's oil and many hair tonics
    He rubbed in both morning and night,
    But when he looked into the mirror
    No more hair grew in sight.
    He fought for his sweet Nellie's honor.
    He cleaned out a hold-up gang's nest.
    He died with his six-guns a smokin' -
    But only two hairs on his chest.

                - Sam Wright 1934

Also, on the shore of this arctic lake, we discussed at length what is currently called "postmodernism." This term "postmodernism" seems to point to a shift in the way artists, social critics, scientists and philosophers have thought about the world. It calls into question ideas and assumptions inherited from what has been called "the modern past." Someone who reviewed my books, KOVIASHUVIK and EDGE OF TOMORROW, referred to me as a "postmodernist."

Since then I have tried to define the term and here we discussed it often over lunch and suppers of grayling, great northern pike or lake trout. We came to "no conclusion," which was one of our definitions of the term. It seems to me to be a search for new ideologies, new scientific recipes, new systems and institutions. In other words, the older modern myths can no longer support us. It is time for a transition.

I guess this is one of the reasons I am writing you these letters into the future. There, you can look back and say, "So that is the way it was? Hard to believe it!" Now I must go cut wood for the Yukon stove or there will be no supper. Can you believe it?

Your Great-Great-Granddad, Sam

EIGHTY-SEVENTH

Dear Great-Great-Granddaughters and Sons,

Here at Koviashuvik we are fulfilling the chores necessary to leave our cabin until we return next summer. Donna spent the morning cleaning and sorting foodstuff to be left over the winter in the high cache, protected from wolves, bear and wolverine.

After lunch we took our boat several miles down the lake to where blueberries are often more plentiful. There we pulled ashore where a grizzly bear had left her huge track in the silt along with those of her cubs. Nearby was her pile of scat full of blueberries.

We had scanned the area before landing. We didn't want to compete with a sow with cubs. Fortunately she and her brood were apparently elsewhere.

When we finished picking berries we trolled for lake trout on our way back. Donna's lure attracted a fine, fat trout that she hooked for supper. Then, before we returned, she also caught a great northern pike in a shallow bay. We brought the pike back alive to put in our lakeside holding pond. It will make our last meal before the bush pilot flies us out day after tomorrow.

As I sit here in our small log cabin writing to you, knowing you are in another place and time that I cannot imagine, I realize how fortunate I've been to have had this isolated place of beauty and quiet. It is still as pristine as it was the year I first hiked into the Brooks Range thirty-eight years ago.

Since then, Gates of the Arctic National Park and Wilderness Preserve, here in the range, have been created. Oil has been piped over the range west of us crossing the state from Prudhoe Bay on the Arctic Ocean south to Valdez on the southern Gulf of Alaska. A highway now accompanies the pipeline across these mountains. There are no other roads this far north, and it is a two-day hike through the mountains to get here. Few venture on foot.

Floatplane is still our usual transportation. Today, fewer planes are chartered to take hunters, campers, or fishermen to northern isolated lakes where there is no fuel supply or lodging for personal comfort. So far this summer, no strange plane has landed on the lake and only the call of birds, wind in the trees and splash of waves on the shore lulls us with nature's music. We feel blessed.

It is time to "hit the sack," as the saying goes, so I will finish this letter later.

It is now "later" than I expected.

Yesterday we were picked up by a floatplane from Bettles Lodge. We then caught a commercial flight south, down the Koyukuk River, to the Village of Alakaket. Then, we flew across the Yukon River flats to the city of Fairbanks. There we spent the night with long time friends, Bev and Syd.

Fairbanks has changed dramatically since I was first here thirty-eight years ago. At that time it was a small town. Today it is definitely a city with several large shopping malls and roads crowded with traffic.

This morning I am sitting on a bench in the sun writing to you outside the Fairbanks Visitor Center. It is swarming with tourists that I could not have imagined that August day I was first here in nineteen sixty-six. I recall looking across the murky Chena River that morning with no idea that some day I would call northern Alaska home.

In front of the bench where I am sitting is a sealed, steel time capsule. It has a bronze plaque, titled: A Step In Time:

"Like these waters that flow to the sea we tread the uncertain path. At this step stone we pause, looking to our past, forward to our destiny and leave these treasures of our time."

I am wondering what the capsule contains? There is this notation: "The opening of this time capsule on January 2059 will commemorate the first century of Alaska Statehood, sealed this day 30 May 1984."

Of course I will not be around in 2059, at the age of one hundred and forty, but you may be here for its opening!

However, you already have the contents of a Time Capsule in my letters to you: "As I have paused: Looking at our past, trying to leave you some of the treasures of our time."

With my love, Your Great-Great-Granddad, Sam

EIGHTY-EIGHTH

Dear Great-Great-Grandsons and Daughters,

I am writing to you today from Chickaloon. This is our other home-site, north of Anchorage, in southern Alaska.

I have written before about these thirty-four acres of aspen, birch and spruce trees between the Talkeetna and Chugach ranges of snow capped mountains that a group of us share.

Here, Donna and I continue preparing a hilltop area where we plan to construct a log home. However, our dwelling at present is in an eight-foot, portable camper that we have parked on our tow-able flatbed trailer.

I wonder if campers and motor homes will be as prevalent in your time as they are today? When I was a kid there were few paved highways and there was no way one could drive to Alaska from the lower forty-eight. I could never have imagined the huge, expandable houses on wheels (usually towing a car behind) that roll up and down the Alaska Highway today.

This afternoon I have been cutting down trees and stacking firewood to give us a view of the white capped, massive pyramid of King Mountain across the defile of the Matanuska River channel. In the opposite direction, Castle Mountain looms with its craggy turrets sheltering Dall sheep, seen through field glasses as white spots against the red-brown cliffs. This view has defined our home site location.

As I think back of the several houses I've constructed and others where we've chosen to live, a view has always been important. Also, a poetic sense of light and sun.

I have friends who feel comfortable in the gullies of freeways, and inside canyons of shopping malls and apartment complexes where I would feel trapped. In some ways I envy them, but not really. I guess I do not want to adapt to that environment.

But from here today, it looks like this may be the environment for most people in your time. If so, I'll not regret missing it. On the other hand, what would I hope to see if I could make a leap into your future?

As a father, I want to believe that my great-great grandchildren, and others long beyond you, will have a beautiful earth to view and walk on – sweet air to breathe – and the chance to see an Arctic tern dive into a lake to retrieve a tasty morsel – to hear loons calling at dusk and perhaps a wolf singing to others from a distant ridge.

What I really hope is that people learn to know that all life on this planet is intimately related. Not just our own kin but beyond them, recognizing that the measure of all things is not just human life but life itself.

As I write you today, ours is the only "living" planet we know. I wonder if it can survive our ignorance. I am reminded of these lines from the poet, Mary Oliver:

....I am noting the way the yellow butterflies
move together, in a twinkling cloud over the field.
And I am thinking: maybe just looking and listening
Is the real world.
Maybe the world, without us,
Is the real poem.

To you, with my affection from Koviashuvik, a time and place of joy in the present moment.

Your Great-Great-Granddad, Sam

EIGHTY-NINETH

Dear Great-Great-Granddaughters and Sons,

Today I am writing to you while sitting in our car on a large commercial parking area in the town of Wasilla, Alaska.

We just finished a fast-food lunch of an oversized hamburger with French fries that I cut in half. We then split a chocolate "bear claw" ice cream scoop, before Donna left to shop for blue jeans in the huge Fred Meyer grocery and department store.

Over thirty-four years ago, when I was in Anchorage, as first minister of the Unitarian Universalist Fellowship, meeting in our little log chapel, Wasilla was a tiny, rural outskirt village in the Matanuska Valley where several members lived. It was considered by some, too long a drive, way around the bay to Sunday meeting.

I recall a funeral here in Wasilla where family and friends constructed a coffin and shared in digging the grave on their home-site. Together, we sang, "So long its been good to know you," as we shoveled the rich soil on to his final resting place.

Today Wasilla is jammed with traffic and with a proposed bridge across the Knik arm of the Cook Inlet. This area will probably become a huge suburb of the city of Anchorage, as Oakland and the east bay are to San Francisco.

In the nineteen sixties, when I was a professor in Berkeley, California living in the Oakland hills, I tried to imagine what it was like before the Golden Gate and Bay bridges were built. I am trying to imagine what this area might be like in your time. It is easy to look back through a rear view mirror, but there is no clear windshield through which to see ahead. Only you will know.

Looking ahead reminds me to have the oil changed in our vehicle before we leave for our thirty-five hundred mile drive south through Canada and the United States to Sonoita in southern Arizona. There, Donna and I will spend the coming winter in our recently acquired home, less than thirty miles from the Mexican border.

Following our trip to south east Asia, my grandson, Rene Henery, purchased the hogan I built in Pleasant Valley. There, he had watched its construction as a youngster, and has warm memories of summers spent there beneath the Mogollon Rim.

Soon, we will be driving to our new dwelling in Sonoita among familiar Emory oaks in the grassland of southern Arizona. I say "familiar" because the rangeland, plants, animals and broken skyline, with its rugged mountains, sing with the same harmony I knew as a child east of there in southern New Mexico over eighty years ago.

Yesterday I acquired my new Alaska Drivers License, "good for five years."

What startled me was the recognition I will be over ninety when it comes up for renewal!

It is a strange experience to know I've been around this long. And still asking myself what this journey is about.

For me, life has not been a journey with the intention of arriving safely at its end in a well preserved body, but rather to finish in a thoroughly used up one, totally worn out and loudly proclaiming, "Wow, what a ride!"

Your Great-Great-Granddad, Sam

NINETIETH

Dear Great, Great Grandsons and Daughters,

This may be my last letter to you, as I look further ahead into this twenty-first century.

Today was Election Day and we chose our first African American, Barack Obama, President Elect of the United States!

Also today, a message with a picture on the computer read: "Here is (son) Silver! 7lbs 7oz, 19 inches healthy boy!" from my grandson, Joaquin. Two beginnings on the same day heralding great expectations for the future!

So, I gathered together all of the letters I have been writing to you about my life and times. I see this as the ninetieth. And with my return from travels, it seems a good time to bundle them up into a form that will be available to you.

When I started writing to you, I was aware that this was a one-way correspondence because you had not been born.

Even though I will be dead when you read this, I hope my letters will have given you a sense of what it was like to be living in the United States during most of the twentieth, and into the twenty-first century.

I've tried to write you as I would like to have been written from a great-great-grandparent who might have written to me from the mid-eighteen hundreds. As I said, when I first wrote to you, I wish I'd had a great-great grandparent tell me about how it was for him in his time.

I have imagined you as young adults. Therefore, any enclosures that have been included are to give you a sense of my formal professional life. They may seem a bit stodgy for your time, but I have included them to give a sense of the way it was in mine.

I tried to imagine one hundred years from now, and what I would have wanted my great-great-grandparent to share with me: the way he saw his world and the essence of his being, his priorities and values.

As I pondered how I could best tell you how it was for me, I began by writing to you a letter, and then another, until this ninetieth seemed to me an appropriate time to call a halt and see that they were mailed.

I'm sorry that you have to receive them all at once, very unlike the way they were sporadically written to you from Arizona, Alaska, Hawaii and south east Asia. But as I pick up a book and put it down and then pick it up as the mood strikes me, I assume it is the same for you.

Before I close this letter I want to share a story I heard about a seeker, who, after years of concentrated effort, gained the power to walk on water. To demonstrate, he invited the Chief and his whole village to gather at the lakeshore. There he gingerly stepped out on one foot, and then the other, until he crossed the surface of the lake and returned.

As he stepped ashore, expecting acclaim, all were silent.

He said to the Chief, "What do you think of that?"

The Chief gave him a puzzled look and said, "We were wondering why you didn't learn to swim like the rest of us?"

At ninety, I am still learning how to become a better swimmer. I'll leave the walking on water up to you.

What I have discovered is that life is a miraculous gift to be honored and treasured. That we honor and treasure life because we have each other, whether in the past or yet to be born.

Each of us arrives with a faith that is not blind belief in what may be, but life in spite of consequences. A faith in our need to affirm the adventure of this sacred journey all share together on this earth that is our home.

My love to you whenever or wherever you are,

Your Great-Great-Granddad, Sam

"A book is not a lump of lifeless paper because from it goes out its own voice as audible as the streams of sound conveyed by electric waves beyond range of our hearing. Just as the touch of a button on our set will fill a room with music, so by opening a book one can call into range a distant voice in time and space and hear it speaking mind to mind, heart to heart."

-Gilbert Highet

ABOUT THE AUTHOR

Born in the mining camp of Santa Rita, New Mexico, Sam Wright grew up among miners, cowboys and Indians and follows a life perspective he calls "an adventure in the exploration of meaning."

After two years away at prep school, Sam returned to the Southwest to earn degrees in biology and anthropology from the University of New Mexico and became a teaching fellow there before being drafted into the Office of Scientific Research and Development during World War ll. After the war, he taught biological sciences at the University of Texas in El Paso and then earned a graduate degree in theology at Starr King School for the Ministry in Berkeley, California where he later held a full professorship.

During a sabbatical leave in 1968, Sam and his wife, Billie, moved into the wilderness of Alaska north of the Arctic Circle. There they built a twelve-foot by twelve-foot log cabin with simple hand tools on a slope above a mountain lake. Their goal was to experience intimately the traditional Eskimo way of life by emulating it as much as possible. Billie Wright's award-winning book, *Four Seasons North: Journal of Life in the Alaskan Wilderness*, was her account of their first year in the cabin that they named Koviashuvik, an Eskimo word for "living in the present moment with quiet joy and happiness." Billie died in December 1987 and asked for her ashes to be scattered at Koviashuvik.

Sam and his present wife, Donna Lee, currently spend their time between Arizona and Alaska.

In 1988, Sam Wright published *KOVIASHUVIK* with Sierra Club Books as the second volume in their new library of nature and natural philosophy. The University of Arizona Press reissued *KOVIASHUVIK* in paperback in late 1997. Since then, Washington State University Press has published his more recent *EDGE OF TOMORROW: An Arctic Year.*

At the turn of this century, Sam Wright began writing letters to his future, unborn Great, Great, Grand Kids: He saw them, not as children, but as comprehending young adults, "Who, like me, would like to have had a great-great grandparent tell me, in personal terms, how it was for him or her before there were paved highways and passenger-planes and before women could vote."